The Material Interests of the Victorian Novel

Victorian Literature and Culture Series

Jerome J. McGann and Herbert F. Tucker, Editors

The Material Interests
of the Victorian Novel

Daniel Hack

UNIVERSITY OF VIRGINIA PRESS

CHARLOTTESVILLE AND LONDON

University of Virginia Press

© 2005 by the Rector and Visitors of the University of Virginia

All rights reserved

Printed in the United States of America on acid-free paper

First published 2005

9 8 7 6 5 4 3 2 1

Library of Congress Cataloging-in-Publication Data

Hack, Daniel, 1965 –

    The material interests of the Victorian novel / Daniel Hack.

      p. cm. — (Victorian literature and culture series)

    Includes bibliographical references and index.

    ISBN 0-8139-2345-x (cloth : alk. paper)

    1. English fiction—19th century—History and criticism.　2. Authorship—

Economic aspects—Great Britain—History—19th century.　3. Literature

publishing—Great Britain—History—19th century.　4. Material culture—Great

Britain—History—19th century.　5. Material culture in literature.　6. Economics

in literature.　I. Title.　II. Series.

PR878.E37H33 2005

823′.809—dc22

                                              2004030848

For Nancy

Contents

Illustrations

Acknowledgments

According to Mayhew's *London Labour and the London Poor,* charitable individuals in Victorian England were sometimes duped into aiding con artists who pretended to be "literary men"; the works described by these supposed authors are perpetually about to go to press but somehow never appear in print. *The Material Interests of the Victorian Novel* has been long enough in the making that I don't blame any of the individuals who provided help along the way for fearing that they had joined the ranks of these gullible souls. I have no hope of repaying the many debts accrued in the writing of this book, but at least, with its publication, I have spared my benefactors this embarrassing kinship.

At the risk of replacing one embarrassing kinship with another, I cannot resist acknowledging individually some of the people who helped bring this book into being. The book began as a dissertation under the exemplary direction of Catherine Gallagher, who was and remains an extraordinary sounding board, shaper of arguments, adviser, and scholarly role model. Thanks, Cathy. Looking back before that beginning to an earlier one, I would also like to thank my first mentors: Jonathan Freedman, who introduced me to George Eliot and has remained a steadfast friend and advocate ever since, and the late, sorely missed James Snead.

Bill Cohen, Tom Laqueur, David Lloyd, Deidre Lynch, and John Plotz all read and commented on one draft or another of the whole book, to its enormous benefit and my lasting gratitude. The outside reader for the University of Virginia Press, Garrett Stewart, was everything one could hope for in a reader. I am also extremely grateful for the generous feedback I received on portions of the manuscript from Rachel Ablow, Gillian Beer, Rosemarie Bodenheimer, Sharon Marcus, Carine

Mardorossian, Robert Patten, the members of the Western New York Victorianist Group, and the members of my dissertation group, including Kate Brown, Laura Green, Michelle Mancini, and Irene Tucker. In addition, Nancy Henry, Claudia Klaver, and Anne Humpherys and Gerhard Joseph were kind enough to invite me to present my work at their schools. Virtually every page of this book was presented at one or more conferences and was altered in some way as a result, and for that I thank the conference organizers and audiences. I also thank the many other friends and colleagues who have talked through my ideas with me, including Amanda Anderson, Ruth Mack, Leah Price, Jennifer Ruth, Hilary Schor, and Blakey Vermeule.

The speaker in Shakespeare's sonnet 111 (which has a totemic presence in this book, as readers will quickly discover) famously asks for "pity" because the conditions of his labor have left his "nature" almost "subdu'd / To what it works in, like the dyer's hand." Me, I can't complain. Whether because my own nature is so fully subdued to what it works in that I don't know any better or because I have been extremely fortunate—it's not for me to say—I have found the conditions remarkably congenial at both the University of California at Berkeley, where I began this project, and the University at Buffalo, where I completed it. I am especially grateful to my department chair, Joseph Conte, for making available time for me to complete the book, and to my many wonderful colleagues at Buffalo for their abundant advice, conversation, and goodwill. Extra thanks to Deidre Lynch for showing me the ropes and being there for me even when she was no longer here with me. I have also benefited greatly from the challenge of teaching my ideas, and I appreciate my students' interest and engagement more than they know. I would also like to thank UB librarians Michael Basinski, Robert Bertholf, Austin Booth, and Laura Taddeo for their invaluable help, and my student Francesca Muscau for her generous research assistance.

While working on this project, my growing interest in the history of the book was matched by a growing fear that if not "the book" as a medium then at least the kind of book I was writing was rapidly becoming "history" itself. I am therefore all the more grateful to Chip Tucker, his fellow Victorian Literature and Culture series editors, and press editor Cathie Brettschneider for their interest in my work, and to the University of Virginia Press for its continued commitment to publication in the field. Thanks also to Ellen Satrom for her expertise and good cheer in guiding the book through production.

Finally, it gives me great pleasure to thank my parents, Elayne and Ray Hack, and my sister, Liz Hack, for their unwavering support and encouragement. Likewise Tracy O'Connell, Tim O'Connell, Phil Davis, Rob Schwartz, Cinda Swanson, and the Bumae. I am more grateful than I know how to say to my sons, Matty and Benjamin, simply for being who they are, and to Nancy Davis for, well, absolutely everything. This is for her.

Earlier versions of two portions of the book have appeared in print: a version of chapter 2 as "'Sublimation Strange': Allegory and Authority in Bleak House," *ELH* 66 (1999): 129–56, © 1999 by The Johns Hopkins University Press; and part of chapter 3 as "Literary Paupers and Professional Authors: The Guild of Literature and Art," *SEL* 39, no. 4 (1999): 691–713, © 1999 by William Marsh Rice University. I am grateful to both journals for permission to reprint the material here.

Introduction

Renewing the Dyer's Hand

THIS BOOK EXPLORES Victorian fiction's engagement with "the material," especially the materiality of writing.

To say this much, or this little, is to invite the question *"materiality" in what sense?* Reference to "the material" and "materiality" *should* invite such questioning, at any rate, as the currency of materiality-talk in literary and cultural studies today reflects less a shared understanding or object of interest than a widespread contest for ownership of this terminology; we are all "materialists" now.[1] Such terms as "the materiality of writing" or "the material text" are used routinely to invoke, at a minimum, any of the following: the specific physical features or sheer physicality of an inscribed surface—and, by extension, the bodily act of writing and the technology of textual reproduction; the socioeconomic or more broadly historical conditions of literary production and circulation; and a distinct "materiality of the signifier," which is linked but not necessarily reducible to the phenomenality of linguistic sounds and marks.[2] Materially minded critics and theorists can differ sharply as to which of these putative forms or registers of materiality takes ontological or methodological priority, and indeed which even merit the title of "materiality." At the same time, *materiality* and its cognates are often used with a vagueness that blurs distinctions and thus evades the question of the relations among the various "modalities of materiality," as Louis Althusser calls them in a classic example of such evasiveness.[3]

Rejecting both conflationary and exclusionary or rigidly hierarchical stances, this study seeks to keep distinct the four primary, contemporary referents of *materiality*—economic, physical, linguistic, and corporeal— while at the same time keeping them all in play, precisely in order to keep open the question of their relationships to one another.[4] My approach is historical and critical rather than theoretical: instead of attempting to decide what should count as "material," I examine how the conditions, components, and consequences of writing now conjured by that term were put into discourse in the mid-nineteenth century.[5] Against the grain of most criticism, whether materialist or idealist, I argue that attention to these "material" aspects of writing does not by itself constitute reading against the grain: on the contrary, such attention corresponds to the Victorians' own, which anticipates and solicits it.[6] As we will see, prominent novels and discussions of authorship often treat the "material" parts and props of writing—including writing designated as "literary"—as neither insignificant and transcendable nor scandalous and regrettable, but rather as potential sources of meaning, value, and power. The investigation and mobilization of writing's putative materialities proves central to efforts to establish the boundaries and relations between textual and extratextual phenomena—the word and the world—and to determine in turn the ethical purchase of the novel as a genre and the literary and cultural authority of its producers.

If "matter," as George Eliot remarks, is a "lofty abstraction,"[7] then the second-order abstraction of "the material" or "materiality" is even loftier. To make the materialities and materialisms at issue here more concrete, let us turn to a brief text to which nineteenth-century writers with the "material interests" I am describing regularly turned, a poem which is itself about the difficulties of abstracting oneself from some material realm.

> O, for my sake do you [with] Fortune chide,
> The guilty goddess of my harmful deeds,
> That did not better for my life provide
> Than public means which public manners breeds.
> Thence comes it that my name receives a brand,
> And almost thence my nature is subdu'd
> To what it works in, like the dyer's hand:
> Pity me then, and wish I were renew'd.[8]

Shakespeare's celebrated complaint puts into play three of the forms of materiality highlighted above: the economic ("public means" of provision), the corporeal ("the dyer's hand"), and the linguistic (as foregrounded here most obviously by the use of rhyme). The crisis the poem describes and responds to results from the first of these, the speaker's economic circumstances. The materiality of the body, by contrast, carries little weight—or, more precisely, the weight it carries is purely rhetorical, since the poem introduces this materiality not as a force to reckoned with but as a figure: "a novel image," as Isaac D'Israeli puts it in his popular study *The Literary Character*, with which the poet "illustrates [his] degradation" as he "pathetically laments [the] compulsion of his necessities which forced him to the trade of pleasing the public" as a playwright.[9] The fact that the poem refers to a body other than the speaker's reinforces this hierarchy, as it implies that the state of the speaker's own body is irrelevant to that of his "nature." At the same time, the speaker's lamented condition seems neither caused nor embodied by "that aspect of language that makes it a part of material reality," in William Keach's phrase;[10] on the contrary, the poem's meter, rhyme scheme, alliteration, and other poetic devices seem to evidence Shakespeare's mastery of this linguistic materiality. This mastery does not render the requested pity superfluous, as it might seem, but rather helps to justify its bestowal. The poem concludes by suggesting that the potential influence of economic circumstances on the writer's character as well as his work can be transcended, with the means of transcendence either affective ("pity") or themselves economic (if "pity" is read as a euphemism for "patronage"): "Pity me then, dear friend, and I assure ye, / Even that your pity is enough to cure me" (lines 13–14).

Different materialisms will have different things to say about the play of materialities in this poem. Consider, for example, the sleight of hand by which the sonnet seems to slight the hand: reference to the stained hand of the dyer elides the reliance of the "speaker" on his own (ink-stained?) hand in his capacity as a writer. One might argue that the speaker's inattention to his own hand helps to keep the focus where it belongs—not on the degree of "intellectual-cerebral elaboration," as opposed to "muscular-nervous effort," involved in his labor but rather on the "specific conditions" and "specific social relations" in which that work is performed.[11] Or, from a slightly different perspective, that through this elision Shakespeare avoids the "fatuous[ness]" and "intellectual dishonesty" that attend efforts to assimilate "the 'production' of texts" to "the experience of the resistance of matter in genuine manual labor."[12] Alternately,

Shakespeare's apparent desire to cover over the physicality of his own labor might be seen to reflect the contempt for manual labor characteristic of culture, along with an idealist refusal to acknowledge the extent to which his own nature is bodily.[13] The poem's reference to the dyer's body rather than the speaker's own also raises the possibility that the condition of "renewal" to which the speaker aspires may require the heightened embodiment of others.[14] Similarly, the very treatment of "(other people's) hands . . . as allegories or symbols" that the sonnet exemplifies may be associated with "the neutralization and distancing which bourgeois discourse about the social world requires and performs."[15]

Taking a different—but also avowedly "materialist"—tack, one might argue that the poem necessarily fails to model the state of transcendence to which the speaker aspires because "what he works in" is language itself. A public means which public meanings breeds, language "prevents individual humans from being able to present their thoughts as the inner contents of their bodies to others in apprehensible form . . . because [it] has a body of its own. If it didn't have a body . . . it wouldn't be perceptible or legible at all. Having a body, it, like material objects, has a perceptibility and opacity of its own that continually exceeds its representative function."[16] The mischief-making materiality of language (so ostentatiously on display in puns) thus leaves us wondering whether the "cure" the speaker envisions in the sonnet's last line ends his predicament or instead preserves it. Like the *pharmakon* of writing in Jacques Derrida's reading of *Phaedrus,* the would-be cure of the sonnet may "worsen the ill instead of remedy it."[17]

Then again, emphasizing still a different kind of materiality, one might argue that all of the preceding approaches reveal an idealizing tendency of their own insofar as they abstract the sonnet from its physical instantiation: not only do they ignore the possible contribution of the work's bibliographic codes to its meaning but they treat "the poem itself" as a stable, fixed entity, despite a textual history that creates uncertainties at the level of orthography, punctuation, and even wording (as in the bracketed "with" in the first line of the poem as quoted above, an emendation of the 1609 quarto edition's "wish"). From this perspective, the use of the dyer's hand as a figure for the poet's nature may be seen to obscure the contributions and corruptions that come from the actual hands of copyists, redactors, and printers.[18]

Or, refusing to be subdued to its syntax, does the vivid image of the dyer's hand instead bring to mind these additional, also stereotypically stained hands? The rhetorical work performed by this trope, in other words, may exceed its author's intentions in such a way as to call attention to—and, by the same stroke, to figure—the bibliographic limits of authorial control. Such a reading partly reconciles—or at the very least combines insights typically afforded by—ostensibly competing materialisms. Similarly, while the pun on "cure," noted above, can be read as suggesting that the threat of subdual stems from the nature of writing itself as what Shakespeare works in, it might also be read as calling into question the difference between reliance on the "public means" of the theater and on "pity"-cum-patronage—or, again, as suggesting a certain analogy between these two double binds.

This latter notion—of the analogous or even common nature of linguistic and economic subdual—comes to the fore in a rescripting of Shakespeare's sonnet by the Victorian era's preeminent writer on authorship, Thomas Carlyle:

> All [Shakespeare's] works seem, comparatively speaking, cursory, imperfect, written under cramping circumstances; giving only here and there a note of the full utterance of the man. . . . Alas, Shakspeare had to write for the Globe Playhouse: his great soul had to crush itself, as it could, into that and no other mould. It was with him, then, as it is with us all. No man works save under conditions. The sculptor cannot set his own free Thought before us; but his Thought as he could translate it into the stone that was given, with the tools that were given. *Disjecta membra* are all that we find of any Poet, or of any man.[19]

Here in "The Hero as Poet" the Globe Playhouse again stands as the primary obstacle to the full unfolding and expression of Shakespeare's individuality. Yet where Shakespeare emphasizes the economically driven, institutional nature of the constraints under which he operates, Carlyle identifies these constraints as more broadly social, or even ontological. For the later writer, that is, the Globe is ultimately a figure not for mere economic necessity but rather for a metaphysical condition. Thus, while Shakespeare proposes an alternative arrangement that will make possible his freedom and wholeness, Carlyle's revisionary account implies that no arrangement could be fully adequate to such a task; for Carlyle, the writer's nature is not almost subdued but always already subdued. Indeed, while Carlyle builds on Shakespeare's example by figuring the effect of "conditions" as a loss of bodily integrity, the body in question now seems as much that of the work as the man. The fallen state described by Carlyle, that is, extends to language, "the stone that [is] given" to writers.[20] Seemingly random sight rhymes that show up in one of Carlyle's sentences—"his great *soul* had to crush itself, as it *could,* into that and no other *mould*"—paradoxically confirm this argument, as they suggest that Carlyle's own attempt to translate thought into words has been corrupted or determined by the very "stoniness" of language that he laments.[21]

One might quarrel, of course, with the manner in which Carlyle seems to conflate economic, physical, and linguistic factors—just as one might quarrel with, say, Althusser's similar tendencies. But the point is that one would be quarreling *with* Carlyle. In other words, and as this passage from Carlyle suggests, nineteenth-century writers are deeply interested in the cluster of issues I have used Shakespeare's sonnet to raise, and are interested in them *as a cluster*—are interested, that is, in exploring the relations among what Carlyle himself might agree to call writing's multiple material conditions. As the passage from Carlyle further suggests, the very use some nineteenth-century writers make of Shakespeare's sonnet itself testifies to this interest: the dyer's hand not only serves as an indelible image of the indelibility of vocational demands but also regularly figures the imbrication of writing's materialities.

Some writers embrace sonnet 111 as an early expression of the Romantic or modern affirmation of creative autonomy, with this autonomy defined above all as freedom from or indifference to economic pressures. Isaac D'Israeli, cited above, uses the poem in this way: quoting the first seven lines of the sonnet (through the words "the dyer's hand"), he warns that "such is the fate of the author, who, in his variety of task-works, blue, yellow, and red, lives without ever having shown his own natural complexion."[22] Carlyle is hardly unique, however, in troping on Shakespeare's trope in ways that complicate this vision of autonomy and highlight the play of multiple materialities. Indeed, despite his famous injunction to "close thy Byron," Carlyle's dual emphasis on the inevitability of authorial subdual and the thingness of language recalls, even as it revises, Byron's own revision of Shakespeare's image in *Don Juan:* after stating that poets "are such liars, / And take all colours—like the hands of dyers," Byron continues, "But words are things, and a small drop of ink, / Falling like dew, upon a thought, produces / That which makes thousands, perhaps millions think."[23] Among the authors treated in this book, Charles Dickens and George Eliot as well as Carlyle rework this iconic image in revealing ways, as we shall see, with Dickens literalizing the figure in *Bleak House* and Eliot revaluing it in both *Romola* and *Daniel Deronda*. The nineteenth-century project of exploring and exploiting writing's several materialities ensures that the dyer's hand is constantly renewed.

Creative appropriations of the dyer's hand, I am suggesting, participate in and exemplify a larger nineteenth-century project of constellating writing's multiple materialities and positioning authors and their works in relation to them. I explore this project by reading the Victorian discourse on authorship and a series of novels from Thackeray's *History of Henry Esmond* to Eliot's *Daniel Deronda* as sustained, reflexive investigations into the meaning and mutual relevance of the physicality of the written or printed word, the exchange of texts for money, the workings and slippages of signification, and the corporealities of character, writer, and reader. The works I focus on do not limit their treatment of these issues to the thematic level, but instead seek to define and bring into play their own material elements; one might call these moments "self-referential," except that the identity and boundaries of the text "itself" are at stake here. To identify and illuminate such moments, the following chapters bring together a range of topics and materials typically treated separately or not at all by literary scholars, including typeface and advertisements bound with novel texts; theories of labor and international trade, arrangements for funding literary production, and begging letters; puns, orthography, and the referential claims of fiction; and the writing, speaking, desiring, suffering—even spontaneously combusting—human body.

Chapters 1 and 2 analyze two contemporaneous novels that in very different ways focus attention on the physical materiality of texts and propose ways of understanding this form of materiality in relation to others. I begin with *The History of Henry Esmond* (1852), asking not how the idiosyncratic physical format of *Esmond*'s first edition frames the novel but instead how the novel (that is, the linguistic text) frames the format. The novel's allegorization of its own passage into print, I argue, transforms both the contingencies of composition and publication and the slippages of signification into paradoxical signs of authorial control; at the same time, though, the novel historicizes the notions of authorship and fictionality that subtend this very question of control. The novelist's authority not over his or her own text but rather outside its ostensible bounds is at issue in *Bleak House* (1852–53), to which I turn next: focusing on the novel's disputed portrayal of spontaneous human combustion, I show that Dickens seeks to expand his sphere of expertise and influence by simultaneously foregrounding writing's presence in the physical world and demonstrating the textuality of that world itself. The stakes and efficacy of Dickens's legitimation strategy emerge most fully with the discovery of similar moves in both the competing discourse of organic chemistry and the advertisements bound with *Bleak House*'s original monthly parts.

Tracking a shift within nineteenth-century economic theory, my third chapter highlights the role of exchange relations as opposed to physical materiality in determining the nature and value of literary labor. I argue that the status of individual authors and of authorship as a profession rides not only or even primarily on authors' perceived relationship to the marketplace (as critics so often emphasize) but also on their perceived relationship to the antithesis of market exchange, begging. The much greater hostility toward this latter form of exchange determines the ultimate shape of such major attempts to imagine and institute forms of nonmarket support for authors as Carlyle's "The Hero as Man of Letters" (1841) and the 1851 founding of the Guild of Literature and Art by Dickens and associates. Continuing to read texts for what they have to say about their own material components and contexts— including what they have to say about the fraught distinction between "component" and "context"—I show that Edward Bulwer-Lytton's play *Not So Bad as We Seem* (1851), written and produced to raise money for the Guild, provides an allegory of the history of authorial remuneration, up to and proleptically including the failed model of the Guild itself.

Building on my argument for the importance of begging in the discourse of authorship, chapter 4 highlights the neglected discourse of begging-letter writing (the writing of letters asking for charity). I focus in particular on novelists' responses to the awkward questions this practice raises about the economic status of literary labor, the significance of writing's physical materiality, the ethics and aesthetics of sympathy, and the power of the written word. The most elaborate and imaginative of these responses, Wilkie Collins's *No Name* (1862), uses the figure of the fraudulent begging-letter writer to collapse distinctions beween bodies and texts even as it finds renewed significance in the *im*materiality of fictional characters. These issues—in particular, the relative nature and power of physical and textual presence—recur in *Daniel Deronda* (1876), which my final chapter reads as a pointed rewriting of Collins's novel. Like *No Name, Daniel Deronda* brings together questions of materiality, sympathy, and authority, but Eliot's novel goes beyond the earlier work to provide the era's most ambitious exploration of word, book, commodity, and body as potentially analogous sites of materiality/ideality. This exploration, I show, is illuminated by such related texts as a contemporaneous tract of political economy, the advertisements published with the novel's original monthly parts, and an unauthorized American sequel. Unlike the other works studied in this book, *Daniel Deronda* finally rejects its provisional alignment of materialities (and idealities) as a misleading category error. Even as it asserts the ultimate incommensurability of different modalities of materiality, however, Eliot's novel remains shaped by the question of their relationship.

As should be clear, this study takes seriously Dickens's complaint against critics who too quickly suppose that authors are "at great pains to conceal exactly what [they are] at great pains to suggest."[24] I want to conclude my introduction by stressing, though, that we should not mistake the frequent self-consciousness and explicitness of the Victorian engagement with writing's materialities for transparency or disinterestedness. On the contrary, the insistence on literature's material ingredients and entanglements has its reasons and effects, and these will be of primary concern in the following pages. We shall see that although authors and texts "suggest" in myriad ways their constitutive and contingent materialities, such suggestions are themselves loaded, even functioning at times as covert claims for the very detachment they seem to abjure. *Daniel Deronda*'s worldly acknowledgment of "the irony of earthly mixtures,"[25] for example, looks quite different when viewed through the lens of

George Gissing's *The Nether World,* where the use of irony itself stands as evidence of superiority to one's working-class milieu—as evidence, as Gissing's narrator puts it, that one's "nature was not subdued to what it worked in."[26] Similarly, my recognition of authorial agency and self-awareness should not be taken as a claim for absolute authorial sovereignty or self-knowledge: authors "suggest," as Dickens says, but they cannot control what their suggestions suggest, as Dickens discovers— nor, as many authors are quick to acknowledge, do they always know what suggests to them what to suggest. This book is accordingly a study of slippage as well as control, and of heteronomy as well as autonomy. In fact, it is a study of the historical contours and uses of these categories themselves.

I   Paratexts and Periwigs

The History of Henry Esmond and the History of the Author

A MILITARY OFFICER, riding a white horse and gloriously appareled in wig, blue sash, red coat, gold buttons, and gold trim, dominates the picture on the cover of the 1985 Penguin Classics edition of William Makepeace Thackeray's *History of Henry Esmond*. According to the credit line on the back cover, this illustration is "a detail from a Tapestry depicting the battle of Blenheim with Marlborough and his Staff, by courtesy of His Grace the Duke of Marlborough and the Marquess of Blandford." [1] At first glance, such an illustration seems entirely appropriate for the fictional memoir of "A Colonel in the Service of Her Majesty Queen Anne," as the work's full title specifies. Ironically, however, not only is Henry Esmond unconscious for most of the Battle of Blenheim, having been "knocked on the head . . . almost at the very commencement of [that] famous day" (279), but also he repeatedly complains that "the stately Muse of History . . . delights in describing the valour of heroes and the grandeur of conquest" while leaving out the "brutal, mean, and degrading" scenes that "form by far the greater part of the drama of war"—namely, "burning farms, wasted fields, shrieking women, slaughtered sons and fathers, and drunken soldiery, cursing and carousing in the midst of tears, terror and murder" (277). Furthermore, Esmond's depiction of Marlborough himself is notoriously hostile: while praising his skill as a soldier, the memoir depicts the great general as "the greatest traitor . . . history ever told of" (337). The illustration is thus misleading by virtue of both its provenance and its treatment of its subject matter— less a paratextual "threshold" of interpretation, in Gérard Genette's metaphor, than a barrier to understanding. [2]

The ironic mismatch of the Penguin edition's bibliographic and lin-

Jocasta.   69

the Second's time, thought the piece, though
not brilliant, had a very pretty moral.

Mr. Esmond dabbled in letters, and wrote a
deal of prose and verse at this time of leisure.
When displeased with the conduct of Miss
Beatrix, he would compose a satyre, in which
he relieved his mind. When smarting under
the faithlessness of women, he dashed off a copy
of verses, in which he held the whole sex up
to scorn. One day, in one of these moods,
he made a little joke, in which (swearing him
to secresy) he got his friend Dick Steele to
help him: and, composing a paper, he had it
printed exactly like Steele's paper, and by his
printer, and laid on his mistress's breakfast-
table the following:—

"Spectator.

"No. 341.   "*Tuesday, April* 1, 1712.
Mutato nomine de te Fabula narratur.—Horace.
Thyself the moral of the Fable see.—Creech.

"Jocasta is known as a woman of learning
and fashion, and as one of the most amiable
persons of this Court and country. She is at
home two mornings of the week, and all the
wits and a few of the beauties of London flock

Figure 1. Sample page of the first edition of The History of Henry Esmond. *(Courtesy of the Poetry Collection of The University Libraries, The State University of New York at Buffalo. Photograph by James Ulrich, University at Buffalo.)*

guistic texts or codes (to adopt Jerome McGann's terminology[3]) stands in sharp contrast to the famously felicitous relationship between these components of the first edition of *The History of Henry Esmond,* published by Smith, Elder in October 1852. This three-volume edition featured a number of striking departures from the bibliographic norms of the day, including unusually wide margins, heavy leading, and an old-fashioned typeface with, for example, a long *s* and a ligature connecting *c* and *t* (fig. 1).[4] Everyone who has commented on the format's idiosyncrasies agrees that they reproduce and thus allude to print practices of the preceding century, when Esmond's memoir was purportedly written, with the typeface in particular serving as "the visual equivalent of Thackeray's pastiche eighteenth-century prose."[5] A review in the *Examiner,* for example, simply pairs these features—"this book is printed in old type, and writ in the manner of the time"[6]—while the *United States Review* calls the combination a "double antiquation."[7] As reviewers, bibliographers, and the odd critic who takes notice of the format further agree, the primary, if not sole, purpose of this simulation is to enhance or extend—enhance by extending—the work's verisimilitude and aura of authenticity. "Infinite pains are taken to beguile us into the notion that we are reading a book written and printed upward of a century ago," comments the *Times*. "Mr. Thackeray has done his part in the matter, and the printers and publishers have done theirs."[8] The first edition's bibliographic features, like Thackeray's style, facilitate the readerly suspension of disbelief and reinforce the fiction that one is reading an eighteenth-century work.[9] Genette himself cites this edition as an exemplary case in which "the graphic realization is inseparable from the literary intention."[10]

Against this consensus, this chapter argues that the tension generated or embodied by the recent Penguin edition is already present in the first edition of *Henry Esmond*—or rather, potentially present and decidedly at issue, present as an issue. For if on one level the relationship between the linguistic and bibliographic texts of the first edition of *Henry Esmond* is transparent, on another it is impenetrable: while the format is presumably meant to signify that Esmond's memoir was not only written but also printed and published in the eighteenth century, it is impossible to determine at what point in the memoir's history these events would have occurred. Whereas the novel's sequel, *The Virginians,* goes so far as to specify that Esmond's funeral sermon was printed "at Mr. Franklin's press in Philadelphia,"[11] in the earlier work Henry Esmond, who addresses his memoirs to his grandsons, makes no mention of having his manuscript printed, let alone published. The clues provided by the editorial apparatus framing his narrative—a preface by his daughter written after his death (and dated 1778), along with footnotes added by his wife, daughter, and grandsons, as well as by Esmond himself[12]—are similarly inconclusive. For example, there is some attempt made to suggest that Rachel Esmond is introducing the very edition the Victorian reader is reading, as her mention in the first edition of the work's three "volumes" is changed (we do not know by whom) to mention of one volume in the one-volume edition of 1858; yet there is no graphic distinction made between footnotes added by Henry, his wife, and his daughter, on the one hand, and those added presumably after the work's printing by his grandsons, on the other. The memoir's implied material state is undeterminable.

Because Henry Esmond's memoir does not unequivocally purport to be an eighteenth-century book, the first edition's typeface can be read as connoting not only "*eighteenth-* (as opposed to nineteenth-) century book" but also "*book* (as opposed to manuscript)." By the same token, the ambiguity attending the memoir's fictive material status distinguishes the text as an abstract entity from any particular material manifestation. As a result, while the first edition's departures from bibliographic norms encourage us to attend to the bibliographic text and find it significant, the novel does not simply establish a relationship between linguistic and bibliographic text but instead raises the question of this relationship and invites readers to consider its significance. Rather than leave these readers to their own devices, moreover, the novel also finds ways to address this topic, as I will show. Thus, if "the graphic realization is inseparable from the literary intention" in the first edition of *The History of Henry Esmond,* as Genette claims, then this is so not in the sense he intends but rather because the work both puts into play and reflects on the relationship between graphic realizations and literary intentions, the physical materiality of texts and authorship.

What difference does a text's material manifestation make? There is striking unanimity regarding the difference it makes for *The History of Henry Esmond* in the recorded comments of three individuals who (like or unlike Rachel Esmond Warrington) had the rare experience of seeing the work first in manuscript and then in print: Thackeray himself; his daughter Anne Thackeray Ritchie, who served as his amanuensis for part of the writing of the novel; and Charlotte Brontë, who was sent the manuscript by George Smith (the publisher of *Henry Esmond* and her own novels). In letters written while the novel was making its way through the press, the author states, "I have got the first sheets of the memoirs of Colonel Esmond in my pocket—printed in a very nice type and looking very handsome,"[13] and "Esmond looks very stately and handsome in print, and, bore as he is, I think will do me credit."[14] Brontë and Ritchie share Thackeray's pleasure at the book's appearance and elaborate the notion of the typeface as costume hinted at in his comments: *Esmond* looks "very antique and distinguished in his Queen Anne's garb," Brontë writes to George Smith in one of the earliest recorded comments on the published novel; "the periwig, sword, lace, and ruffles are very well represented by the old *Spectator* type."[15] Similarly, in her introduction to the volume of the 1898 Biographical Edition of Thackeray's complete works containing *Henry Esmond,* Ritchie writes, "'Esmond' was the only book of my father's that was published in all the dignity of three volumes. It came out in periwig and embroidery, in beautiful type and handsome proportions."[16]

These comments suggest that the transformation from manuscript to printed page and then bound book makes manifest or even increases the novel's stature and authority; Thackeray himself goes so far as to say, "I like it better in print than in writing."[17] *Pace* Walter Benjamin, mechanical reproduction here seems to give the text an aura it otherwise lacks. Ritchie's statement in particular makes clear, moreover, that this novel's "dignity" or cultural distinction is enhanced not simply by virtue of its printing or publication but by the specific form its publication takes, namely, a three-volume edition. The use of this format takes on special significance in the context of Thackeray's career, since *Henry Esmond,* as Ritchie also notes, was his only novel published in this form rather than serially, in monthly numbers or a magazine. As such, it is the sole novel Thackeray wrote that did not begin publication before he finished writing it. Both implicitly and explicitly, this fact has long underwritten the novel's reputation as Thackeray's most carefully constructed work, a unique exception to his usual improvisatory, if not careless, practice.[18]

Yet while *Henry Esmond*'s mode of publication has played a key role in the establishment of the novel's author effect, it has done so in part because of Thackeray's own descriptions of his writing and publishing practices. Thackeray most fully cultivated the persona of the disaffected, lazy, even bored author later in his career, and publication of his judgment of *Esmond* as his most polished work occurred only after his death. Nonetheless, the reader coming to the newly published *History of Henry Esmond* after having read Thackeray's previous novel, *The History of Pendennis,* would have had ample reason to view the novel's three-volume format not merely as a generalized sign of cultural cachet but also as a specific indication that the novel will stand out from the author's preceding works for its coherence, consistency, and shapeliness. *Pendennis* was published in monthly parts from November 1848 to December 1850, with a three-month hiatus at the end of 1849 due to Thackeray's illness—the hiatus itself a dramatic indication of the novel's status as ongoing performance rather than self-contained, *finished* (in both senses) artifact. The novel earned immediate notoriety for its portrayal of authors as hacks, but equally important to the construction of Thackeray's authorial image was the novel's "Preface," which accompanied the final monthly number.[19] There Thackeray reflects on publication in monthly numbers, "this kind of composition" that involves "constant communication with the reader." He emphasizes the importance of honesty and intimacy over artistry, while acknowledging, "Many a slip of the pen and the printer, many a word spoken in haste, [the writer] sees and would recall as he looks over his volume." He goes on to state that "this book began with a very precise plan, which was entirely put aside," and claims that even on the last day of composition he was still changing his mind over how to end the novel: "Nay, up to nine o'clock this very morning, my poor friend, Colonel Altamont, was doomed to execution, and the author only relented when his victim was actually at the window."[20]

The History of Henry Esmond constitutes a clear departure from this representation of authorial practice. Initial publication of the work in its entirety shifts attention away from the temporality of composition to the spatiality of form, a spatiality whose shapeliness is embodied in turn by the three volumes of equal size into which the novel is divided. The very presence of "front matter," such as a table of contents, at the actual front of the novel (rather than at the end of the last monthly part) reinforces this emphasis on finished product over creative process, as does the shift from the authorial retrospection of the "Preface" to *Pendennis* to the represented retrospection of the "Preface" by Henry Esmond's daughter with which the later novel begins. The effect is one of heightened textual unity and autonomy, and therefore heightened authorial control. The very material form of the first edition thus promotes an understanding of the novel as free from the deforming (let alone determining) influence of material contingencies.

The first edition's departures from the bibliographic norm enhance the cultural work performed by the three-volume format itself in the context of Thackeray's career. Most obviously, by subsuming the book's materiality within the novel's representational project and thus within the realm of aesthetic intentionality, the first edition highlights the work's organic, autotelic nature. In addition, as Ritchie's yoking together of the novel's three-volume format and its antiquarian flourishes makes clear ("'Esmond' was the only book of my father's that was published in all the dignity of three volumes. It came out in periwig and embroidery . . . "), the very grandeur of the eighteenth-century practices replicated by the first edition reinscribes the prestige of the nineteenth-century format in which it is published. The book's specific departures from nineteenth-century bibliographic norms, including its heavy leading and wide margins as well as the antiquarian typeface, reinforce the qualities of spaciousness, luxury, and gentility that the "three-decker" connotes.[21] The typeface thus encodes both *Henry Esmond*'s status as a three-decker and the cultural status of the three-decker itself. "More than most writers of fiction," according to Walter Bagehot, Thackeray "felt the difficulty of abstracting his thoughts and imagination from near facts which *would* make themselves felt";[22] here, though, where the typeface makes readerly abstraction difficult, the near facts that make themselves felt are not the tawdry "accompaniments of an early literary life" that Bagehot has in mind but rather signs of authorial command and cultural distinction. Returning once more to Gérard Genette's contention, we might conclude then that if the first edition of *Henry Esmond* is a classic case "in which the graphic realization is inseparable from the literary intention," it is also a case in which the effect of a text fully determined by literary intentionality is created in part by that graphic realization.

A very different picture emerges, however, if instead of viewing the format through Brontë and Ritchie's eyes we view their comments through the lens provided by the novel. For the imagery they use recalls—perhaps is borrowed from—an episode late in the story, when Henry Esmond directs an elaborate plot to bring the Stuart Pretender to England in the last days of Queen Anne's reign, a plot that involves disguising the Pretender as Esmond's kinsman, Frank Castlewood. Laying the groundwork for this impersonation, Esmond buys a portrait of the Pretender by "the famous French painter Monsieur Rigaud," a portrait "whereof the head only was finished"; Esmond himself paints in Frank's uniform, "with a light-brown periwig, a cuirass under his coat, a blue ribbon, and a fall of Bruxelles lace" (450). The novel itself, in the Brontë-Ritchie reading, becomes a very similar picture: "The periwig, sword, lace, and ruffles are very well represented by the old *Spectator* type"; "it came out in periwig and embroidery." But Henry Esmond's story ends with his renunciation of the Jacobite cause served by the painting, and he begins his memoir with a call for "familiar rather than heroic" history, a preference he figures specifically as a rejection of the aggrandizing style of court painters such as Rigaud; the periwig, in particular, serves as the very emblem of this rejected style: "I wonder shall History ever pull off her periwig and cease to be court-ridden?" (45). Read the way Brontë and Ritchie read it, then, the format of the first edition—not unlike the cover of the modern Penguin edition—contradicts Henry Esmond's stated political beliefs and corresponding aesthetic ideals. Given how characteristically Thackerayan Esmond's antiheroic rhetoric is, we might well conclude that the monumentalizing format contradicts Thackeray's own project too.

On this account, then, rather than reinforcing the work of the linguistic text, the bibliographic text instead subverts it. Given the usual critical disregard of bibliographic texts, this outcome threatens to render the foregoing analysis self-defeating: if the material form of the first edition of *Henry Esmond* interferes with a proper understanding of the novel proper, then one might as well (continue to) ignore it. The apparent gap between the novel's design and the novelist's confirms us in our habitual indifference to a text's material manifestation. You can't judge a book by its cover. At best, rather than dismissing the bibliographic text as heteronomous, we might read it as a sign of heteronomy, of the inevitable limits or constraints on an author's ability to realize his or her vision.

Alternately, but with similarly dismissive results, one might argue that it is less the format of the first edition itself than the Brontë-Ritchie reading of it that brushes against the grain of the novel. After all, Brontë is a notoriously poor reader (or strong misreader) of Thackeray's work, and, given Ritchie's role as amanuensis, we might even suspect her of a sly show of ressentiment; is there not a hint of wickedness in this passage from her unpublished reminiscences: "I said to Papa that I thought he was very like Esmond and Papa said he thought he was perhaps only Esmond was a little bilious fellow"?[23] It is crucial to notice, however, that the potential subversiveness of Ritchie's introduction is uncannily anticipated within the novel: like the Biographical Edition of Thackeray's novel, Henry Esmond's memoir is prefaced by a seemingly dutiful introduction by the author's daughter, and, as a number of critics have shown, Rachel Esmond Warrington's preface subtly conflicts with the paternal narrative it presents. The preface, as Christina Crosby argues, is where "this extension of the novel's irony [to Esmond himself], of the work of unmasking, is most evident": "This fulsome preface is evidence of a family life disturbed by jealousy and repressed desires, the site of unsettling repetitions in which the daughter, named after her mother, comes 'to supply the place' quitted by Rachel when she dies, a family in which Esmond's grandsons are divided by 'fatal differences' in political allegiance, and Esmond himself is shown to be remote and unforgiving."[24] Insofar as it is subversive, then, Ritchie's introduction extends a pattern established within the novel; our very perception of Ritchie's account as subversive is promoted by the text she introduces. More strongly, we might say that Ritchie's contradictoriness seems scripted in advance by that which it would contradict. It is as if she is still taking her father's dictation.

Just as *Henry Esmond* anticipates and thereby subverts the subversiveness of Anne Thackeray Ritchie's reading of its format, so too does the novel neatly capture—and thereby complicate—the view of the material limits of authorial sovereignty her reading produces. For the very episode that provides the terms of the Brontë-Ritchie reading can also be read as an allegory of the novel's bruising passage into print—that is, an allegory of this passage as bruising: Rigaud creates a work of art that other hands "complete" by tricking out in a falsifying costume, and this fate, we might infer, is also Thackeray's. As an artist, Rigaud is a ready figure for the author; more important, though, while the narrative of artistic production Thackeray recounts is exceptional with regard to painting, this narrative better reflects the sociality of the process by which books are typically made (or novels are made into books). The use of a painter here instead of a writer promotes an understanding of this nonauthorial contribution as neither an organic component of the work's production nor an incidental act of reproduction that does not impinge upon the work's essential identity, but rather as an act of appropriation and arbitrary transformation.

Yet the very presence of this allegory changes the equation. For if the contingency of the bibliographic text is represented or encoded as such within the linguistic text, the bibliographic text thereby loses its contingency—or rather, its contingency loses its contingency. The allegorization of the contradiction between bibliographic and linguistic texts dissolves this contradiction, transforming it into a textual effect reflecting a higher-level consistency. By representing, however elliptically, the process by which he loses control over the form his work takes, Thackeray regains control, if not over the novel's materiality itself, then over the meaning of that materiality.[25] In other words, the unlikely fate of this decapitated portrait of a would-be sovereign allegorizes Thackeray's own loss of sovereignty, and thereby manages to transform the evidence of that loss into evidence of that sovereignty. Indeed, this paradoxical operation suggests an alternative reading of the Rigaud episode: rather than aligning Thackeray with Rigaud as someone whose work, once sold, is simultaneously completed and corrupted by others (let alone aligning him with the Pretender), we might instead identify Thackeray with Henry Esmond as someone who knowingly exploits the gap between his own contribution to a work and that work's (type)face.

Yet *The History of Henry Esmond* also makes available another, more transparent allegory of its own passage into print, one with different implications than the Rigaud-Esmond portrait. In this instance, Thackeray conjures a scenario in which the physical form of a work is fully determined by an author and intrinsic to its identity. Paradoxically, however, an episode that seems to demonstrate the extension of authorial dominion and affirm the significance of bibliographic texts ends up doing neither. Instead, the episode identifies a different and more fundamental threat to the authorial construction and control of meaning, a threat that emerges despite—and all the more visibly because of—Henry Esmond's success in achieving the bibliographic fidelity to which the first edition of Thackeray's novel ostensibly aspires. Again here, however, Thackeray seems to control, or at least control for, his own text's uncontrollability by representing this lack of control.

Book 3, chapter 3, "A Paper out of the 'Spectator,'" recounts "a little joke" Henry Esmond plays on his cousin Beatrix Esmond, who rejects Henry's persistent attempts to marry her and openly shops for a wealthy husband. Esmond, "smarting under the faithlessness of women," enlists the aid of "his friend Dick Steele," and, "composing a paper, he had it printed exactly like Steele's paper, and by his printer, and laid [it] on his mistress's breakfast-table" (388). Bearing the telltale epigraph,

Mutato nomine de te Fabula narratur.—Horace.
Thyself the moral of the Fable see.—Creech,

Esmond's imitation *Spectator* consists of two letters (388). The first, signed "Oedipus," seeks Mr. Spectator's help in identifying a fellow admirer of one "Jocasta," "a woman of learning and fashion" (388). Jocasta, the letter explains, has met a young gentleman in the country who "made a considerable impression upon her, and touched her heart for at least three-and-twenty minutes" (389). Unfortunately, however, when Jocasta again sees this man—who, we might note, "has a blue ribbon to his cane and sword, and wears his own hair"—she realizes that "she has forgotten his name," and no one else present knows it either (389). Explaining that "if balked in anything, [Jocasta] is sure to lose her health and temper; and we, her servants, suffer, as usual, during the angry fits of our Queen" (391), Oedipus pleads for Mr. Spectator's help. This letter is followed by one to Mr. Spectator from the gentleman in question, who recounts the same sequence of events from his perspective. Having been "greatly fascinated by a young lady of London," he writes, he becomes "entirely her slave" (392). Over time, however, the writer realizes "that this fair creature was but a heartless worldly jilt, playing with affections that she never meant to return, and, indeed, incapable of returning them" (392). Recounting her failed attempt to learn his name, he signs his letter "Cymon Wyldoats."

After reproducing this sham *Spectator* paper in its entirety, Henry Esmond immediately goes on to explain that "the above is a parable, whereof the writer will now expound the meaning" (393). Jocasta, of course, "was no other than Miss Esmond, Maid of Honour to her Majesty," who had told Henry "this little story of having met a gentleman, somewhere, and forgetting his name." "As for Cymon," Esmond goes on to explain, "he was intended to represent yours and her very humble servant, the writer of the apologue and of this story, which," he repeats, "we had printed on a 'Spectator' paper at Mr. Steele's office, exactly as those famous journals were printed, and which was laid on the table at breakfast in place of the real newspaper" (393). The material manifestation of the text thus appears here as an element over which the author exercises absolute control, and indeed an essential part of the work as conceived by its author. The very word *paper* captures this relationship, as Esmond uses it to refer to both text and object, even slipping from one meaning to the other within the space of the single sentence quoted above: "composing a paper, he had it printed exactly like Steele's paper" (388).

An obvious *mise-en-abyme,* this episode would seem to promote a similar understanding of the novel's own bibliographic text as a fulfillment of Thackeray's intentions, consistent with or even integral to the novel "itself." Yet Esmond's absolute control over the physicality of the sham *Spectator* and the material conditions of its production does not translate into control over the text's reception. Interpreting his own parable, Esmond explains that "this sham 'Spectator' was intended to convey to the young woman that she herself was a flirt, and that Cymon was a gentleman of honour and resolution, seeing all her faults, and determined to break the chains once and for ever" (393). Although, as Esmond intends, Beatrix recognizes herself in the story—"you have been telling my story to Mr. Steele—or stop—you have written the paper yourself to turn me into ridicule" (398)—the incident nonetheless does not mark a turn in their relationship: she does not change her ways, and he himself fails to live up to his resolution to "break the chains."[26] Nor, crucially, does Esmond exercise complete control over the meaning of his own text, or restrict it to the single meaning he assigns it. Crosby notes, for example, that "the appearance of Oedipus and Jocasta in *Esmond* has only a mocking relation to the ancient drama, and none at all to the 'Oedipal' plot of the text."[27] Going further, and with an eye on the "de te Fabula" epigraph, J. Hillis Miller argues that we can read both the *Spectator* paper and the novel as a whole "one way according to Henry's intention and in another way according to its application to Henry himself"; on this second reading, Miller suggests, "Henry is indeed an Oedipus, but an Oedipus manqué whose eyes remain blinded."[28]

Even as the episode underscores Henry's control over the material form his text takes, then, that text continues to represent breakdowns in communication and proliferations of meaning. The sham *Spectator* paper itself identifies an alternative, seemingly more fundamental, cause for these events: not the materiality of the book but that of language itself, and the concomitant gap between sign or signifier and that which is signified. For not only does Esmond's very appropriation of *Oedipus Rex* highlight the arbitrariness with which one set of terms can be mapped onto another, but the paper itself focuses explicitly on the nature and effects of such arbitrariness. Thus, in her effort to learn the name she has forgotten, Jocasta artfully turns the conversation to spelling: "'We were discoursing,' says she, 'about spelling of names and words when you came. Why should we say goold and write gold, and call china chayny, and Cavendish Candish, and Cholmondeley Chumley? If we call Pulteney Poltney, why shouldn't we call poultry pultry—and—'" (391). In its graphic representation of the phonetic representation of both phoneme and grapheme, this passage manages both to render and to blur the difference between the two forms of linguistic materiality. This demonstration of the arbitrary materiality of the signifier is met in turn with an example of the polysemy made possible by this materiality, as the unsuitable suitor responds by stating, "'Such an enchantress as your ladyship . . . is mistress of all sorts of spells.'" Pun intended, of course, but the speaker's control over the disparate meanings of his words does not overshadow the larger prospect of uncontrollability or dissemination his double meaning makes visible. This prospect is reinforced here, even as it is resisted, by the immediate identification of the pun as purloined: "But this was Dr. Swift's pun, and we all knew it" (391).[29] The sham *Spectator* paper ends, finally, by crossing the matter of spelling with that of punning: frustrating Jocasta's efforts to learn his name, the unidentified man replies to the question "And how do you spell your name?" by saying only, *"I spell my name with the y"* (391). He ends his own letter to Mr. Spectator, however, by signing his name as "Cymon Wyldoats" and adding a postscript: "You know my real name, Mr. Spectator, in which there is no such a letter as *hupsilon*. But if the lady, whom I have called Saccharissa, wonders that I appear no more at the tea-tables, she is hereby respectfully informed the reason *y*" (393).

Not only are letters figural, as the antique typeface insistently reminds the reader, but they are figurative too. This slippage between the figurative and the literal is further emphasized later in the same chapter. Expatiating on his faithful devotion to Beatrix, Henry comments, "How long was it that Jacob served an apprenticeship for Rachel?" to which Beatrix responds, "For mamma! . . . Is it mamma your honour wants, and that I should have the happiness of calling you papa?" (401). Esmond responds in turn as if Beatrix had mistaken his figuration of her as the biblical Rachel for a literal reference to Beatrix's mother, also named Rachel: "I spoke of a Rachel that a shepherd courted five thousand years ago. . . . And my meaning was. . . ." The reader realizes, however, that Beatrix is offering an alternative, and ultimately more accurate, reading of his figure, or rather is vexing the distinction between literal and figurative, as

ultimately it is "mamma your honour wants," and gets. Indeed, the proliferation of Rachels in the novel combines with the slipperiness of such
distinctions to heighten the intimations of incest that readers have found
so discomforting: first, Esmond marries a Rachel who is not literally his
mother but who has said, "I am your mother, you are my son" (292);
then, when she dies, their daughter Rachel, on her own account, comes
to "supply the place which [her mother] was quitting" (39).

How much of Esmond's narrative, and of Thackeray's novel, then, is
at the mercy of the play of the signifier? To what extent does such play
generate meaning, to what extent undo it? "Cymon," for example, is
clearly a rough anagram of "Esmond," and as such signals the former's
status as a stand-in for the latter. But whence "Wyldoats"? Within the
sham *Spectator* paper, this name is ironic at best, since the pseudonymous
Cymon is left "wondering at the light-heartedness of the town-people,
who forget and make friends so easily"; his closing, "your constant
reader," is precise (393). The constant reader of the novel, however, will
recognize the phrase "wild oats" as one that has appeared several times,
including in the two chapters immediately preceding this one, the third
of book 3. On both of those occasions, however, the phrase is used by
Beatrix's brother Frank, who first tells Henry that "for the next three
years, . . . I'll sow my wild oats" before settling down (361), and soon
thereafter writes to tell Henry of his marriage: "The young scapegrace,
being one-and-twenty years old, and being anxious to sow his 'wild
otes,' as he wrote, had married" (370). Esmond's intentional misspelling
of the phrase recalls this transcribed misspelling, which Esmond himself
is careful to highlight—but to what end? The allusion does not create
meaning, and in fact rebuffs efforts to be found significant.

This is no isolated incident. For example, another of the novel's several references to spelling, and to bad spelling in particular, works similarly: commenting on a letter he has received from the Dowager Vis-
countess Castlewood, Esmond observes that "spelling was not an article
of general commodity in the world then, and my Lord Marlborough's
letters can show that he, for one, had but a little share of this part of
grammar" (220–21). This aside reflects Esmond's enmity toward Marlborough, yet the military commander plays no role in this chapter of the
novel. His sudden, gratuitous appearance here—occurring as it does in
a passage that already focuses attention on language—therefore seems

prompted less by psychological considerations than by the polysemy of the word *general.* If the novel can be read as suggesting that its ironies, contradictions, and inconsistencies are the result of the material conditions of publication, then it also offers reason to believe that they are the result of textuality, or the materiality of the signifier.[30]

The History of Henry Esmond, I have argued, makes available two competing understandings of the source of its own ironies and inconsistencies, indeed of the ways in which meaning is both constituted and corrupted: the material conditions of authorship and the materiality of language—in brief, history and textuality.[31] My discussion of the novel's allegorization of these processes has not failed to plunge us, if by an unfamiliar route, into a familiar thicket in *Esmond* criticism: To what extent does Thackeray intend the meanings and apparent breakdowns in meaning I have identified, and to what extent do they escape his control? Similarly, to what extent do the novel's ironies come at Henry Esmond's expense rather than Thackeray's? At this late date, such concerns may seem passé, thanks to the ascendancy of posthumanist discourses of materiality; as Michel Foucault famously put it in "What Is an Author?": "No longer the tiresome repetitions: 'Who is the real author?' 'Have we proof of his authenticity and originality?' 'What has he revealed of his most profound self in his language?'"[32] But whether or not reports of the death of the author have been greatly exaggerated[33]—whether or not, that is, we are still interested in answering specific questions about authorial intention, authority, or personality—we are more interested than ever in the history of such questions and the beliefs that underwrite them; the death of the author implies his or her birth. *Henry Esmond* not only rewards this interest but in fact shares it. In other words, not only does *Henry Esmond* insistently float or prompt the kinds of questions about the nature of authorship that critics now tend to historicize rather than address, but it too treats these questions historically. While the novel may therefore be said to "choose" history over textuality, it does not grant priority to the material conditions of authorship over the materiality of language. Instead, it charts the history of interest in both these categories.

The first point to be made here is one that I take to be relatively uncontroversial: the kinds of questions we have been asking of *The History of Henry Esmond* have a history, and this history is largely that of print culture. As Elizabeth Eisenstein asks rhetorically, in a sentence that has achieved the dissemination she herself identifies as one of the distinctive features of the culture made possible by print technology, "Until it became possible to distinguish between composing a poem and reciting one, or writing a book and copying one; until books could be classified by something other than incipits; how could modern games of books and authors be played?"[34] The very identification of a text as an abstract entity distinct from its material manifestation derives from print, or is at least given currency by it, since, as Catherine Gallagher argues, "the potential for seemingly infinite reproduction obviated the possibility of equating the text with any, or for that matter all, of its instantiations."[35] Moreover, this distinction between abstract text and physical embodiment is crucial to the notion of literary property that underwrites copyright law, which, as Mark Rose has demonstrated, is central to our understanding of authorship: "The distinguishing characteristic of the modern author . . . is proprietorship; the author is conceived as the originator and therefore the owner of a special kind of commodity, the work."[36] According to Rose, this notion of copyright, and thus of authorship, underwrites the pre–poststructuralist "concern for the integrity of the individual work as an aesthetic artifact" and commitment "to establishing what an author *really* wrote (as if there were always a single theoretically determinable literary object)."[37] While focusing more on the effects of print technology itself, Walter J. Ong argues similarly that print increases the possibility and importance of "conscious control" on the part of the writer, who "finds his written words accessible for reconsideration, revision, and other manipulation until they are finally released"; print itself, then, has the effect we associated earlier with the three-decker, because it encourages a conception of the work "as a self-contained, discrete unit, defined by closure."[38]

Going further, Ong credits the kind of unstable irony we have found in *Esmond* to print as well, since "the typographic distances between writer and reader" radically expand "the possibilities of ironic indirection."[39] Print may also facilitate attention to and a conception of the materiality of language, insofar as "typography makes words out of pre-existing objects (types) as one makes houses out of bricks."[40] More generally, the kind of meticulous close reading that can identify a novel's subtle patterns and echoes and show *Henry Esmond* in particular to be, as Elaine Scarry puts it, "a tissue of small, almost imperceptible contradictions" (107), is consistent with and even promoted by the very logic of print technology. Thackeray himself hints at this linkage in a letter to his publisher: "I beg pardon about Esmond. The blunders are only such as a P[roof]reader will see."[41]

The kinds of questions we have been posing about *Henry Esmond* are thus characteristic of print culture. This point is worth making here, because Thackeray's narrative takes place at a crucial historical moment in the emergence of this culture from an earlier, oral-scribal one. As a number of scholars have argued, a dominant print culture, and in particular the modern literary system it underwrites, takes shape only once "a certain level of production and consumption of printed materials [has been] attained," and this level was reached in the eighteenth century.[42] The Statute of Anne (8 Anne c. 19), England's first copyright law, and as such a crucial watershed in Rose's account, was enacted in 1710. By the middle of the century, as Alvin Kernan argues, "an older system of polite or courtly letters—primarily oral, aristocratic, amateur, authoritarian, court-centered—was swept away . . . and gradually replaced by a new print-based, market-centered, democratic literary system in which the major conceptions and values of literature were, while not strictly determined by print ways, still indirectly in accordance with the actualities of the print situation."[43] *The History of Henry Esmond, Esq., A Colonel in the Service of Her Majesty Queen Anne* is therefore set during a transitional, formative period, when the groundwork for the modern literary system was being laid but this system was not yet fully in place.

Even the novel's interest in the materiality of language, or rather its representation of such interest, is as specifically situated historically as, say, its representation of Jacobite plots. Reversing our earlier emphasis, for example, we might note that even as Esmond's comment that "spelling was not an article of general commodity in the world then" (220) jumps its metonymic rails to generate an attack on Marlborough, it also makes a valid historical claim. The standardization of orthography is tied to the spread of printing and the eighteenth-century rise of the dictionary, and the specific spelling variant the *Spectator* paper highlights, the use of *i* vs. *y*, is one that persisted into the eighteenth century.[44] In a more precise act of historicization, the novel's sham *Spectator* is dated only a month before Swift's "Proposal for Correcting, Improving, and Ascertaining the English Language," which called for the establishment of an Academy with authority to regulate matters of spelling, grammar, and the like. Swift—who, as we have seen, is cited in the sham *Spectator* paper for his pun on "spells"—might as well have been referring to Esmond's Jocasta when he complains of "a foolish Opinion, advanced of late Years, that we ought to spell exactly as we speak."[45] (Punning itself, for that matter, is a subject the actual *Spectator* takes up on more than one occasion.[46])

Henry Esmond is thus located at a critical moment in the historical transition from scribal to print culture, a moment when modern notions of authorship and literary property were being formulated, when the marketplace was beginning to replace patronage as the dominant system of literary production, when the distinction between abstract text and material manifestation strongly emerged, and when the significance of various forms of linguistic materiality was a topic of debate. But the novel is not simply located at this juncture: rather, it explicitly locates itself there. Perhaps the key marker of the novel's literary-historical self-consciousness is its treatment of Joseph Addison. Thus, I argued earlier that the indeterminate material status of the memoirs Rachel Esmond Warrington introduces—are they handwritten? printed? published?—raises the question of the significance of these very distinctions. Within the novel, we might further notice, these distinctions are foregrounded and linked to the subject of authorship: not only does Henry Esmond produce the sham *Spectator* paper, for example, but he then refuses to allow its publication, despite Steele's willingness to "let the piece pass into his journal and go to posterity as one of his own lucubrations" (397–98). Similarly, Esmond writes a comedy, *The Faithful Fool*, which is performed for three nights and published, but "his name was never put to the piece," "only nine copies were sold," and he "had the whole impression burned one day in a rage," although "the prompter's copy lieth in my walnut escritoire" (387–88). What is particularly telling, though, is that on both these occasions when Esmond discusses his own literary production, he goes on to praise Joseph Addison's work at the expense of his own: "Esmond had tried to imitate as well as he could Mr. Steele's manner (as for the other author of the *Spectator,* his prose style I think is altogether inimitable)" (397); Addison "was bringing out his own play of

'Cato' at the time, the blaze of which quite extinguished Esmond's far-thing candle" (387). Esmond clearly sees himself as writing in the Age of Addison—and this age, the novel makes clear, is a transitional one.

In Addison's most sustained appearance in the novel, his writing of the poem *The Campaign* serves to exemplify a vanishing model of literary production. Governed by a different aesthetic from Esmond's (or indeed Thackeray's), this poem reflects and promotes a different conception of authorial investment and intention, differences that are in turn bound up (pun intended) with the material manifestation of the author's work and its mode of circulation. Thus, book 2, chapter 11, "The Famous Mr. Joseph Addison," shows an impoverished Addison at work in 1704 on his poem about the Battle of Blenheim, a poem he is writing to curry favor with the Whig government; as Addison himself explains to his friend Henry Esmond, he has been "engaged as a poetical gazetteer" (295). Esmond, who participated in the battle (as noted earlier), complains, "You hew out of your polished verses a stately image of smiling victory; I tell you 'tis an uncouth, distorted, savage idol; hideous, bloody, and barbarous. . . . You great poets should show it as it is—ugly and horrible, not beautiful and serene. Oh, sir, had you made the campaign, believe me, you never would have sung it so" (297). In response, Addison does not dispute that his writing of *The Campaign* depends upon his not having made the campaign, but instead suggests that the nature of his muse renders this lack of personal experience and emotional involvement an advantage: "It hath been, time out of mind, part of the poet's profession to celebrate the actions of heroes in verse, and to sing the deeds which you men of war perform. I must follow the rules of my art, and the composition of such a strain as this must be harmonious and majestic, not familiar, or too near the vulgar truth" (298). The poem is not a reflection of its writer's personality. In addition, while the writer's control, understood as his command of his materials, is important here, such command does not reflect a greater autonomy, such as the determination of subject matter and approach. Thackeray explicitly depicts this regime as one in which printing and publication are of secondary importance, at best. Thus, we see Addison interrupted by a "gentleman of the Court" who exclaims, "Trust me with the papers—I'll defend them with my life. Let me read them over to my Lord Treasurer," and then "seize[s] the manuscript pages" (300). "Within a month after this day," Esmond recalls,

"Mr. Addison's ticket had come up a prodigious prize in the lottery of life. All the town was in an uproar of admiration of his poem, the 'Campaign,' which Dick Steele was spouting at every coffeehouse in Whitehall and Covent Garden, [and] the party in power provided for the meritorious poet" (302). "Mr. Addison got the appointment of Commissioner of Excise" before his poem is even published (302).

The novel hints at a contrast between Addison's poetic practice here and the authorial practice soon to emerge in the *Spectator:* not only does the *Spectator* circulate in print form in a nascent literary marketplace— and its status as a printed text is of course highlighted by Esmond's imitation—but also, as that imitation again suggests, it is typically less directly political, and focuses on the everyday rather than the heroic or extraordinary.[47] To be sure, Esmond specifically claims to be copying the style of Steele, not Addison, but this is precisely because he finds the latter's "prose style . . . altogether inimitable" (397). Given the attention the narrative has paid to the writing of *The Campaign,* we might read the emphasis of this statement as falling on Addison's *prose* style, as opposed to his earlier verse style, which does not aspire to inimitability, because it does not derive its value from the imprint of the author's unique personality.

Esmond's own writing is intensely personal in both motivation and content: "When displeased with the conduct of Miss Beatrix, he would compose a satire, in which he relieved his mind. When smarting under the faithlessness of women, he dashed off a copy of verses, in which he held the whole sex up to scorn" (388). This is the state of mind in which he writes the sham *Spectator* paper, and his play, *The Faithful Fool,* fits the same pattern: "All this comedy was full of bitter satiric strokes against a certain young lady. The plot of the piece was quite a new one. A young woman was represented with a great number of suitors, selecting a pert fribble of a peer, in place of the hero . . . , who persisted in admiring her" (388). Nonetheless, the relationship of author to text in Esmond's depicted writings is not yet the emergent one in which, as Rose describes it, a work is seen as "the objectification of a writer's self," "a representation in which the originality of the work, and consequently its value, becomes dependent on the individuality of its author."[48] Esmond's liminality is marked most obviously by his deep ambivalence toward publication: as we have seen, he publishes his play but then buys up and destroys all the copies, he prints but does not publish his *Spectator* paper, and he expresses no intention to publish his autobiography.

More subtly, Esmond's liminality is also reflected by the nature of his characters. For the eighteenth-century change in the material conditions of literary production is accompanied by both a change in the perceived materiality of the literary work itself (which now comes to seem fundamentally immaterial) and a change in the materiality of the literary referent. According to Rose, the eighteenth century sees the development of a conception of literature and authorship whereby "the commodity that changed hands when a bookseller purchased a manuscript or when a reader purchased a book was as much personality as ink and paper," a personality which is either that of the author or of the fictional characters populating the new genre of the novel.[49] Rose does not explore the relationship between these two sources or loci of personality, which hardly seem equivalent. As Catherine Gallagher explains, however, the existence of the latter personality—that is, the fictional character— provides evidence of the inventiveness of the former, the author: stressing the difference between "stories [that] claimed to be about somebody" and "the stories of people who never actually lived," or "nobody's story," Gallagher argues that "the fictionality of the novel . . . simultaneously, if somewhat paradoxically, allowed both the author and the reader to be 'acquisitive without impertinence.' That the story was nobody's made it entirely the author's; that it was nobody's also left it open to the reader's sentimental appropriation."[50] Unlike the modern author-proprietor, however, Henry Esmond's stories are not entirely his own: his claim for the originality of his play's plot is presumably ironic, but even if it is not, the characters in both the play and the *Spectator* paper are not quite fictional. Nor, for that matter, are they historical—that is, both real and historically important—like those of Addison's *Campaign:* rather, Esmond's characters are transparent representations of specific individuals. Not only, that is, are the characters based on these actual individuals but they refer to them as well. As such, they embody a premodern version of literary interest and value.

With the writing of his memoirs, however, Esmond produces a text that does derive its value from the personality of its author. Within the narrative itself, Esmond's attempt to influence Beatrix by writing and printing the *Spectator* paper seems designed to move between fictional and referential registers, or, more specifically, to move ("backwards," historically speaking) from the former to the latter. For this hoax to have its full effect on Beatrix, in other words, she must first identify *with* the character portrayed before identifying herself *as* that woman. Indeed, even as Beatrix is at first being taken in, she herself seems to want the text to be more novelistic: "How stupid your friend Mr. Steele becomes! . . . Will he never have done with . . . Jocastas and Lindamiras? Why does he not call women Nelly and Betty, as their godfathers and godmothers did for them in their baptism?" (398). The degree of sympathetic identification she nonetheless does achieve works to enhance her mortification when, arriving at the phrase "Spell my name with a y," she realizes she is reading "my story" (354).[51] At the same time, although she continues to read, "her face rather flushed," it is not clear whether she in fact reaches the end before switching to musing over the possible motivation of the presumed author, Steele, for telling the story—motivation Beatrix locates in his stormy relationship with his wife: "Whenever I see an enormous compliment to a woman . . . I always feel sure that the Captain and his better half have fallen out over-night, and that he has been brought home tipsy" (398).

If Beatrix starts out being "acquisitive without impertinence," then, she winds up being impertinently inquisitive. As such, is Beatrix still reading like a novel reader? To read the *Spectator* paper as referring to actual people and actual events is to read as a scandal reader; to read it as a story about nobody in particular would be to read as a novel reader; but what kind of reader seeks to locate authorial motivation in specific events in the author's life? What kind of text is neither a point-by-point or individual-by-individual translation of real people and events nor the pure product of the author's inventiveness? One set of answers to these questions is surely the Thackerayan reader and the Thackerayan novel: "If the secret history of books could be written," runs the well-known passage in *Pendennis,* "and the author's private thoughts and meanings noted down alongside of his story, how many insipid volumes would become interesting, and dull tales excite the reader! Many a bitter smile passed over Pen's face as he read his novel, and recalled the time and feelings which gave it birth" (432). Thackeray conceives of others' novels as well as his own as on some level autobiographical—"Mother, you must allow me to introduce you to Jane Eyre," he said, much to Charlotte Brontë's mortification[52]—and he encourages his readers to do the same. While it is in a letter to his mother that he calls Esmond "a handsome likeness of an ugly son of yours"[53] (a likeness, as we have seen, that Anne Thackeray Ritchie also notes), an anonymous reader of the novel might find similar food for thought in the joint departure of author and protagonist for the United States: Esmond's emigration to Virginia is announced at the beginning of his daughter's preface and narrated in the novel's final paragraph, while Thackeray's dedication to Lord Ashburton states, "My volume will reach you when the Author is on his voyage to . . . America" (36).

This sort of teasing invitation to identify author with protagonist *on some level* is perhaps typical of the novel as a genre. For Thackeray, though, the tug of the referential on the fictional seems unusually strong, and we might identify this tug as part and parcel of the same nostalgia for—or, more neutrally, identification with—the early days of print culture that the novel depicts and that is embodied by the first edition's resistance to the conceptual separation of text from embodiment. Along with its antiquarian format, the first edition of *Henry Esmond* even features an explicitly allegorical (that is, referential) passage of the sort characteristic not of fiction but of scandal. The ostensible topic of this episode, moreover, is the authorship of a *Tatler* paper. As in Esmond's *Spectator* paper, however, and as is appropriate for the early eighteenth century, the matter of getting a name right here is less a question of proprietorship than of propriety. At issue in this passage is the authorship of the *Tatler* paper featuring the line "to love her is a liberal education" (351). The mistaken belief has arisen that "that paper was Mr. Congreve's," because, as its real author, Richard Steele, says, "Tom Boxer said so in his *Observator.* But Tom's oracle is often making blunders" (537). Justifying her husband's hostility, Mrs. Steele says that when his "last comedy came out, Mr. Boxer took no notice of it—you know he is Mr. Congreve's man, and won't ever give a word to the other house," whereupon Steele himself asserts that "Mr. Congreve has wit enough of his own. . . . No one ever heard me grudge him or any other man his share" (538). As Gordon Ray has explained, this passage stems from a mistake made by John Forster when reviewing Thackeray's lectures entitled *The English Humourists of the Eighteenth Century* in the *Examiner:* thus, Tom Boxer is Forster, Steele is Thackeray, and Congreve is Dickens.[54] Rendering curiously irrelevant the promiscuous intermingling of fictional and historical characters that has long bothered critics of the novel, this passage uses both as markers for actual, mid-nineteenth-century individuals, and at least momentarily transforms a historical novel into a scandalous allegory.

Thackeray removed this passage from the 1858 edition of the novel, also the first English edition not to feature the antique typeface.[55] Together, these changes suggest that we can read the novel's publication history as embodying the history of publication itself, as from one edition to the next *Henry Esmond* detaches itself as a text from its material instantiation and ephemeral, specific referentiality. Returning one last time to the Rigaud/Esmond portrait, we can see that this narrative too is anticipated within the novel. For if we accept the Ritchie-Brontë reading of the original format, then the change from that format to a standard one corresponds to the movement from the portrait Henry Esmond helps paint to the anti-aggrandizing theory of portraiture he comes to embrace. Within the novel, this movement reflects the eventual shift in Esmond's political loyalties from Tory to Whig, since his introductory (that is, retrospective) attack on court painting links this style to the doctrine of divine-right monarchy, with Louis XIV and Charles II the examples he provides.

More strikingly, Esmond's political progress is not only signaled by this change in aesthetic ideals but is also accompanied by, even enacted through, the exchange of one model of textual-material relations for another. When he renounces the Jacobite cause, Esmond burns the documents that establish his right to the Stuart-bestowed title of Viscount, and he renounces this title precisely by burning the documents: "'These are my titles . . . and this is what I do with them: here go Baptism and Marriage, and here the Marquisate and the August Sign-Manual, with which your predecessor was pleased to honour our race.' And as Esmond spoke he set the papers burning in the brazier" (507). In place of an identity constructed and guaranteed by specific pieces of paper, he chooses the identity he carves out for himself and memorializes in his memoir— a text, as we have seen, that is transmitted in an indeterminate material form. The novel ends, then, with a transition from texts that cannot be separated from their material instantiation to a text so distinct from its materiality that this materiality cannot be specified, and Thackeray couples this transition with one from a sovereign-authorized identity to a self-authorized one, the latter characterized by ostensibly sovereign authorship. The climax of Henry Esmond's political narrative thus constitutes a virtual allegory of the emergence of the modern literary system.

In a final twist, however, even as the first edition of *The History of Henry Esmond* forecasts its own obsolescence, a ghostly trace of this edition lingers on in all later ones, thanks to the incomplete effacement of the privately allegorical Tom Boxer. Although Thackeray removed the main, coded passage about Boxer/Forster, Steele/Thackeray, and Congreve/Dickens from the 1858 edition of *Henry Esmond,* he neglected to omit a further, now inexplicable reference—or rather, a reference explicable only by reference to the earlier edition—to poor Dick Steele "weeping about the treachery of Tom Boxer" (353). This omitted omission is typically considered a sign of neglect on the author's part, a trace of the artistic treachery of Thackeray; or at best, given the lack of evidence "that Thackeray even saw proofs of the cheap edition,"[56] a sign of his text's corruption by the material conditions of publication— another sign, as the famous image in *Pendennis* has it, that "Pegasus trots in harness, over the stony pavement" (380). However, we might also see this trace of the trace of John Forster as one final sign of the incompleteness of Thackeray's capitulation to the normatively abstract texts and fictional referents of print culture.

Indeed, even as Thackeray removed the body of his coded attack on Forster from the 1858 edition of the novel, he inserted a new, more heavily coded one into the sequel to *Henry Esmond, The Virginians,* which was coming out in monthly numbers at the time. In the 1850 "dignity of literature" dispute, Forster wrote disparagingly that "Mr. Thackeray is continually doing himself wrong by a *tone of persiflage* which is seldom in perfect good taste" (emphasis added);[57] in his review of *Henry Esmond,* Forster had also found fault with that novel on a number of grounds and described Beatrix, in particular, as "a being perfectly impossible."[58] It is with these comments in mind that we should read—because it is evidently with these comments in mind that Thackeray wrote—a passage in *The Virginians:* speaking to one of Henry Esmond's grandsons, who has been paying compliments "to a rich young soap-boiler's daughter," the former Beatrix Esmond, now an aging baroness, remarks, "You court her with infinite wit and esprit, my dear, . . . but she does not understand half you say, and the other half, I think, frightens her. This *ton de persiflage* is very well in our society, but you must be sparing of it, my dear nephew, amongst these *roturiers* [commoners]."[59] Given this sly poke by Thackeray, we might choose to see the preserved reference to Tom Boxer in *Henry Esmond* as a sign of the author's continued loyalty to scandalous as opposed to fictional referentiality, and, more generally, to a premodern model of authorship and letters.

Or we might instead choose to reconsider our labeling of certain strategies and preoccupations as "premodern." For while the forms taken by Thackeray's incomplete capitulation to the pressures and norms of abstraction, immateriality, and fictionality are distinctive, his resistance is not. Thackeray's simultaneous activation and exploration of the potential meaningfulness of writing's multifaceted materiality is by no means exceptional in Victorian fiction, but rather is one of its defining features. This is true even or especially of the work of the novelist whom we have seen Thackeray allegorically identify as the leader of "the other house" (538), and never more so than in the "house" Dickens was building when Thackeray wrote those words: *Bleak House,* to which we now turn.

Reading Matter in *Bleak House* and
the "Bleak House Advertiser"

No Victorian novelist devotes more attention to the physical materiality of writing and signs than does Charles Dickens. From the "multifarious documents" of the first sentence of *The Pickwick Papers* (not to mention that work's title) to the "add[ing of] one thick line to the score" with a "bit of chalk" in the last completed sentence of *The Mystery of Edwin Drood,* Dickens's novels are filled with references to the presence, creation, appearance, physical features, and sheer tangibility of marked, written, printed, and inscribed surfaces and objects.[1] Pip may confidently report that "my first fancies regarding what [my parents] were like, were *unreasonably* derived from their tombstones" (emphasis added)—"The shape of the letters on my father's, gave me an odd idea that he was a square, stout, dark man, with curly black hair"—but Dickens's enduring fascination with such "odd idea[s]" suggests that he does not find them so odd after all: again and again his novels explore the potential significance of writing's physical materiality, asking just what can be "reasonably" derived from "the shape of . . . letters."[2]

Within Dickens's oeuvre, the most varied and sustained engagement with these questions occurs in *Bleak House,* not least but not only through that novel's famous depiction of Chancery as an institution dedicated to the production and proliferation of documents. In *Bleak House,* the process Jean-Joseph Goux calls "the indifferentiation of matter"[3] is constantly and multifariously halted, sidetracked, and called into question, as both of the narrators and numerous characters frequently note or discuss the appearance, physical form, or sheer materiality of documents and other surfaces on which there is writing, from "the dust" to a "tarnished brass plate," "tissue-paper" to chalked walls, "a stained discoloured paper, which was much singed upon the outside, and a little burnt at the edges" to "immense masses of papers of all shapes and no shapes," a "wilderness of desk bespattered with a rain of ink" to "an immense desert of law-hand and parchment," "the entanglement of real estate in meshes of sheep-skin, in the average ratio of about a dozen of sheep to an acre of land" to "a bit of the printed description of [the] house at Chesney Wold" used as "the wadding of the pistol with which the deceased Mr. Tulkinghorn was shot."[4] There is reference in the novel to the handwriting or writing activity of no fewer than twenty named characters. In short, *Bleak House* is less "a document about the interpretation of documents," as J. Hillis Miller argued in a groundbreaking essay, than it is a document about the materiality of documents.[5]

Or rather: a document about the materiality of documents and the interpretation of that materiality. For the foregrounded materiality of writing in *Bleak House* does not always or even typically block access to meaning, as one might expect, but on the contrary often proves legible and meaningful. It therefore cannot be viewed solely as an emblem of the deferrals of interpretation that the Chancery system generates and profits from, although at times it plays that role too.[6] Handwriting, in particular, acquires immense importance in the novel, as at various moments it comes to indicate the gender, moral character, physical and psychological condition, or identity of a writer. Most tellingly, the novel relies on attention to the "shape of letters" to set in motion its scandal plot, as Lady Dedlock recognizes the hand in which an otherwise inconsequential legal document has been copied as that of her lover Hawdon (whom she thought dead). The very improbability of this scenario—"What fate pursued [Dickens] that he could not, in all the resources of his brain, hit upon a device for such a simple end more convincing than this?" complained George Gissing[7]—attests to the importance of the pattern it typifies.

How might we account for this emphasis on the meaningful materiality of writing? If we take the novel's practice as a model for our own and attend to the physical manifestation of *Bleak House* as its first readers would have encountered it, one answer immediately presents itself: the "fate" that "pursued" Dickens was simply his alertness to the signs of his times. *Bleak House*'s engagement with the physical materiality of writing may well be the most intensive of any Victorian novel, but even a rapid survey of its original monthly numbers shows that this engagement reflects widespread cultural practices. Like other Dickens novels published in parts, each monthly number of *Bleak House* included advertisements printed before and after the novel text, and these advertisements are as filled with the products and paraphernalia of writing as is the novel itself.[8] There are, of course, advertisements for books of all kinds—more ads for books, in fact, than anything else. In addition to these advertisements, though, as well as those for such goods as waterproof overcoats, "parasols made of China crepe," bedsteads, tea and coffee, "Ne Plus Ultra Needles," water-purifying filters, cough lozenges, milk of magnesia, and "the gentleman's real head of hair, or invisible peruke," one finds numerous advertisements for stationers, printing presses, inks (including "Encre à la Violette, the ladies' writing ink" and "Waterlows' Instantaneous Communicative Ink"), and handwriting lessons (from "Mr. Carstairs, Son of the inventor of the celebrated System of Writing") (fig. 2).[9] An interest in the information to be gleaned from the specific appearance of writing emerges both in an advertisement for handwriting analysis (by "Mr. Warren," who "continues with great success to delineate the Character of Individuals from their Handwriting"[10]) and in ads for several miscellaneous products that admonish the reader/buyer to attend not only to a label's precise wording but also to the color of its ink for indications of the product's authenticity:

> N.B. Be sure to ask for "Sir James Murray's Preparation," and to see that his name is stamped on each label *in green ink,* as follows:—"James Murray, Physician to the Lord Lieutenant."

> CAUTION: A. R. and Sons have complaints repeatedly from parties who have materially suffered from the use of spurious imitations [of a hair dye]; and to frustrate to some extent such impositions, they here add a small copy in outline of their genuine label . . . on which will be seen the names and addresses of the Proprietors in full (these are in red ink on the label), any deviation from which will always prove a spurious article.[11]

Pace Pip, then, both *Bleak House* and the "Bleak House Advertiser" suggest that much can be "reasonably derived" from the appearance of writing.

Dickens himself suffered from the publication of pirated issues and

MUDIE'S SELECT LIBRARY
is removed from No. 28, Upper King-street, Bloomsbury, to
510, NEW OXFORD-STREET, AND 20, MUSEUM-STREET.

AN ample supply is provided at this Library of all the principal New Works as they appear. The preference is given to works of History, Biography, Religion, Philosophy, and Travel. The *best* works of Fiction are also freely added.
Single Subscription one guinea per annum. First Class Country Subscription two guineas and upwards, according to the number of volumes required. Literary Institutions and Book Societies supplied on liberal terms.
The Addenda for 1850—1 is now ready, and will be sent in answer to all applications inclosing 12 stamps.
CHARLES EDWARD MUDIE, 510, New Oxford-st.

CHARACTER FROM HAND WRITING.

MR. WARREN, of 9, Great College-street, Westminster, continues with great success to *delineate the Character of Individuals from their Handwriting.*—All persons desirous of testing his art are invited to forward a specimen of their ordinary writing, together with 13 postage-stamps, and a mention of their sex and age, to the above address.

THE TOILET OF BEAUTY furnishes innumerable proofs of the high estimation in which GOWLAND'S LOTION is held by the most distinguished possessors of brilliant complexions. This elegant preparation comprehends the preservation of the complexion both from the effects of cutaneous malady and the operation of variable temperature, by refreshing its delicacy and sustaining the brightest tints with which beauty is adorned. 'Robert Shaw, London," is in white letters on the Government stamp of the genuine. Prices, 2s. 9d. and 5s. 6d.; quarts, 8s. 6d.

WRITING RAPIDLY IMPROVED.

MR. CARSTAIRS (Son of the inventor of the celebrated System of Writing), continues to give LESSONS to LADIES and GENTLEMEN of all ages, in his highly improved method, which will impart a command and fluency of the hand and pen seldom, if ever, equalled, in every size and variety of penmanship, even to the worst writer, in the shortest possible time. Arithmetic and Book-keeping taught practically.—PROSPECTUSES of terms, &c., may be had at his establishment, 81, LOMBARD-STREET, CITY.

SIR JAMES MURRAY'S FLUID MAGNESIA.

PREPARED under the immediate care of the Inventor, and established for upwards of thirty years, by the PROFESSION, for removing BILE, ACIDITIES, and INDIGESTION, restoring APPETITE, preserving a moderate state of the bowels, and dissolving uric acid in GRAVEL and GOUT; also as an easy remedy for SEA SICKNESS, and for the febrile affection incident to childhood it is invaluable.—On the value of Magnesia as a remedial agent it is unnecessary to enlarge; but the Fluid Preparation of Sir James Murray is now the most valued by the profession as it entirely avoids the possibility of those dangerous concretions usually resulting from the use of the article in powder.
Sold by the sole consignee, Mr. WILLIAM BAILEY, of Wolverhampton; and by all wholesale and retail Druggists and Medicine Agents throughout the British Empire, in bottles, 1s., 2s.6d., 3s.6d., 5s.6d., 11s., and 21s. each.
☞ The Acidulated Syrup, in Bottles 2s. each.
N.B.—Be sure to ask for "Sir James Murray's Preparation," and to see that his name is stamped on each label *in green ink*, as follows :—" James Murray, Physician to the Lord Lieutenant."

Figure 2. Advertisements in the "Bleak House Advertiser" (no. 1, March 1852). (Courtesy of the Poetry Collection of the University Libraries, The State University of New York at Buffalo. Photograph by James Ulrich, University at Buffalo.)

"spurious imitations" of his works, so perhaps it is no wonder that his novels model the skills needed by the discriminating consumer. A closer look at both *Bleak House* and the "Bleak House Advertiser" reveals, though, that more is at stake in the novel's insistent attention to the physical materiality of writing. Whereas in *Henry Esmond,* as we saw in the last chapter, the foregrounded physical materiality of the printed text raised questions concerning the text's linguistic and economic materiality, *Bleak House* stresses instead the relationship between the physical materiality of writing and that of the human body. The novel insistently links these materialities, I will argue, to demonstrate their shared ontological status and primacy. This common status is called upon to author-ize—even as this primacy renders urgent—the efforts of a writer such as Dickens to describe and analyze the workings of the body in particular and the natural world in general.

Like *Henry Esmond's* unconventional format, then, *Bleak House's* insistence on writing's physical materiality engages the question of novelistic authority. *Bleak House* replaces *Esmond's* diachronic orientation, how-

ever, with a synchronic one: at issue is not the history of authorial authority over texts or the novelist's own such authority as viewed through
the lens of this history, but rather the relative authority of different contemporary discourses and different kinds of experts. The publication for-
mats of the two novels reflect this divergence, insofar as the antiquarian
trappings of *Henry Esmond* point back in time, whereas the sandwiching
of Dickens's text between numerous pages of advertisements (including
several for *Henry Esmond,* which was published in the middle of *Bleak
House*'s nineteen-month run) bespeaks cultural simultaneity and conti-
guity.[12] It is in the "Bleak House Advertiser" rather than *Bleak House* per
se, moreover, that Dickens's legitimation strategy—which can seem ec-
centric or even misguided—will find its appropriate context, and indeed
its vindication.

Lady Dedlock's fateful recognition of her lover's handwriting, noted
above, adumbrates *Bleak House*'s alignment of the materialities of writing
and the human body. When the lawyer Tulkinghorn begins to read a legal document to Sir Leicester and Lady Dedlock, the notoriously com-
posed and detached lady "carelessly and scornfully abstracts her attention" (16). When the document catches her eye nonetheless and she
realizes who its writer is, she is overcome by what she calls a faintness
"like the faintness of death" (16). The recognition of the handwriting
thus reminds Lady Dedlock of her experience of forbidden physical passion and results in an experience of vulnerable embodiedness. Heightened consciousness of writing's materiality leads to a threatened loss of
all consciousness and corresponding reduction to the sheer materiality of
a corpse.

  The role of writing's materiality in this incident may seem fortuitous:
surely it is what Lady Dedlock learns, not how she learns it, that determines her traumatic reaction. Yet *Bleak House* quickly confirms and elab-
orates this link between the noticed or unnoticed materiality of writing,
on the one hand, and that of persons, on the other, through its depiction
of the "telescopic philanthrop[ist]" Mrs. Jellyby and her downtrodden
daughter and amanuensis, Caddy. Their relationship reifies the dynamic
of Lady Dedlock's transformation, with each firmly occupying one of
the poles between which Lady Dedlock moves: Lady Dedlock's act of
"abstract[ing] her attention" from a document becomes the habitually

"abstracted air" (296) of a mother who constantly dictates but never puts pen to paper, while the accentuated physicality of Lady Dedlock's swoon becomes the "inky condition" (57) of a daughter who "can't do anything hardly, except write" (44). Mrs. Jellyby's refusal to engage directly with writing's materiality typifies her detachment from and disregard of her immediate material surroundings, starting with her own body and those around her, while Caddy's inkiness both causes and reveals her "nature" to be, in the Shakespearean image discussed in my introduction, "subdued / To what it works in, like the dyer's hand"—lines quoted by Dickens himself in the novel's preface to introduce the novel's exploration of professional deformation or, more broadly, the shaping influence of one's livelihood on one's personality or identity.[13]

Unlike Shakespeare's sonnet, however, which shows no interest in the dyer's nature, in Dickens's portrayal of Caddy the damaged person is the one whose hand is stained. Caddy eventually frees herself from her "state of ink" (38) by marrying, but her own child virtually embodies her erstwhile markedly somatic and somatically marked state: the baby is born "deaf and dumb" (768), with, as Esther remarks, "curious little dark veins in its face, and curious dark marks under its eyes, like faint remembrances of poor Caddy's inky days" (599). Mother and daughter (and granddaughter) thus occupy what Elaine Scarry, in her reading of the capitalist/worker relationship according to Marx, calls "disparate levels of embodiment," with the former achieving "bodily evaporation" at the expense of the latter's "bodily magnification";[14] here, though, it is specifically one's degree of engagement or contact with the physical materiality of writing that enacts and reveals this quasi-ontological condition.

Esther's reading of Caddy's daughter's mysterious marks suggests further that just as texts have a materiality akin to that of bodies in *Bleak House,* so too do bodies have a legibility akin to that of texts. Indeed, bodies are as much inscribed as they are magnified in Dickens's novel: to become more emphatically material here is to become more textual. The life-threatening illness that leaves Esther scarred confirms this pattern, even though Esther herself offers it as a counterexample, an instance of materiality blocking meaning. That is, Esther claims to take solace in the fact that her scarring protects her mother—who refuses to publicly acknowledge their relationship—by obscuring their resemblance: "I was so changed as that I never could disgrace her by any trace of likeness; as that nobody could ever now look at me, and look at her, and remotely think of any near tie between us" (449). Yet if the marking of Esther's face ostensibly renders her relationship to her mother illegible, the novel encourages us to read the marks themselves as evidence of Esther's mother's denial of their relationship. Caddy's daughter again helps make this dynamic visible: Caddy names her daughter Esther, and the marks on "little Esther's" face thus recall not only her mother's past but also her namesake's scars; just as Esther Turveydrop's marks symbolize maternal neglect and mistreatment, a mother's "bodily evaporation" at the expense of her daughter's "bodily magnification" or inscription, so too do Esther Summerson's.[15]

Esther's illness in fact follows upon, and thus seems to be precipitated by, a scene in which Lady Dedlock's own participation in this dynamic of embodiment and disembodiment is figured in especially vivid terms. When the law clerk Guppy discloses that Esther Summerson's real name is Esther Hawdon—and thus, though Guppy himself does not know all this, that Lady Dedlock's child with Captain Hawdon did not die in infancy, as she believed—Lady Dedlock exclaims, "My God!" and then "sits before him . . . for the moment, dead" (362). As in the earlier scene, a reminder of her affair with Captain Hawdon restores Lady Dedlock to a sense of embodiedness even as it reduces her to a corpselike state. A remarkable simile captures the effect of her quick return to consciousness and composure: "Her exclamation and her dead condition seem to have passed away like the features of those long-preserved dead bodies sometimes opened up in tombs, which, struck by the air like lightning, vanish in a breath" (362). Such is Lady Dedlock's usual detachment that its reestablishment is figured not as the body's reanimation but rather its dematerialization. As with the Jellybys, however, this dematerialization leads to the intensified bodiliness of another, as Esther almost immediately thereafter contracts her life-threatening illness. Lady Dedlock symbolically causes Esther's scars to appear, and she causes them to appear symbolic.

By emphasizing the materiality of texts and the semiotics of bodies, *Bleak House* reduces the difference between texts and bodies. This chiastic convergence has ethical implications, as the mother-daughter relationships reveal. As the novel also stresses, however, this convergence has epistemological implications as well, in that it aligns the activities and protocols of interpreting and manipulating linguistic signs, on the one hand, with those of observing and interpreting corporeal phenomena, on the other. This alignment suggests in turn that expertise and thus authority in one of these spheres extends to both, and this question of authority comes to the fore in the fallout (in both senses of the word) from the event that occurs immediately after Esther falls ill. This event—which follows from Guppy's interview with Lady Dedlock and is strongly foreshadowed by that scene's image of a dissolving body—is the death of the character in the novel who attends most closely to the shapes of letters, and who is unable or unwilling to derive anything from these shapes, especially on anyone else's say-so: Mr. Krook, the illiterate owner of a rag-and-bottle shop and literary history's most notorious victim of spontaneous human combustion.

Krook's initial appearance in the novel comes in the chapter following that which introduces the Jellyby household and quickly produces an even more extreme version of the split between absorption in and separation from the materiality of documents on display there; indeed, Krook's house provides a virtually allegorical schematization of degrees of attention (or inattention) to the materiality of writing. The lodger on the top floor, Miss Flite, exhibits complete blindness to the materiality of writing: she puts great stock in the importance of what she calls her "documents," but these turn out to be "principally . . . paper matches and dry lavender" (7). By contrast, Krook himself, who lives in his shop on the ground floor, shares Miss Flite's belief in the power of written words but acts on this belief by focusing intensely on their tangible and visible form: he amasses large numbers of (actual) documents and spends his time tracing letters on his walls in a vain attempt to teach himself to read and write—refusing "to be taught by someone" on the grounds that "they might teach me wrong!" (181). On the middle floor, in between these two, lives the pseudonymous Nemo, who barely and briefly subsists by copying legal documents. It seems plausible to annex this no-man's-land to the realm of either his upstairs or his downstairs neighbor: on the one hand, copying seems to confirm the fundamentally abstract identity of a text and thus drain its particular material instantiation of significance; on the other hand, the fact that the words Nemo copies seem to mean little to anyone foregrounds the mere physical existence of the document as an object. In fact, though, the occupant of the building's middle story comes to be identified with neither of the extremes represented by his neighbors—the extremes, as it were, of indecipherably krooked shapes and untethered flites of fancy—but instead helps to stake out the novel's middle ground of meaningful materiality, for it is Nemo's handwriting that Lady Dedlock recognizes.

Thus established as a privileged site for the consideration of writing's materiality, Krook's house becomes a privileged site for the consideration of the body's as well. This occurs first when Nemo's corpse is discovered, and then, more dramatically, when Krook dies halfway through the novel, in the final chapter of the tenth number. The novel's third-person narrative returns to Krook's house at this point in the story, immediately after Lady Dedlock's encounter with Guppy (interrupted by the two chapters of Esther's narrative that culminate in Esther's falling ill), because Guppy himself returns there to try to secure the bundle of Nemo/Hawdon's letters he has promised to bring to Lady Dedlock. Krook—whose hoarding ways lead his neighbors to think of him as a parodic version of Chancery's Lord Chancellor—has possession of these letters, having taken them when Nemo died, and he is to show the letters at midnight to Guppy's friend Tony Weevle (aka Jobling), whom Guppy has installed in Nemo's former room. Yet instead of poring over the traces Krook makes and those he has agreed to produce, the characters spend their time puzzling over the mysterious and disgusting traces to which, as they will eventually learn, he has been reduced:

> "Tony," says Mr. Guppy, uncrossing and recrossing his legs; "how do you suppose he spelt out that name of Hawdon?"
>
> "He never spelt it out. . . . He imitated it—evidently from the direction of a letter; and asked me what it meant."
>
> "Tony," says Mr. Guppy. . . "should you say that the original was a man's writing or a woman's?"
>
> "A woman's. Fifty to one a lady's—slopes a good deal, and the end of the letter 'n,' long and hasty."
>
> Mr. Guppy . . . happens to look at his coat-sleeve. It takes his attention. He stares at it, aghast.
>
> "Why, Tony, what on earth is going on in this house to-night?

> Is there a chimney on fire? . . . See how the soot's falling. See here, on my arm? See again, on the table here! Con-found the stuff, it won't blow off—smears, like black fat!" (398)

Although Krook's demise recalls the figure of the dead body "struck by the air like lightning," he most definitely does not "vanish," and the "stuff" into which he is transformed—"a dark greasy coating," "a smouldering suffocating vapour," "a thick, yellow liquor," "a stagnant, sickening oil"[16]—clings to the narrative as it clings to Guppy's sleeve. As we see in this passage, this "stuff" repeatedly or ostensibly draws the characters' attention away from their discussion of Krook and the letters they are trying to obtain from him.

Yet physical remains and documents are linked, not opposed, on what the narrator describes as "a fine steaming night to turn the slaughter-houses, the unwholesome trades, the sewerage, bad water, and burial-grounds to account, and give the Registrar of Deaths some extra business" (393). The shapes of letters and the nauseous matter permeating the air are equally clues to be analyzed, traces loaded with information. Appropriately, then, the subject of the characters' plotting and the apparent distraction from it soon come together, or rather are shown to be one and the same, as Tony Weevle returns from a visit to Krook's room to report that "'the burning smell is there—and the soot is there, and the oil is there—and he is *not* there!'" (402). The two descend together, and Tony points to the spot where, earlier in the evening, "'I left him turning the letters over in his stand, standing just where that crumbled black thing is upon the floor'" (402). At this point, the narrative voice merges with that of the characters as they come to make sense of what they observe:

> Here is a small burnt patch of flooring; here is the tinder from a little bundle of burnt paper, but not so light as usual, seeming to be steeped in something; and here is—is it the cinder of a small charred and broken log of wood sprinkled with white ashes, or is it coal? O Horror, he IS here! and this from which we run away, striking out the light and overturning one another into the street, is all that *represents* him. (403; emphasis added)

The pointed use of the word *represents*—as opposed to, say, *remains of*—at this climactic moment highlights the convergence here of empirical

observation and semiotic decoding, inference and interpretation: in discovering Krook's remains, the characters discover what is at once a clue
and a sign.

While Guppy and Weevle flee from their gruesome discovery, the
narrator continues with the work of interpretation to establish what the
"all that represents him" represents in turn. The cause and meaning of
Krook's death are established simultaneously:

> The Lord Chancellor of that Court, true to his title in his last act,
> has died the death of all Lord Chancellors in all Courts, and of all
> authorities in all places and under all names soever, where false
> pretences are made, and where injustice is done. Call the death by
> any name Your Highness will, attribute it to whom you will, or
> say it might have been prevented how you will, it is the same death
> eternally—inborn, inbred, engendered in the corrupted humours
> of the vicious body itself, and that only—Spontaneous Combus-
> tion, and none other of all the deaths that can be died. (403)

The emphasis shifts here from how little is left of the shopkeeper to how
much his demise encompasses—from *all* as token of paucity and lack to
all as indicator of plenitude or universality. Yet the synecdochic logic remains the same as that which permitted the identification of Krook's
charred bone. Just as the "little bundle of burnt paper" on the floor is
steeped in Krook's residue, so too is this residue steeped in allegorical
meaning.

This convergence of bodies and signs and of the concomitant forms of
scrutiny they require is reinforced by the scene in the novel that most
closely resembles Krook's death. Just as "The Appointed Time" builds to
the discovery of Krook's remains, chapter 48, "Closing In," builds to the
discovery of Tulkinghorn's corpse. Like Krook, the lawyer Tulkinghorn
has been closely identified with Chancery, and both characters are
known for secrecy and accumulative, hoarding ways (the lawyer collecting secrets and the shopkeeper miscellaneous objects, including documents). Both die sudden, violent deaths on the brink of committing the
uncharacteristic act of revealing a secret: Krook, by showing documents
to Tony Weevle, and Tulkinghorn, by exposing Lady Dedlock to her
husband. In fact, it is the *same* secret that each almost exposes, that of
Lady Dedlock's affair with Captain Hawdon (alias Nemo). Most strik-

ingly, just as the discovery of Krook's remains prompts an allegorical turn
on the part of the narrator, the discovery of Tulkinghorn's corpse produces a turn to Allegory—that is, to the allegorical painting on Tulkinghorn's ceiling, which is sometimes referred to as "the Roman," sometimes simply as "Allegory":

> A little after the coming of day, come people to clean the rooms.
> And either the Roman has some new meaning in him, not ex-
> pressed before, or the foremost of them goes wild; for, looking up
> at his outstretched hand, and looking down at what is below it,
> that person shrieks and flies. The others, looking in as the first one
> looked, shriek and fly too, and there is an alarm in the street.
>
> What does it mean? . . . All eyes look up at the Roman, and all
> voices murmur, "If he could only tell what he saw!" (585)

The Roman now points "with far greater significance than he had in
Mr. Tulkinghorn's time, and with a deadly meaning," because, the chapter ends by revealing, "Mr. Tulkinghorn's time is over for evermore; and
the Roman pointed at the murderous hand uplifted against his life, and
pointed helplessly at him, from night to morning lying face downward
on the floor, shot through the heart" (586–87).

This scene not only literalizes the earlier scene's turn to allegory but
also, like the earlier scene, narrows the gap between the figurative and
the physical. To shift one's gaze from Tulkinghorn to the Roman is to
turn from one body to another, equally uncommunicative one. More
precisely, of course, it is to shift one's gaze from a body to a representation of a body, yet the very way Dickens reminds the reader of this distinction serves to minimize it: he alludes to the representation's materiality, noting that the Roman "shall point, so long as dust and damp and
spiders spare him" (585). Again, that is, *Bleak House* calls attention to the
material aspects of a sign, and treats this materiality as comparable if not
identical to that of the human body. This conflationary tendency reaches
a logical, if humorous, extreme in Dickens's assertion that "I shall not
abandon the facts [concerning the existence of spontaneous human com-
bustion] until there shall have been a considerable Spontaneous Combustion of the testimony on which human occurrences are usually received" (4). This flourish comes in the novel's preface (first published

with the final monthly number), a text Dickens distinguishes from "the body of this book" (3).

Dickens defends the existence of spontaneous human combustion in the novel's preface because his depiction of that event was challenged immediately upon its publication. I revisit this well-known dispute here because it most fully reveals the cultural stakes of *Bleak House*'s treatment of bodies and texts. In what are probably the first, and certainly the most influential, published comments on Krook's notorious death, the critic George Henry Lewes used his weekly "Literature" column in the 11 December 1852 issue of the *Leader* to protest that spontaneous human combustion is "absolutely impossible, according to all known laws of combustion, and to the constitution of the human body."[17] Declaring that spontaneous combustion is "only admissible [in literature] as a metaphor," Lewes accuses Dickens of "overstepping the limits of Fiction" and "giving currency to a vulgar error."[18] At stake in the dispute as Lewes frames it, then, is not simply the possibility of spontaneous human combustion but also the authority to pronounce upon such a possibility: the novelist, Lewes suggests, "has doubtless picked up the idea among the curiosities of his reading from some credulous adherent to the old hypothesis," but belief in the possibility of spontaneous combustion constitutes "a scientific error, which we doubt if [Dickens] can find one organic chemist of any authority to countenance now." Thus, whereas Krook's fear that someone will teach him reading and writing "wrong" seems paranoid, Lewes suggests that Dickens has received just such a miseducation about the physical world—a miseducation that puts Dickens in the position Krook himself comes to represent, that of an authority making false pretenses.

Dickens himself ensured the prominence of Lewes's objection by immediately incorporating it into the novel's next number, where the narrator mocks "authorities (of course the wisest) [who] hold with indignation that the deceased had no business to die in the alleged manner" (413). While Dickens was always quick to defend his novels' verisimilitude, he did not often incorporate such defenses (or challenges) into the novel in this way; in addition, as we have seen, he returned to the issue in the preface, and also responded privately in letters to Lewes, with whom he was acquainted. This insistence on confronting Lewes tends to baffle or disappoint later critics, virtually all of whom dismiss Lewes's complaint as pedantic and superfluous, especially in light of the explicit symbolic meaning the narrator assigns Krook's death; at worst, Dickens is seen as guilty of a slightly embarrassing but ultimately insignificant error, a harmlessly wild surmise akin to Keats's famous confusion of Balboa and Cortez.[19] Yet this critical consensus relies upon the very distinctions between bodies and signs and between empirical and symbolic explanations that *Bleak House* persistently calls into question. In other words, the logic of the novel virtually demands that Dickens respond as he does.

Turning this last point around, we might better say that Dickens's desire to respond to criticism such as Lewes's dictates the logic of the novel: that is, *Bleak House* weakens the distinctions it weakens in order to legitimize Dickens's interventions in questions of public policy having to do with physical matter, in particular the disposal of dead bodies and the circulation of noxious substances.[20] The reference to "the sewerage, bad water, and burial-grounds" cited earlier explicitly locates the spontaneous-combustion episode in this context. Indeed, whatever its exotic overtones, spontaneous combustion itself is also a version—albeit a vastly accelerated one—of the corruption, decomposition, and dissemination that the narrator angrily describes as originating in the "pestiferous and obscene" graveyard in which Nemo is buried, "whence malignant diseases are communicated to the bodies of our dear brothers and sisters who have not departed" (137). Even the comic gruesomeness of the spontaneous-combustion scene recalls an article advocating the reform of burial practices that Dickens ran in *Household Words* two years earlier: "Science . . . has shocked and disgusted people by showing them that they are drinking their dead neighbours. It has taught parties resident in large cities that the very air they live in reeks with human remains, which steam up from graves; and which, of course, they are continually breathing. . . . It reveals how the whole of the defunct party is got rid of, and turned into gases, liquids, and mould."[21]

Nemo's unsanitary graveyard itself, it is worth recalling, is identified in the novel as the actual or "scientific" source of Esther's illness (with the streetsweep Jo and then Esther's maid Charley as the infectious intermediaries). Again, though, even as *Bleak House* claims authority to describe the disease's literal as well as symbolic cause, the novel minimizes the difference between these registers: the image of a crumbling corpse to describe Lady Dedlock's recovery of her self-possession echoes the earlier, physical decomposition of her lover's corpse—"sow him in corruption, to be raised in corruption" (137)—and in both cases the trail leads back from Esther to one of her parents. Insofar as motherhood is typically associated with literality and paternity with the symbolic, the chiastic crossing of these associations here further blurs the difference between realms, again facilitating Dickens's effort to extend his authority over both.[22]

Dickens's eagerness in *Bleak House* to assert and defend his authority to describe the fate of bodies is anticipated revealingly in a review article he wrote a few years earlier. In 1848, the novelist reviewed Robert Hunt's *The Poetry of Science, or, Studies of the Physical Phenomena of Nature,* a book designed, in Dickens's words, "to show that the facts of science are at least as full of poetry, as the most poetical fancies ever founded on an imperfect observation and a distant suspicion of them."[23] In language anticipating the "Preliminary Word" in the first issue of *Household Words,* Dickens praises the book for aiming to show "that Science, truly expounding Nature, can, like Nature herself, restore in some new form whatever she destroys; that, instead of binding us, as some would have it, in stern utilitarian chains, when she has freed us from a harmless superstition, she offers to our contemplation something better and more beautiful, something which, rightly considered, is more elevating to the soul, nobler and more stimulating to the soaring fancy" (135–36).[24]

Yet if Dickens is capable of lauding such a project and even claiming it as his own, he is also attuned to its status or use as a threat to his own authority as an imaginative writer. "The sublime creations of the most gifted bard," writes Hunt, "cannot rival the beauty of . . . the highest and truest poetry of science."[25] The topic Dickens finds most interesting when approached from Hunt's perspective is also the one he is most eager to defend from Hunt's exclusivist gestures; not surprisingly, this topic is bodily decomposition. Dickens excerpts the following passage from Hunt's chapter entitled "Chemical Phenomena," labeling it "How We 'Come Like Shadows, So Depart'":

A Plant exposed to the action of natural or artificial decomposition passes into air, leaving but a few grains of solid matter behind it. An animal, in like manner, is gradually resolved into "thin air." Muscle, and blood, and bones having undergone the change, are found to have escaped as gases, "leaving only a pinch of dust," which belongs to the more stable mineral world. Our dependency on the atmosphere is therefore evident. We derive our substance from it—we are, after death, resolved again into it. We are really but fleeting shadows. Animal and vegetable forms are little more than consolidated masses of the atmosphere. The sublime creations of the most gifted bard cannot rival the beauty of this, the highest and truest poetry of science. (137–38)

The lengthy quotation ends with Hunt's statement that

when Shakespeare made his charming Ariel sing—
Full fathom five thy father lies,
Of his bones are coral made,
Those are pearls that were his eyes,
Nothing of him that doth fade,
But doth suffer a sea-change,
Into something rich and strange
—he little thought how correctly he painted the chemical changes, by which decomposing animal matter is replaced by siliceous or calcareous formation. (138)

Choosing to take offense, Dickens comments: "Why Mr. Hunt should be of opinion that Shakespeare 'little thought' how wise he was, we do not altogether understand. Perhaps he founds the supposition on Shakespeare's not having been recognized as a practical chemist or palaeontologist" (138).

In this instance, at least, the polemical edge Dickens detects does not seem to be intended by the author, judging by the minor revision the passage undergoes in a later edition, where the words right after the Shakespeare quotation become "he painted, with considerable correctness, the chemical changes. . . ."[26] Yet Dickens's tart response may seem particularly curious when one recalls that, Ariel's song notwithstanding, Ferdinand's father has not in fact died: it could easily be argued that what

Shakespeare is really "thinking" here primarily concerns the power of the mind over the material world, in the face of which power the importance of actual bodily dissolution pales.

A few years earlier, at any rate, Ralph Waldo Emerson had turned specifically to *The Tempest* to illustrate just such a view of the relationship of man to nature. Describing the "transfiguration which all material objects undergo through the passion of the poet" (in the service of which "all objects shrink and expand"), Emerson quotes Prospero: "The strong based promontory / Have I made shake, and by the spurs plucked up / The pine and cedar."[27] According to Emerson, "the poet . . . uses matter as symbols. . . . [He] conforms things to his thoughts," and "Shakspeare possesses the power of subordinating nature for the purposes of expression, beyond all poets."[28] The ideal Emersonian has "transferred nature into the mind, and left matter like an outcast corpse."[29] Yet this felicitous image identifies exactly how Dickens's understanding of the relationship of the mind to the material world differs from that of an idealist such as Emerson—or from the nineteenth-century's leading theorist of the imagination, Samuel Taylor Coleridge, who similarly and just as resonantly asserts that the "poetic imagination . . . turns bodies / To spirits by sublimation strange, / As fire converts to fire the things it burns."[30] In *Bleak House,* by contrast, the strange sublimation of spontaneous human combustion, like the communication of disease from the graveyard where Nemo is buried, demonstrates the absolute refusal of matter—and especially corpses—to be taken leave of. The narrator's assignment of symbolic significance to Krook's death may seem to support an Emersonian or Coleridgean reading of the episode, but in fact the chapter's overwhelming emphasis is on physical transformation and persistence, not expressive transfiguration or sublimation. Krook's remains linger in the reader's mind just as surely as they linger in the air (and on the windowsill, and on sleeves . . .). For Dickens as much as for George Henry Lewes, "the body remains an obstinate fact."[31]

The degree to which the narrator's reading of Krook's death approximates a Coleridgean sublimation does account, however, for the novel's hints of uneasiness with that reading: the fruitless turn to mute Allegory in a literal-minded appeal for "higher meaning" upon the discovery of Tulkinghorn's corpse might be seen to parody the earlier scene's symbolic reading of Krook's death—especially since Tulkinghorn is a more powerful and appropriate representative of the evils of Chancery than is Krook. Furthermore, the narrator's apocalyptic reading of Krook's death bears an uncomfortable resemblance to the laughably "rapid logic" (397) of Sir Leicester Dedlock, who can turn almost any event into a sign that "'the floodgates of society are burst open, and the waters have—a—obliterated the landmarks of the framework of the cohesion by which things are held together!'" (571). At the same time, the motives of Tulkinghorn's murderer, Mlle. Hortense, are egregiously slim, whereas Sir Leicester is correct that society is changing in ways he disapproves of, so symbolic readings are hardly discredited here. As we have seen, moreover, one of the primary items in Dickens's ongoing indictment of the political authorities both in and out of *Bleak House* is the shameful state of graveyards. The warning Krook's disembodiment is made to embody therefore does not dispose of the question of dead bodies, à la Emerson, but instead encompasses the question of their disposal.

Bleak House, I have argued, emphasizes commonalities between documents and bodies, symbolic and material processes, and reading and empirical analysis in order to extend Dickens's authority from the realm of texts and tropes to that of physical phenomena—including, paradigmatically, spontaneous human combustion. While these efforts provoke a response from George Henry Lewes, Lewes's response indicates even more clearly than Hunt's book that Dickens himself is responding to prior provocations. Turning to the work of the main authority Lewes cites, the prominent German chemist Justus von Liebig, we discover in fact that even before Dickens takes up the topic, spontaneous human combustion already serves as a site for the contestation and consolidation of cultural authority. We also discover that the conflationary strategy Dickens employs is already in circulation in this very context.

Liebig's debunking of the notion of spontaneous human combustion appears in his popularizing and popular work *Familiar Letters on Chemistry,* where he raises the question of spontaneous combustion not for any intrinsic interest it might possess but precisely as a "striking instance of the difference between the present and former modes of investigating and explaining natural phenomena."[32] "The descriptions of cases of death from spontaneous combustion, which belong to the last century," he argues, "are not certified by highly cultivated physicians; they commonly proceed from ignorant persons, unpractised in observation, and bear in themselves the stamp of untrustworthiness" (297). For Liebig, and for Lewes after him, the most basic criterion of (un)trustworthiness is obviously class. In one of his open letters to Dickens, for example, Lewes writes, "Not to lay stress on the chief testimony [concerning a supposed instance of spontaneous combustion] being a toll-keeper and a herd-boy, persons from whom one would little expect accurate descriptions, let me only refer to these points. . . ."[33] Repeating this argument in a later article on spontaneous combustion, Lewes even dispenses with his earlier, coy preterition to assert flatly that "in the first place, the testimony is that of a tollkeeper and a herd boy, surely not the most reliable sources to which one would look for accuracy in description."[34] Such comments strongly recall an event in the novel that Lewes himself clearly does not recall, the treatment of the streetsweeper Jo at Nemo's inquest:

> "This won't do, gentlemen!" said the Coroner, with a melancholy shake of the head.
>
> "Don't you think you can receive his evidence, sir?" asks an attentive Juryman.
>
> "Out of the question," says the Coroner. "You have heard the boy. 'Can't exactly say' won't do, you know. We can't take *that,* in a Court of Justice, gentlemen. It's terrible depravity. Put the boy aside."
>
> Boy put aside. (134–35)

Viewed in this context, Dickens's defense of spontaneous combustion can be seen to function as part of the novel's more general argument against the silencing or discrediting of individuals lacking what those in positions of authority deem sufficient cultural capital.[35] Yet Liebig and Lewes clearly seek to assert the authority of experts in "investigating and explaining natural phenomena" not only against illiterate figures such as Jo—whose cultural disenfranchisement is already all but absolute—but against nonspecialists such as Dickens as well. Indeed, the full title of Liebig's book makes extremely clear this interest in extending the reach of the chemist's authority: *Familiar Letters on Chemistry, in Its Relations to Physiology, Dietetics, Agriculture, Commerce, and Political Economy.* Liebig devotes much of the book to establishing and celebrating the chemist's high level of professional training and expertise; it is these claims that reverberate in Lewes's discussion. "There is," Liebig explains, "no art so difficult as that of observation; it requires a cultivated, sober mind, and a well schooled experience, which is only acquired by long practice" (28). He further argues that "the study of Chemistry is profitable, not only inasmuch as it promotes the material interests of mankind, but also because it furnishes us with insight into those wonders of creation which immediately surround us, and with which our existence, life, and development, are most closely connected" (1). At his most extravagant, Liebig claims that "without the knowledge of natural phenomena, and of the laws by which they are regulated, the human mind is incapable of forming an adequate conception of the greatness and unfathomable witness of the CREATOR; for all the images which the most inexhaustible fancy or the most cultivated intellect can form will appear, when compared with the reality, but as glittering, variegated, unsubstantial bubbles!" (21). Liebig promotes the paramount authority of the scientist within his proper realm, but this realm turns out to be the entirety of God's creation.

What is most striking about Liebig's work in the present context is that even as the chemist devalues the expertise of imaginative writers, he describes the processes of observation and analysis in ways that co-opt their skills. He begins his book with an extended analogy comparing the natural world—or, alternatively, our observations of it—to language: "All our observations, taken collectively," he writes, "form a language. Every property, every alteration which we perceive in bodies, is a word in that language" (8). The chemist performs experiments to render the properties of "the invisible material world . . . as intelligible as the black lines and characters which convey to a far distant friend our invisible thoughts" (9). To understand "the book of nature," one must learn its "language," its "alphabet," and its "signs or symbols," and the chemist must then "be able to express all his conclusions—all his results—in the form of phenomena. Every experiment is a thought thus rendered perceptible to the senses" (11–12). Experiments, Liebig explains, constitute "the *interpretation* of phenomena at will" (12; emphasis added). Those who deny the value of chemistry, on the other hand, "can no more read its language than they could a work written in Hebrew characters" (13). Liebig embellishes the familiar image of the book of nature to the point where it is no longer clear whether the chemist's expertise lies in the

realm of books or that of nature—or whether there is in fact any significant difference between the two.

Strategically analogizing or conflating linguistic and physical objects
and methods, Liebig's *Familiar Letters* thus anticipates *Bleak House* while
pressing in the opposite direction, to legitimize and expand the authority of scientists. Fittingly, the proximity of these two works, both of
which emphasize the proximity of the physical and discursive realms, is
physical as well as discursive: an advertisement for a new edition of
Liebig's popular work appears in the pages of the first monthly number
of *Bleak House*.[36] Returning to the "Bleak House Advertiser," in fact, we
discover that just as many advertisements share the novel's interest in the
materiality of writing, as noted earlier, so too does a conspicuous series
of advertisements reinscribe the novel's yoking together of attention to
matter, attention to texts, and questions of authority. These advertisements play out a controversy which uncannily parallels that over spontaneous human combustion in its subject matter, its trajectory, and, remarkably enough, the key role played by Justus von Liebig. Concerns
over vulnerable bodies, documents, and the authority to describe and
control either or both take center stage here on the margins of *Bleak
House* just as they do within the novel itself, offering dramatic confirmation of the presence and importance of this constellation in the culture
at large.

In the fifth number of *Bleak House,* published in July 1852, immediately following Dickens's text—which ends with Jo pointing out
Nemo's rat-infested burial place to the disguised Lady Dedlock—is
a several-pages-long advertisement for "Allsopp's Pale or Bitter Ale"
(fig. 3). Asserting that "in consequence of the reported adulteration of
Bitter Beer, Messrs. Samuel ALLSOPP and SONS have received numerous incidental TESTIMONIALS to the excellence, purity, and salu-
tary effects of their ALES," the advertisement quotes from some three
dozen "testimonials," the first of which is "FROM BARON LIEBIG."
In a statement dated 6 May, Liebig writes, "The specimens of your Pale
Ale sent to me afforded me another opportunity of confirming its valuable qualities. I am myself an admirer of this beverage, and my own experience enables me to recommend it, in accordance with the opinion
of the most eminent English physicians, as a very agreeable and efficient

tonic, and as a general beverage, both for the invalid *and the robust.*"[37] This advertisement runs again in the September number (no. 7). In November (no. 9), a much longer extract from the same letter appears, also occupying the prime space facing the last page of *Bleak House* novel text:

ALLSOPP'S PALE OR BITTER ALE. REMARKS UPON THE ALLEGED USE OF STRYCHNINE IN THE MANUFACTURE OF PALE ALE. BY BARON LIEBIG. (IN A LETTER TO HENRY ALLSOPP, ESQ., BURTON-ON-TRENT.)

The unguarded remark of a French chemist, that the strychnine imported into England is employed as a substitute for hops in the manufacture of beer, has lately spread alarm among the lovers of pale ale. *Having been appealed to by you, to express my opinion on this subject,* which appears to me to be, in a dietetic point of view, one of considerable public interest, I now offer the following brief statement.

. . . Nobody, at all acquainted with the great breweries of that country [England], could seriously entertain the suspicion of an adulteration of beer with strychnine or any other deleterious substance. It is practically impossible that any operation of a doubtful character could be carried out in these extensive establishments on account of the large number of workmen employed in them.

Uncertain, perhaps, of the force of this latter consideration—the assertion of which, in any event, hardly requires a celebrated scientist— Liebig adds that "I have farther assured myself, by an analysis of several specimens of pale ale obtained from London houses, supplied by your establishment, of the utter groundlessness of the imputation, that this beer was poisoned with strychnine."

As in the Dickens-Lewes controversy, then, Liebig's authority is called upon to help settle a question of corrupted matter. The ale controversy, however, proves no easier to lay to rest than that over spontaneous combustion: immediately following the advertisement just cited (which again follows Liebig's letter with several pages of additional testimonials) appears an ad headed "Baron Liebig on Certain Late Anonymous Advertisements." Here we learn—in a manner exquisitely in keeping with the novel that gives us Jarndyce and Jarndyce, on the one hand, and that

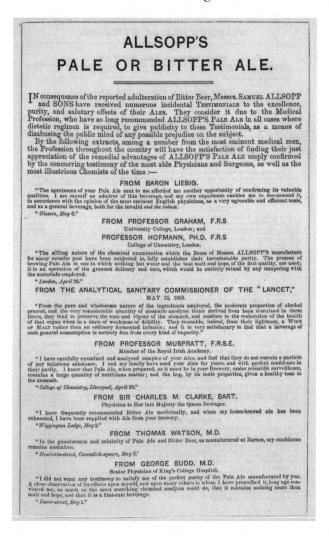

Figure 3. Advertisement facing the final page of Bleak House, *chapter 16, "Tom-All-Alone's" (no. 5, July 1852). (Courtesy of the Poetry Collection of the University Libraries, The State University of New York at Buffalo. Photograph by James Ulrich, University at Buffalo.)*

emphasizes the convergence of questions concerning matter and those concerning signs, on the other—that a controversy has broken out surrounding Liebig's statements in the strychnine controversy. The advertisement provides an extract of a letter from Liebig to Allsopp, dated 12 September 1852, in which Liebig reports, "To my great astonishment and concern, my attention has lately been called to several anonymous articles and advertisements headed by my name, such as in the——[this dash an odd adoption of a novelistic device], whose author altogether misrepresents the motives of my remarks, and even goes so far as to say 'that I had never analysed your beer, nor, perhaps, ever tasted it in my life,' and to allege a retraction on my part of the original statement." Liebig tells Allsopp that "in every respect I adhere to the statement made in my letter to you," adding "which certainly you have, and are at perfect liberty to publish."

This dispute shifts, then, from a question of scientific analysis to one of textual evidence and interpretation. Unlike Liebig, the reader of *Bleak House* will hardly be "astonish[ed]" by the course this scandal runs—and runs: the tenth number of the novel, which concludes with the spontaneous-combustion episode, contains yet another letter from Liebig, this one dated 24 July 1852, in which Liebig denies that the praise in his original letter to Allsopp was, as the advertisement suggested, "exclusively confined to Mr. Allsopp's beer; THIS WAS NOT THE CASE: my remarks referred to that CLASS of beer." Appended is a note: "N.B. The Baron's original letter is in the hands of Mr. Miller, at the Jerusalem Coffee House, Cornhill, where it may be seen by any one taking an interest in the matter." Below which, on the same page, is *yet another* advertisement from Messrs. Allsopp and Sons, who now recommend that "parties applying to Mr. Miller . . . for any information in the above subject . . . ask to see a letter from Baron Liebig addressed to Mr. Bass, and dated Giessen, 23rd August 1852." "Copies of which letter," add the Allsopps, without disclosing its contents, "are already in the possession of all the Brewers at Burton-upon-Trent." Discussion of the purity of ale gives way entirely here to discussion of the authenticity, location, and meaning of documents. Eventually, the dispute disappears from the pages of the "Bleak House Advertiser"[38]—presumably, Jarndyce-and-Jarndyce-like, having collapsed under its own weight.

Both *Bleak House* and the "Bleak House Advertiser" thus offer striking, and strikingly similar, examples of a process of corruption or slippage whereby questions about matter become questions about signs and vice versa. In the "Bleak House Advertiser," at least, this process works not to extend the scientist's authority, as Liebig would have it in his *Familiar Letters,* but rather to undermine it. By contrast, the extent to which this controversy reads as if it were scripted by Dickens—as if it were an excerpt from *Bleak House* rather than an adjunct to it—testifies to the novelist's command of his material, and of his work's materiality. Ultimately, then, through a feedback loop as serendipitous as the circulation of "corrupted humours" (403) in Krook's body is catastrophic, the novel's attention to the meaningful materiality of texts models attention to—say, advertises the potential significance of—the "Bleak House Advertiser," and the "Bleak House Advertiser" ends up advertising the authority of *Bleak House* itself.

This chapter began by treating Lady Dedlock's recognition of her lover's handwriting not as an unconvincing plot device, as Gissing would have it, but rather as an emblem of the novel's project of asserting the meaningful materiality of documents and exploring this materiality in relation to that of bodies. Within the novel itself, however, Lady Dedlock's recognition of the handwriting also provokes incredulity, on the part of her husband, and we do well to consider his response. Sir Leicester can conjure only one plausible scenario to explain this recognition: after Tulkinghorn reports that the handwriting belongs to a recently deceased copyist of unknown identity who went by the name "Nemo," Sir Leicester "renews his stately protest, saying, that . . . it is quite clear that no association in my Lady's mind can possibly be traceable to this poor wretch *(unless he was a begging-letter writer)*" (150; emphasis added). Sir Leicester is of course wrong about Nemo. Yet this ostensibly casual, parenthetical suggestion identifies an occupation and kind of writing that, like Krook's traces, become fraught sites for the articulation of writing's multiple materialities and the concomitant establishment of novelists' cultural authority. The next two chapters of this study track this road flagged but not taken in *Bleak House,* focusing first on the relationship between authorship and begging in general, and then on that between novelist and begging-letter writer in particular. These chapters will show, among other things, that literary references to begging in the nineteenth century can rarely afford to be casual and that, Sir Leicester's parentheses notwithstanding, the figure of the begging-letter writer is never easily contained.

3   As Bad as They Seem?

Professional Authors and Literary Paupers

TRACKING THE PLAY of multiple materialities in *The History of Henry Esmond* and *Bleak House,* we have seen that both novels devote special attention to the physicality of the written or printed word, especially as this bears on authors' literary and cultural authority. While this acute interest in writing as a medium is obviously overdetermined, we might identify as a proximate cause both authors' immersion in a different medium immediately preceding and during the composition of these novels: Thackeray, who wrote *Henry Esmond* between August 1851 and May 1852, delivered his lecture series *The English Humourists of the Eighteenth Century* over a dozen times from May 1851 to April 1853; Dickens, who began work on *Bleak House* in November 1851, directed and played the lead role in Edward Bulwer-Lytton's play *Not So Bad as We Seem* from March 1851 through September 1852. For both authors, these activities represented a new level of participation in forms of public, spoken, embodied performance: lecturing was an entirely new and somewhat traumatic experience for Thackeray, and although this was not the first time Dickens had performed in amateur or benefit theatricals, it was the most prolonged and consuming such experience of his life to that point (with his public readings still to come). The explorations of writing's physical materiality in *Henry Esmond* and *Bleak House* thus constitute reflective returns to form.

In shuttling between the activities of authorship and public performance, Thackeray and Dickens were also moving back and forth across an important economic divide—a divide marked precisely by the physical materiality of the written or printed word. According to the political-economic orthodoxy of the day as expressed in John Stuart Mill's

Principles of Political Economy (first published in 1848), materiality plays a crucial role in the fundamental distinction between productive and unproductive labor—that is, labor that does or does not produce wealth (or, sometimes, capital). Updating Adam Smith's classic definition of productive labor as labor that "fixes and realizes itself in some particular subject or vendible commodity, which lasts for some time at least after that labour is past," Mill defines productive labor as "those kinds of exertion which produce utilities embodied in material objects."[1] Anyone interested in classifying the several activities Thackeray and Dickens engage in would not have to go to the trouble of extrapolating from this definition, as Mill gives "the labour of the musical performer, the actor, the public declaimer or reciter, and the showman" as examples of unproductive labor, while stating explicitly that "the labour of the author of a book is equally a part of its production with that of the printer and binder" (1:46, 41).

The distinction between productive and unproductive labor carries great weight with a broad spectrum of mid-nineteenth-century thinkers and writers, including many hostile to the values and policies associated with political economy. This power stems not only from the commanding prestige and influence of political economy but also from the tendency of the productive/unproductive binary to shade into such morally charged oppositions as industriousness vs. idleness and independence vs. parasitism; Mill complains that even some political economists treat "unproductive" as "synonymous with wasteful or worthless" (1:44). Because of these associations, virtually all authors strive to establish their credentials as productive laborers, or at least avoid the stigma of unproductiveness. Strategies to achieve this end are rarely straightforward, as we shall see. However, for an unusually explicit avowal of the desire to promote an understanding of literary labor as productive, we need look no further than the text announcing the performances of the play Dickens participated in while writing *Bleak House: Not So Bad as We Seem* was written and performed on behalf of the newly founded Guild of Literature and Art (more on which below), and the Guild's Prospectus declares that "[the Guild's] originators have agreed to exhibit certain Dramatic Representations in London, during this year 1851,—so as to place before the public, at a time when the other producers of the country will receive a memorable attention, the claims of a class whose productions form not the least honour to England in the eyes of the foreigner."[2] In a crystal-clear rhetorical maneuver, this passage aligns the performances of *Not So Bad as We Seem* with the Great Exhibition of the Works of Industry of All Nations, and it does so less to promise the future display of "claims" than to stake its own claim to the specifically economic rank of "producer" for author and artist.[3]

Viewed in this context, the attention to the physical materiality of texts paid and solicited by *Henry Esmond* and *Bleak House* serves to remind the reader of the productiveness of literary labor. Yet authors feel the need to assert their standing as producers precisely because of their uncertain hold on this status. In *The Wealth of Nations,* Adam Smith had unequivocally classified "men of letters of all kinds" as unproductive laborers. Smith does not explain this classification, but his larger argument suggests that it is based on the belief that the author's work, "like the declamation of the actor, the harangue of the orator, or the tune of the musician, . . . perishes in the very instant of its production."[4] The author's involvement in the making of books is mediated or attenuated compared to that of the printer or binder, and the very transformation of manuscript into book requires the separability of the author's contribution from its original material form. Both *Bleak House* and *Henry Esmond* register—not least, by attempting to compensate for—what we might call these *counterproductive* aspects of authorship. Thus, even as *Bleak House* makes the materiality of writing into a source of authorial leverage over the material world, the novel creates its overwhelming impression of writing's tangibility by highlighting written documents and the physical act of writing, not the printed work of the author. The first edition of *Henry Esmond,* by contrast, does call attention to itself as a printed book, but the novel as a whole ends up highlighting the normally immaterial nature of modern literary property, with its own departure from this norm serving less to dramatize Mill's dictum than to reverse it: the labors of printer and binder, like that of the author, contribute to the production of meaning. Mill's own reclassification of authors, as shown in that dictum, depends upon an extension of the bounds of what counts as "exertion which produce[s] utilities embodied in material objects": "I shall not refuse the appellation productive to labour which yields no material product as its direct result," he asserts, "provided that an increase of material products is its ultimate consequence" (1:48). This detachment of productiveness from immediate material results helps secure authors' place in the fold.[5]

Also emerging within Mill's discussion, however, are indications that the creation of a material product, whether immediate or deferred, may not be sufficient—nor perhaps even necessary—to make labor productive.[6] This complication will have profound importance for authors attempting to establish their credentials as productive laborers. Although Mill never addresses or even openly acknowledges it, his own dissatisfaction with the theory he is refining—and, as Karl Marx points out, ambiguities within the theory itself as first articulated by Adam Smith[7]— leads him to place increasing emphasis on circumstantial considerations rather than any inherent feature of an activity or the result of that activity. This shift occurs in the section where he aligns the labor of author with that of printer and binder, as he moves from one justification to another for viewing labor "usually classed as mental," in particular that of "the inventors of industrial processes," as productive (1:40). At first, this classification turns on the fact that "there is some bodily ingredient in the labour most purely mental, when it generates any external result": "Newton could not have produced the Principia without the bodily exertion either of penmanship or of dictation; and he must have drawn many diagrams, and written out many calculations and demonstrations, while he was preparing it in his mind." Apparently unconvinced by his own argument, Mill quickly sets it aside and introduces an entirely different consideration: "Whether mental, however, or bodily, [inventors'] labour is a part of that by which the production is brought about." Even here, though, as he replaces Newton with the more promising example of James Watt, Mill does not rely solely on the direct path leading from Watt's idea to the production of a material object: "The labour of Watt in contriving the steam-engine was as essential a part of production as that of the mechanics who build or the engineers who work the instrument; and was undergone, no less than theirs, in the prospect of a remuneration from the produce" (1:41). Almost as an afterthought, Mill adduces the circumstances of—in particular the motives for—Watt's invention as evidence of his labor's status.

The significance of these extra factors grows as Mill continues. Although "mere thought," he argues, is important "even in a purely productive and material point of view," the thinkers of such thoughts are not to be classed as producers—except of "the books, or other useable or saleable articles, which directly emanate from them." Mill justifies this restriction on the grounds that the "material fruits" of their thoughts "are seldom the direct purpose of the pursuits of savants, nor is their remuneration in general derived from the increased production which may be caused incidentally and mostly after a long interval, by their discoveries" (1:41–42). Again here, Mill gestures toward the purpose and payment of labor even as he excludes these from his formal definitions of productive and unproductive labor. Productive labor is not simply (if at all) labor that fixes value in material objects, but labor performed in return for payment.

In the manner of a Derridean supplement, this added factor of remuneration threatens to supplant the determinant it is introduced to support. This prospect emerges most clearly in Mill's *Principles* when he acknowledges that labor "employed for purposes of production" is sometimes "wasted" (1:51). Whereas the significance of the distinction between productive and unproductive labor had seemed to be that the latter, "however largely or successfully practised, does not render the community, and the world at large, richer in material products, but poorer by all that is consumed by the labourers while so employed" (1:49), it turns out that productive labor too "may render a nation poorer, if the wealth it produces, *that is, the increase it makes in the stock of useful or agreeable things,* be of a kind not immediately wanted; as when a commodity is unsaleable, because produced in a quantity beyond the present demand; or when speculators build docks and warehouses before there is any trade" (1:51; emphasis added). The sheer materiality of the thing produced here renders it "wealth," but—as the interpolated definition implicitly acknowledges—this designation comes to border on the nonsensical when no one, either individually or collectively, profits from the desirable-but-not-desired object's production. In both its concessions and its resistance, then, Mill's work registers the importance of context—in particular, the context of exchange—in determining the productiveness or unproductiveness of particular actions.

The example of Mill suggests that it is scarcely possible to determine authors' status as productive or unproductive without taking into account the question of remuneration. This point is driven home in analyses of political economy that dispense entirely with the criterion of ma-

teriality, from Karl Marx's attempt to clarify the orthodox distinction between productive and unproductive labor to Stanley Jevons's attempt to
demolish it: in his *Theories of Surplus Value* (written in 1862–63), Marx
emphasizes that for labor to be productive from the standpoint of capitalist production it must generate capital, not simply revenue, and on this
basis he argues that the productiveness of labor depends solely on the circumstances in which the labor is performed: "These definitions are . . .
not derived from the material characteristics of labor (neither from the
nature of its product nor from the particular character of the labor as
concrete . . .), but from the definite social form, the social relations of
production, within which the labor is realized. An actor or clown is a
productive laborer if he works in the service of a capitalist."[8] "A writer
is a productive laborer," he continues, "not in so far as he produces ideas,
but in so far as he enriches the publisher who publishes his works, or if
he is a wage-labourer for a capitalist"; or again, "the writer who turns
out stuff for his publisher in factory style, is a productive laborer."[9]
Jevons, in his *Principles of Economics* (which he was at work on when he
died in 1882), dismisses the materiality-based distinction between productive and unproductive labor as "absurd and artificial," but notes that
"to write a book which nobody will buy; to arrange a play which nobody cares to hear—such are truly cases of unproductive labour."[10] All
individual authors need do to establish their standing as productive, then,
is point to their success in the marketplace.

But of course it is not so simple, and not only because Marx and
Jevons go further than most midcentury writers in insisting that productiveness is determined circumstantially. Rather, these two critics of orthodox political economy make plain a potential conflict that is less obvious but still discernible in Mill's account: the aspects of labor that take
on heightened significance—the expectation of remuneration and the
presence of an existing market for one's goods—are precisely those
against which a broadly Romantic model of authorship defines itself. According to this familiar view, the creation of literary works of art should
proceed in a state of indifference to (if not defiance of) the expectations
and demands of the marketplace, and the failure to achieve immediate commercial success serves as evidence of artistic integrity and originality. Although it is easy to overstate the currency of this model in the
mid-nineteenth century, there is no doubt that many leading Victorian

writers do seek to distinguish authorship from wage labor and the products of their exertions from "mere" commodities. What has been insufficiently recognized, however, is that this goal rarely—if ever—supersedes that of avoiding the stigma of being labeled unproductive. Efforts to position authors economically so as to enhance their prestige and cultural authority thus face two distinct and potentially contradictory imperatives.

The most spectacular collisions between these two aspects of midcentury authorial legitimation strategies occur when authors seek to institute or even simply imagine alternatives to the literary marketplace. As we will see in some detail, such alternatives must be distinguished from charity, yet the solicitation of charity—in a word, begging—epitomizes both nonmarket exchange, on the one hand, and unproductive idleness, on the other. By tracing the treatment of beggars and begging in the discourse on authorship, then, we can see how the effort to distance authors from the marketplace and the effort to show that authors are productive laborers come together—and how they fall apart. This chapter will focus primarily on this dynamic as it unfolds in the era's most influential call for an alternative to the literary marketplace, Thomas Carlyle's "The Hero as Man of Letters," and the most elaborate effort to establish such an alternative, the founding of the Guild of Literature and Art.

Paying the Man-of-Letters Hero

The Victorian era's best-known celebration of authorship comes from the era's leading critic of the market economy. It is therefore no surprise that "The Hero as Man of Letters" (delivered as a lecture in 1840 and published the following year) evinces abundant hostility toward the marketplace and the writer's reliance on it. Yet Carlyle's status as paradigmatic spokesman for this position has obscured the actual contours of his argument. As several recent critics have shown, Carlyle is urgently interested in constructing a model of masculine identity for male writers. One component of this identity, however, is engagement in productive labor, and the difficulty of detaching this status from market exchange forces Carlyle to rethink a position these critics tend to take for granted: that the model he constructs must be located outside the marketplace.[11]

"The Hero as Man of Letters" argues that "since it is the spiritual always that determines the material, [the] Man-of-Letters Hero must be

regarded as our most important person. He, such as he may be, is the soul of all. What he teaches, the whole world will do and make." [12] From this premise, Carlyle reasons that "the world's manner of dealing with [the Man-of-Letters Hero] is the most significant feature of the world's general position" (134). His discussion therefore focuses on the merits and failings of the current arrangement, whereby "the inspired wisdom of a Heroic Soul [is] sold and bought, and left to make its own bargain in the marketplace" (133). According to Carlyle, this market-based system is unequivocally "the worst" of all possible arrangements of "furtherance and regulation," for it leaves authors "at the mercy of blind Chance" (143 –44). This "chaotic" (137) state of affairs is objectionable for two reasons: first, in the "whirl of distracted atoms, one cancelling the others," worthy authors are forced to struggle for their subsistence and often get "lost by the way" (144); second, and more important, this chaos signals the disorganization of society as a whole, its failure to "set its *light* on high places, to walk thereby" (145). Carlyle describes the literary marketplace as a realm of mutual indifference if not antagonism, with the commodification of literature signaling the lack of genuine connection between author and audience: "To a certain shopkeeper, trying to get some money for his books, if lucky, [the man of letters] is of some importance; to no other man of any" (137–38). [13]

After thus denouncing the status quo, Carlyle turns to the question of "the best possible organisation for the Men of Letters in modern society; the arrangement, of furtherance and regulation, grounded the most accurately on the actual facts of their position and of the world's position" (143). While claiming that "the problem far exceed[s] my faculty," he nonetheless asserts that there is "one remark I must not omit, That royal or parliamentary grants of money are by no means the chief thing wanted! To give our Men of Letters stipends, endowments and all furtherance of cash, will do little towards the business." The immediate problem with these would-be cures, apparently, is that they too closely resemble the disease itself in their focus on finances: "On the whole," he continues, "one is weary of hearing about the omnipotence of money"; in fact, "for a genuine man, it is no evil to be poor; . . . there ought to be Literary Men poor,—to show whether they are genuine or not!" (143).

In thus praising poverty as a crucible for the literary prophet, Carlyle invokes a version of the "charismatic economy" that Pierre Bourdieu,

following Max Weber, sees structuring the realms of both prophecy and "the literary and artistic world": "Like prophecy, especially the prophecy of misfortune, which . . . demonstrates its authenticity by the fact that it brings in no income, a heretical break with the prevailing artistic traditions proves its claim to authenticity by its disinterestedness."[14] Strikingly, however, Carlyle does not use this model to mystify or dismiss as irrelevant the question of how authors should subsist. Instead, having rejected first the marketplace and then governmental patronage as fundamentally flawed forms of support, Carlyle arrives at the logical telos of this line of argument: alms. Immediately after announcing that authors ought to be poor, he reminds his audience that "Mendicant Orders, bodies of good men doomed to *beg,* were instituted in the Christian Church; a most natural and even necessary development of the spirit of Christianity." Carlyle rhapsodizes about the "priceless lessons" imparted by the "Poverty" and "Degradation" of such an existence, and he concludes by forcefully declaring, "To beg, and go barefoot, in coarse woollen cloak with a rope round your loins, and be despised of all the world, was no beautiful business;—nor an honourable one in any eye, till the nobleness of those who did so had made it honoured of some!" (143). Begging, he suggests, represents the way of life best suited to the heroic vocation of authorship.

While presented in provocative fashion, Carlyle's vision of mendicant orders of men of letters builds on a traditional identification of authors with beggars. Historically, this identification—which has been variously celebrated and regretted—rests on the vagabondlike mobility and marginality of bards and minstrels (Homer is often the exemplary figure in this regard[15]) and the shared poverty of beggars and writers (the former's implicit, the latter's proverbial). Adam Smith, in his discussion of "that unprosperous race of men commonly called men of letters" in *The Wealth of Nations,* goes so far as to claim that "before the invention of the art of printing, a scholar and a beggar seem to have been terms very nearly synonymous."[16] "This melancholy fact that man of genius discovered," as Isaac D'Israeli would later complain, "without the feather of his pen brushing away a tear from his lid—without one spontaneous and indignant groan!"[17]

After the invention of printing, as Smith also notes, the potentially "profitable employment" of "writing for a bookseller"[18] emerges. None-

theless, the possibility of kinship or identity between beggars and scholars, poets, men of letters, and the like does not therefore disappear; on the contrary, with the rise of a market-based system of literary production and circulation, this convention gains new prominence. This is the case not only because men of letters largely remain an unprosperous race but also because the concept of begging itself acquires new importance within the emerging and, in the first half of the nineteenth century, increasingly hegemonic discourse of political economy. Begging plays a key role in this discourse, as a famous passage in *The Wealth of Nations* makes evident: "It is not from the benevolence of the butcher, the brewer, or the baker, that we expect our dinner, but from their regard to their own interest. We address ourselves, not to their humanity but to their self-love, and never talk to them of our own necessities but of their advantages. *Nobody but a beggar* chuses to depend chiefly upon the benevolence of his fellow citizens."[19] Unlike the wealth of potential motives for human action that Smith implicitly brackets, benevolence retains a place as self-interest's binary opposite. Begging—the appeal to benevolence—therefore emerges as the form of behavior precisely antithetical to normative, socially beneficial participation in a market economy.

On the whole, *The Wealth of Nations* says very little about begging; in fact, this passage constitutes the book's sole mention of the phenomenon other than that in the section on men of letters (a coincidence, as the saying goes, that is surely no accident). Yet this very reticence paradoxically underscores begging's crucially marginal—that is, margin-establishing—position in the system Smith describes: begging constitutes the type of exchange against which market exchange is defined, the exception that proves the rule of barter, purchase, and sale. The very recognition of a transaction as an instance of market exchange thus entails distinguishing it from a charitable encounter.[20]

In the eighteenth century, as *Henry Esmond* dramatizes, reliance on the market replaces reliance on patronage for authors (and others), but in the nineteenth century, thanks to the influence of political economy and the growth of the capitalist society that it legitimizes, charity replaces patronage as the market's primary diacritical term. (Indeed, it is presumably patronage that Smith is really attacking in the guise of begging, precisely by equating the former with the latter.) Once this understanding of begging as the market's other achieves the status of both common sense and official policy, begging and almsgiving also necessarily serve to structure the field of nonmarket forms of support. In other words, even if writers searching for supplements or alternatives to the marketplace disdain begging itself, they cannot help but define their preferred mechanism—their alternative alternative—in relation to it. Advocates of such alternative procedures for supporting authors must take care to distinguish these alternatives from the eleemosynary transactions they reject; indeed, they must distinguish the very act of making their proposals from that of making a request for alms. As I show in the second half of this chapter, these rhetorical and theoretical challenges often prove as daunting, not to say disabling, as any of the logistical ones these advocates face.

Yet such challenges await only those intent on charting a course between market exchange and begging. For critics of political economy from the late eighteenth century on, however, the Smithian conception of begging can also serve as reason to defend begging in the face of its ever-increasing stigmatization, criminalization, and attempted suppression. That is, while many opponents of the laissez-faire system point to the continued existence of beggars as an indication of that system's inadequacy or immorality, some go further to praise begging in the very terms it is attacked, as an attempt to evade the grasp of the invisible hand. Not merely marginal but rather oppositional, begging becomes a symbol and repository of communal values perceived to be under assault.

George Meredith's 1861 poem "The Beggar's Soliloquy" provides a particularly explicit articulation of this pro-begging logic (even as Meredith's irony tempers the poem's endorsement of this position). The poem presents the musings of a vagrant lounging in fields near a church during Sunday service. After extolling the pleasures of life on the heath, the speaker directly addresses the politics of begging:

> I'm not a low Radical, hating the laws,
> > Who'd the aristocracy rebuke.
> . . . .
> On the contrary, I'm Conservative quite;
> > There's beggars in scripture 'mongst Gentiles and Jews:
> It's nonsense, trying to set things right,
> > For if people will give, why, who'll refuse?

That stopping old custom wakes my spleen:
    The poor and the rich both in giving agree:
Your tight-fisted shopman's the Radical mean:
    There's nothing in common 'twixt him and me.
He says I'm no use! but I won't reply,
    You're lucky not being of use to him![21]

Begging stands on the side of custom, religion, and generosity, against atomization, selfishness, and the ascendancy of a utilitarian calculus. By putting this defense of begging in the mouth of a beggar, Meredith gives it an amusingly self-serving quality, but the speaker's situation does not necessarily discredit the argument he voices.[22] Ultimately, in fact, the poem's sympathies seem to lie with the beggar, who becomes less roguish and more reflective as his soliloquy progresses. He argues:

Now, giving and taking's a proper exchange,
    Like question and answer: you're both content.
But buying and selling seems always strange;
    You're hostile, and that's the thing that's meant.
It's man against man—you're almost brutes;
    There's here no thanks, and there's there no pride.
If Charity's Christian, don't blame my pursuits,
    I carry a touchstone by which you're tried.   (lines 75–82)

Adopting Smith's description of begging as the antithesis of market exchange but drawing opposite conclusions, Meredith's philosophically savvy speaker makes absolutely clear the anti–political-economic—indeed, anti-Hobbesian—nature and appeal of mendicancy.

By virtue of the logic Meredith's poem so fully displays, begging can be seen to embody forms of social interaction that industrial capitalism (or related avatars of modernity, such as urbanization) stand accused of devaluing and destroying. As such an embodiment—and as Meredith's serendipitous use of the word *touchstone* may suggest to the alert post-Arnoldian reader—begging resembles nothing so much as *culture*, which famously serves as "the normal antithesis to the market" for writers in England's influential "culture and society" tradition.[23] From this perspective, beggars and charitable transactions perform functions similar if not identical to those of authors and aesthetic experience; like culture, in Raymond Williams's apt phrase, the beggar's appeal to benevolence functions as "the court of appeal, by which a society construing its relationships in terms of the cash-nexus might be condemned."[24]

To see this ideological affinity between begging and culture most fully exploited, we need to go back to the turn of the century, to the work of William Wordsworth. While vagrancy, in particular, constitutes one of the central tropes of Wordsworth's entire oeuvre, most salient here are his interest in the beggar as a potential figure for the poet or poetry itself, and his use of this figure to capture and criticize the political and economic transformations of contemporary society.[25] "The Old Cumberland Beggar" exemplifies this strategy, as in this poem Wordsworth conjoins begging with literature in explicit opposition to the ideology and policies of political economy. Written, as Wordsworth later recalled, around the time "the political economists were . . . beginning their war upon mendicity in all its forms, and by implication, if not directly, on alms-giving also,"[26] the poem directly addresses "Statesmen! ye / Who are so restless in your wisdom, ye / Who have a broom still ready in your hands / To rid the world of nuisances" (lines 67–70). The poet argues that the beggar's recurrent appearances save his benefactors from succumbing to "selfishness and cold oblivious cares" (line 95); Wordsworth's beggar has provided even the poor with the opportunity to "have been kind to such / As needed kindness, for this single cause, / That we have all of us one human heart" (lines 151–53).

Wordsworth's defense of begging in this poem functions simultaneously as a defense of poetry, or, more specifically, of his own poetic practice. For the old Cumberland beggar, like "The Old Cumberland Beggar," is a text: "the villagers in him / Behold a *record* which together binds / Past deeds and offices of charity" (lines 88–90; emphasis added). The poem itself provides a record of this record, and therefore beggar and poem are not only both texts, they are comparable texts. This implicit analogy becomes more conspicuous when, on behalf of the beggar, the speaker asks (begs?) of the "Statesmen": "while life is his, / Still let him prompt the *unlettered* villagers / To tender offices and pensive thoughts" (lines 168–70; emphasis added). The detail of illiteracy here prompts the reader to infer the source of such prompting for the *lettered* villager, and by extension for the reader as well. Indeed, the beggar's influence on his benefactors both resembles that of a poem and makes these individuals more like poets, insofar as a poet is a "man . . . endued with more lively sensibility, more enthusiasm and tenderness, who has a greater knowledge of human nature, and a more comprehensive soul, than are supposed to be common among mankind."[27] According to Wordsworth, then, as forms of ethical action, begging and poetry are nearly interchangeable.

Returning from this excursion to "The Hero as Man of Letters," we can see that Carlyle's attraction to the notion of the author as beggar makes perfect sense: the preexisting alignment of begging with culture in opposition to the market combines with Carlyle's intense hostility toward the cash nexus to render this notion irresistible. It turns out, however, that Carlyle does resist this notion, and in fact refuses to recommend that authors support themselves by begging. For no sooner does he conjure a vision of mendicant orders than he abandons it: "Begging is not in our course at the present time," he asserts, while still musing, "but for the rest of it, who will say that a [Samuel] Johnson is not perhaps the better for being poor?" (143). Mention of a "monastic order" (144) briefly recurs, but not begging itself as an attractive or even acceptable option.

Carlyle presents this retreat as a capitulation to present possibilities. Nonetheless, the force of his statement is clearly prescriptive rather than descriptive, for while there are no mendicant orders of authors, there are certainly many authors and would-be authors actively engaged in begging (a point to which I will return). Why, then, does Carlyle reject the very means of subsistence his own argument leads him to and seems almost to demand?

Even in the supplied context of poems that present a rationale for supporting begging, some ambivalence on Carlyle's part would not be entirely surprising: together these poems suggest that the very attempt to advocate begging on behalf of oneself or others is almost inevitably vexed. By making a beggar his poem's speaker, for example, Meredith throws into relief Wordsworth's instrumentalizing treatment of his beggar (although the relative spryness of Meredith's beggar prevents us from reading his monologue as "The Old Cumberland Beggar's Soliloquy"): Wordsworth largely excludes consideration or even acknowledgment of the beggar's own thoughts and feelings. Even if this lack is taken to indicate not the sort of callousness on Wordsworth's part that he himself decries but rather the actual diminished state of the beggar's subjectivity, the prospect of such diminishment hardly recommends begging as a suitable way of life for the poet or man of letters. Yet the distinctive voice and intellectual agility of Meredith's beggar are also troublesome, as we have already seen. By having a beggar defend alms, the poem foregrounds the self-serving nature of this defense and the acquisitive nature of begging itself; the beggar's interest in legitimizing acts of benevolence, in other words, stems all too clearly from his own self-interest.[28] By arguing his own case with such verve, moreover, the beggar raises the question of whether he himself truly needs or deserves aid, an issue that much exercised the Victorians.

In short, if Wordsworth's beggar is barely human, Meredith's is all too human, and the pitfalls they represent are perhaps reason enough for Carlyle to step gingerly around the subject of begging. Carlyle, however, is not the type to step gingerly, and in fact he does not simply flirt provocatively with the idea of mendicant authors and then let it drop: instead, he reverses course to treat begging as anathema. Faced with the prospect of authors as beggars, Carlyle turns on a dime.

Carlyle's newfound hostility toward begging, along with the reasons behind this change in attitude, emerge most fully later in the lecture, in his biographical sketch of Samuel Johnson. As evidence of the "giant invincible soul" of this prototypical modern man of letters, Carlyle fondly recounts "that story of the shoes at Oxford": when a "charitable Gentleman Commoner" discreetly leaves a pair of shoes outside the impoverished young Johnson's door, Johnson refuses the gift by throwing the shoes out the window. Carlyle could not approve more strongly of this gesture:

> Wet feet, mud, frost, hunger or what you will; but not beggary: we cannot stand beggary! Rude stubborn self-help here; a whole world of squalor, rudeness, confused misery and want, yet of nobleness and manfulness withal. It is a type of the man's life, this pitching-away of the shoes. An original man;—not a secondhand, borrowing or begging man. Let us stand on our own basis, at any

rate! On such shoes as we ourselves can get . . . not on . . . the thing [Nature] has given another than us! (154)

It is wrong to depend on others, Carlyle declares, wrong to accept something one has not earned for oneself. Nobility lies in the refusal of charitable offers.

This object lesson accords somewhat awkwardly with Carlyle's habitual demand for a society governed by "mutual helpfulness," but it fully reflects other Carlylean values. In particular, Carlyle is intent here on affirming what Herbert Sussman calls "the manliness of literary 'Labour,'" a manliness under threat from "the bourgeois model of manhood as active engagement in the commercial and technological world," on the one hand, and an influx of women authors, on the other.[29] Thus, while Carlyle's hostility to the cash nexus draws him to a vision of mendicant orders, he cannot reconcile this mendicancy with a "manfulness" conceived in terms of "rude stubborn self-help." Indeed, Sussman usefully explains Carlyle's ongoing interest in the all-male, celibate community of the monastery in terms of a desire for a masculine vocational model, but in "The Hero as Man of Letters" this concern over masculinity better accounts for his abandonment of the monk-model.

The Johnson anecdote makes clear that, even as male Victorian authors seek to articulate styles of manhood that can "be affirmed outside the economic arena,"[30] manliness retains as its sine qua non an economic self-sufficiency conceived in the first instance as a refusal to solicit or receive charity. Moreover, the near-universal desire to attain and display this independence almost invariably outweighs any desire to enhance literature's "moral authority" by asserting its "(putative) distance from the 'masculine' sphere of alienation and market relations," as Mary Poovey puts it.[31] Thus, Poovey's own influential reading of *David Copperfield* in terms of this latter project underestimates the crucial importance of David's market success to Dickens's effort to "enhance the social status of the literary man":[32] insofar as Dickens represents authorship as a form of "nonalienated labor," he does so to legitimize the alienation—the sale—of the fruits of that labor; at the same time, the very fact that one can make a living and support a family through this activity does much to enhance, indeed establish, its social legitimacy. In *Bleak House,* by contrast, Dickens portrays the artist truly intent on maintaining his distance from the marketplace—the proudly "amateur" and shamelessly improvident Harold Skimpole—as contemptibly irresponsible toward both his family and his art.[33]

Carlyle is at least nominally more willing than Dickens to challenge conventional notions of respectability, and, as we have seen, he began his discussion by dismissing the market system as the worst of all possible arrangements. Yet opponents of political economy such as Carlyle are at least as committed to an ideal of productive labor as the political economists they disdain, and—as the rhetoric of the Johnson anecdotes suggests—begging stands in opposition to productive labor as well as to market exchange. In identifying self-help with *originality* and opposing this originality to begging and borrowing, Carlyle draws on a labor theory of value that privileges production over exchange as the source of value, with exchange relegated to "an epiphenomenal status."[34] Thus Johnson, an "original man," pitches away the shoes because he, as or like a productive laborer, intends to bring something new and valuable into the world. "A begging man," by contrast, is as "secondhand" as the shoes Johnson refuses, because he engages only in parasitic acts of exchange. Begging's difference from productive labor here trumps its difference from market exchange.

To make matters worse, begging's status as a form of unproductive exchange tends to shade into an identification of begging with *idleness* as opposed to *work* of any kind. Begging, that is, is widely seen not merely as the quintessential recourse of the idle but as tantamount to idleness itself.[35] By definition, beggars are not workers, but rather occupy the ranks of "Those Who Cannot Work" or "Those Who Will Not Work," as Henry Mayhew puts it.[36] As the foremost preacher of the gospel of work, Carlyle hates idleness even more than he hates the cash nexus: "Idleness is worst, Idleness alone is without hope: work earnestly at anything, you will by degrees learn to work at almost all things. There is endless hope in work, were it even work at making money."[37] From this perspective, it is remarkable that Carlyle ever comes as close as he does to endorsing begging. And indeed, Carlyle himself seems somewhat surprised by his attraction to begging, for, as we saw earlier, no sooner does he raise the idea than he drops it. In turning away from begging, moreover, Carlyle radically transforms his argument, as he now focuses on describing alternatives to begging instead of alternatives to commodification. How should authors live, he asks, if not by begging? How should authors live in order to avoid becoming or resembling beggars?

While itself striking, this reorientation of Carlyle's argument has truly startling effects: he proceeds to go over the same ground he has already covered, only this time in reverse. Thus, immediately after declaring that "begging is not in our course at the present time," he repeats the praise of poverty that had led him to celebrate the mendicant orders of monks: poverty tests the potential author and teaches him "that outward profit, that success of any kind is *not* the goal he has to aim at" (143). But what if the goal is not so much success as survival? In embracing poverty but ruling out begging, Carlyle no longer has an explanation of how struggling authors are to be kept from starving. In implicit response to this objection, he allows that "money, in truth can do much" even if "it cannot do all." Backpedaling furiously, he reconsiders one possibility he has already rejected, a system of grants or stipends. "Besides, were the money-furtherances, the proper season for them, the fit assigner of them, all settled," he now asks, "how is the [Robert] Burns to be recognised that merits these?" (144).

This question of "recognition" troubles Carlyle, but it does not stymie him. With a logic as parsimonious as his authentic man-of-letters hero will need to be, Carlyle answers his own question by declaring that "he must pass through the ordeal, and prove himself. *This* ordeal; this wild welter of a chaos which is called Literary Life: this too is a kind of ordeal!" (144). In other words, the marketplace itself may be the one thing needed, precisely by virtue of its neglect and mistreatment of authors. As a site and source of resistance, Carlyle suggests, the marketplace presents an appropriate test of merit. The very qualities that condemn the marketplace also redeem it.

By making a living in the alien, chaotic marketplace and thereby proving that he is not beggarly, the author also shows that authorship itself is not beggarly, not a form of unproductive idleness. Indeed, the priority Carlyle places on gaining this point accounts not only for his rapprochement with the marketplace but also for his otherwise mysterious refusal even to entertain the notion that writing should be a leisure-time activity, as Samuel Taylor Coleridge among others famously argues.[38] Carlyle's vision of an economy of scarcity further reinforces this linkage of market success to productive labor, as does the neat symmetry of his argument's movement from the marketplace to begging and back again. Such reinforcement is necessary, however, precisely because the effectiveness of market success in distinguishing an author from a beggar is by no means assured. The lecture's symmetry is in fact false, for while Carlyle starts out by treating market exchange and begging as opposites, when he considers begging in relation to productive labor this earlier opposition dissolves: the operative distinction becomes instead that between production and exchange, with begging and selling both versions of the latter. From this perspective, begging epitomizes exchange divorced from production, a subcategory that can encompass versions or instances of market exchange itself. Market success by itself, in other words, does not necessarily reflect or impart the anti-beggarly qualities of industriousness, "originality," and independence that Carlyle seeks to demonstrate; at best, such success may serve to mark a nominal distinction between author and beggar, but it does not foreclose the possibility of their fundamental kinship as unproductive parasites.

Despite Carlyle's efforts, then, the marketplace may fail to provide the distance from begging he seeks to ascribe to it. For this reason, perhaps, he is finally no more willing to embrace the marketplace than he was begging. Instead, the course of his argument having returned him to his starting point—the spectacle of the author abandoned to the whims of the market—he considers simply beginning anew: "For Men of Letters, as for all other sorts of men. How to regulate that struggle? There is the whole question" (144). Unwilling to go (or continue to go) in circles, however, he takes refuge in a vision of utopia: "By far the most interesting fact I hear about the Chinese is . . . that they do attempt to make their Men of Letters their Governors!" (145). Short of this millennium, Carlyle finds himself at a loss. Far from concluding, however, that if authors' material conditions cannot be improved they must therefore be transcended, Carlyle calls into question the very possibility of such transcendence by declaring these conditions symptomatic of a spiritual crisis. Thus, looking at the eighteenth century, he announces mournfully that "the evil that pressed heaviest on those Literary Heroes of ours was not the want of organisation for Men of Letters, but a far deeper one; out of which, indeed, this and so many other evils for the Literary Man, and for all men, had, as from their fountain, taken rise[:] the *spiritual paralysis* . . .

of the Age" (146–47). Carlyle here reasserts the philosophical idealism that formed the basis for his claims concerning the heroic status of authors in the first place, but the metaphysical hierarchy that made authors' material conditions crucially important now sets a limit to that importance. Coming as it does on the heels of his failure to imagine a satisfactory literary system, this potentially dialectical reversal constitutes little more than an admission of defeat.

Uncharitable Interpretation and the Guild of Literature and Art

As we have seen, "The Hero as Man of Letters" displays a striking ambivalence toward begging: as the opposite of market exchange, begging is appealing, but as the opposite of productive labor, it is contemptible. In the mid-nineteenth-century discourse of authorship more generally, however, these attitudes are rarely so evenly balanced: although the long-standing scholarly emphasis on writers' efforts to distance culture from the marketplace might lead one to expect otherwise, it is the second, antibegging orientation of Carlyle's account and not its earlier, anti-market/pro-begging orientation that proves typical. As the example of Carlyle suggests, when the aversion to begging and hostility to the marketplace clash, the antibegging imperative tends to prevail. While attitudes toward the role and influence of the marketplace vary, virtually everyone who discusses how writers should live rejects begging as a legitimate option.

Writers on the subject reject begging for much the same reason Carlyle eventually does: begging epitomizes unproductiveness, a status that implies dependency and a resistance to work. There are also a great many authors who do not share Carlyle's desire to challenge conventional notions of respectability, and who are unwilling to embrace (even rhetorically) the poverty and dislocation associated with begging. Yet rather than simply discard or ignore begging as an option, authors work to cultivate their individual and collective identity as specifically, emphatically *not* beggars. This project is made particularly pressing and difficult by a factor that "The Hero as Man of Letters" obscures: the existence of authors actively engaged in begging. Carlyle portrays begging as the market's conceptual alternative rather than its supplement—that is, as the voluntary but no longer viable behavior of medieval monks rather than a practice individuals continue to turn to when they fail in the labor market. Thus, he shows authors struggling and suffering, but he never acknowledges the simple reality that, even as he speaks, authors and would-be authors are soliciting, and sometimes receiving, charity.[39] This situation leads many who address the economics of authorship to ask not whether authors should spurn the market and turn to begging but rather what if anything should be done for authors whom the market spurns. As a result, many participants in this discourse pay much greater attention than Carlyle does to possible alternative sources of income: whereas Carlyle only gestures toward generic "money-furtherances" (144), they investigate a range of possibilities between charity and market rewards. Writers evaluate the few established extramarket resources, such as royal pensions and the Royal Literary Fund; they discuss expanding or resurrecting older forms of support, such as aristocratic patronage, government sinecures, and publication by subscription; and they plan more innovative arrangements involving lectureships, stipends, subsidized housing and the like, often to be administered under the auspices of newly envisioned professional organizations.[40]

Yet the challenges authors face in finding alternatives to begging are not only logistical but also rhetorical, conceptual, and finally ideological: not only must authors establish systems of support, they must establish that this support is truly an alternative to, rather than a version of, alms to beggars. To keep authors from begging—as opposed, say, merely to keeping them from starving—means keeping their activities and transactions from being easily characterized or widely perceived as begging. While such a project *may* involve changes in the economic conditions of authorship, it *must* involve persuasive acts of description and interpretation. The point is not that participants in this discourse are interested solely in matters of "mere" perception as opposed to the actual material conditions of authors, but rather that they are interested in questions of legitimacy as well as practicality, and the legitimacy of any given form of support rests largely on its difference from alms. With regard to this difference, perception *is* reality. Moreover, this legitimization plays a crucial role in securing actual, material support.

Thus, just as dismay at the idea of authors receiving charity motivates efforts to create extramarket systems of support, this anticharity orientation also plays a crucial role in determining the form such efforts take.

Activists go to great lengths to guard themselves "from being supposed to wish that a mere money-service, a system of flattery and beggary, should replace that of the booksellers," as John Forster puts it (writing of Oliver Goldsmith but thinking of the challenges he and his colleagues face).[41] In order to dignify the transfers of cash they advocate, proponents of nonmarket forms of authorial support therefore engage in what I will call *uncharitable interpretation:* the categorization of a suspect transaction as tribute or market exchange or the repayment of a debt or nearly anything, in short, except charity.

Uncharitable interpretation mirrors—that is, resembles and reverses—the more familiar conceptual or ideological operation encapsulated in the notion of the gift. Gift giving, according to Marcel Mauss's influential theory, commonly occurs within a cycle of reciprocity involving the imposition and fulfillment of obligations; gifts, in other words, are not really free—and therefore not really gifts, as various commentators have noted.[42] Like a market economy, then, a gift economy employs a calculus of debt and credit, but the gift economy typically disavows this calculus. Uncharitable interpretation, by contrast, typically seeks to foreground this calculus, so as to represent apparent gifts as acts of equivalent exchange. William Dorrit, the Father of the Marshalsea, exemplifies this strategy when, after receiving his inheritance, he transforms Arthur Clennam's earlier gifts into loans: "I shall repay the— hum—the advances I have had from you, sir, with peculiar pleasure."[43] Here we do not find the notion of the gift being used to disguise a market transaction, but rather the reverse.[44]

Ironically and not unproblematically, in other words, schemes to supplement the literary marketplace often end up relying on a rhetoric and logic of debt, credit, and exchange similar if not identical to that of the marketplace itself. This reinscription of a market logic is ironic and problematic, it should be stressed, not because advocates of market supplements disdain the marketplace, but rather because their efforts are premised on an assertion of its inadequacy. That is, the more a transaction resembles market exchange, the less it resembles charity, but an emphasis on the former similarity also tends to obscure any rationale for supplementing the market in the first place: after all, the best measure of market value is the market itself. And—to reverse my earlier emphasis— even though these advocates do not believe that authors should shun the marketplace, they *are* arguing that the market value of one's work should not be the sole basis for its remuneration. Indeed, the very attempt to supplement the marketplace both presupposes and reinforces the view that literary value, or, more broadly, the value of artistic and intellectual pursuits, cannot be reduced to exchange value—otherwise there would be little reason to aid commercially unsuccessful writers (other than the benevolence that motivates charity). Again, this rejection of the marketplace as the sole or ultimate index of value neither constitutes nor implies a complete disavowal of market competition and payment, let alone a modernist embrace of market failure as a source of artistic legitimacy.[45] Nonetheless, the very establishment of a category of nonmarket, noncharitable funding for authors does work subtly to redefine the meaning of authorial participation in the marketplace itself, by implying that even authors *in* the marketplace are not necessarily *of* it.

In the two decades immediately following Carlyle's lecture, the effort to save authors from begging reaches its highest profile and fullest manifestation in the writings and activities of the father of the Father of the Marshalsea, Charles Dickens, and two of his close friends, Edward Bulwer-Lytton and John Forster. These writers' efforts to defend and establish systems of support that will stave off the threat of begging dovetail with their well-known desire to enhance the "dignity of literature." Indeed, the two goals are best considered together, for each serves as a means to the other's end: by saving authors from begging, extramarket support improves the image of authorship as a profession; at the same time, raising the image of the profession helps make it possible to institute such support and to distinguish it from alms to beggars.

The practice—and, along with it, the impasses—of uncharitable interpretation characterize both the defense of existing forms of authorial support and the advocacy of new ones. Uncharitable interpretation plays a key role, for instance, in the best-known episode in the midcentury debate over the "dignity of literature," the dispute involving John Forster, William Thackeray, and the *Morning Chronicle*. This dispute's notoriety stems largely from Thackeray's participation, as he writes a letter to the *Morning Chronicle* defending his negative portrayal of authors in *Pendennis*.[46] The exchange begins, however, with an attack on the awarding of civil-list pensions to authors and revolves around the question of whether or not the marketplace should be the sole source of funding for literary and intellectual endeavors. This battle over the legitimacy of extra-market support for authors is waged largely through competing efforts to assimilate this support to, or distinguish it from, alms to beggars.

In an editorial occasioned by the death of a literary pensioner, the *Morning Chronicle* disparages civil-list pensions as a mischievous form of "protection."[47] Advocating a laissez-faire system of literary production, the article asserts that the "self-dependence [of 'genius']—its capacity for making its own way against all obstacles—is the best criterion of its genuineness" (487). In fact, the *Chronicle* maintains, thanks to "the love of notoriety inherent in mankind, combined with the common distaste for continuous or unexciting labour," there will never be a shortage of writers (488). Nonetheless, the article suggests that "national aid" may be justified if it is conferred not on the basis of "poverty, coupled with ordinary merit, in a man of letters" but rather "as the spontaneous expression of national gratitude, as the promise and forerunner of immortality" (488). As a rule, however, pensions are unnecessary and even invidious, for "one ill-bestowed pension . . . is quite sufficient to spread injurious and ill-founded notions regarding the claims of literary paupers upon the State" (488).

Responding two days later in *The Examiner* (which he edited), John Forster seizes on this last phrase, complaining that "it is a degrading view of the claims of men of literary and scientific eminence to call them the 'claims of literary paupers on the State.'"[48] Not only degrading, this epithet is also inaccurate: "The State is not asked to support 'literary paupers,' and is not asked to 'protect' literature." Forster argues,

> There is no parallel between commercial protection and the recognition of services done to the State by literary men. Services done to the State by distinguished efforts in art, literature, and science, are as unequivocal, and at the least as important, as services done by professors of arms, law, divinity, and diplomacy. The claims of literature and science are for a due recognition and recompense of such valuable service rendered to the State. They are advanced, not in behalf of individuals, but of the class. They are not beggars' petitions, but demands for justice. (489)

The logic of this argument is clear: from the premise that the efforts of "literary men" are "services done to the State," it follows that the state is indebted to these men, and therefore that any payment it makes to them constitutes repayment of that debt. Pensions and the like are not charity, nor even supererogatory tokens of gratitude or esteem (or what Mr. Dorrit would call "Testimonials"[49]), but simply "due . . . recompense." Less clear, however, is the exact nature of the "services" literary men provide, and Forster has little to say on this score. Perhaps he does not feel the need to, given the *Chronicle*'s concession that "an exciseman's place was [not] good enough for BURNS; [and] a pension was [not] wasted upon SAMUEL JOHNSON" (488); nonetheless, his argument soon slips to a weaker claim: "There are many modes in which men of science and literature can render available services to the State—as the teachers and managers of educational institutions; as curators and directors of public museums, libraries, and gardens; as members of scientific associations, supplied by the State with funds for the prosecution of experiments and observations" (490). Thus, rather than continue to maintain that literary men render valuable service to the state by the very act of pursuing their literary labors, Forster here makes the very different assertion that these individuals have skills the state can tap for its own purposes. This switch suggests an implicit acknowledgment that a demand for "recompense" for authors' "service" *as authors* may be a demand for something for nothing, after all—or, at least, that it may continue to be perceived as such.

Despite this slippage, however, Forster goes on to advocate not only the rewarding of already-completed efforts—"retiring pensions," as he puts it at one point (491)—but also the funding of those efforts as they occur, or in order that they may occur. He argues that it is not enough to pay authors for service rendered to the state, because often they cannot render that service without first receiving support: "In acquiring scholastic treasures, the man of letters is more likely to miss than to obtain the means of providing against daily wants" (491). This likelihood stems from the very nature of the writer's activity: whereas for "the votaries of commerce . . . gain is the object of their efforts," for "the votary of intellectual labour," by contrast, "learning, or the mastery of art, is the object of effort" (491). The disjunction between intellectual pursuits, on the one hand, and commerce and the provision of daily wants, on the other, explains why men of letters require extramarket support. Implicitly, this disjunction also explains why men of letters *de-*

serve such support—that is, for their very indifference to or transcendence of commercial values. Forster's interest, however, lies not in critiquing these values but rather in justifying his project to those who hold them, and he therefore portrays "study" itself as a form of acquisitive labor (albeit in a noncommercial economy) and the relationship between "the industrial member of society" and "the man of letters" as complementary, not antagonistic: "For enlightenment and refinement the industrial class are in great measure dependent on the literary, and for the means of subsistence the literary are in equal measure dependent on the industrial class" (491). Forster here adopts a classic trope of political economy, the division of labor. This strategy of normalization seems canny, yet it threatens to succeed too well, by transforming the argument into, or allowing it to be easily mistaken for, an affirmation of existing free-market arrangements. "But," he therefore hastens to add, "the making of books is only a small part of literary labour . . . and to leave this class entirely and exclusively dependent on book-making for subsistence is to deny them time and opportunities to study." Rhetorically, however, the effect of this statement is to undermine the model of equivalent exchange it ostensibly clarifies. In implicit acknowledgment of this failure, Forster again abandons the "strong" version of his argument to call instead for the provision of public-sector jobs that would "provide for men of literature the means of at once prosecuting their studies and of actively serving the public" (491).

For the second time in the course of a brief article, then, Forster slides from arguing that literary men serve the public by writing to arguing that literary men should be allowed to serve the public, in part so that they can write. The stakes are much higher the second time this slippage occurs, however, for the discussion as a whole has moved from a consideration of "the recognition of services done" to the "desireable means of properly providing for literary men" (491), from the question of "justice" to that of "subsistence," and with this new focus the article has begun to resemble the "beggar's petitions" it disavows. Forster, at least, seems to think so, as—in a textbook example of protesting too much—he concludes by flatly rejecting this comparison yet again: "In asserting the claims of literature to public employment and distinction, we have no idea of suing *in formâ pauperis*." To shore up the distinction between author and beggar, he moves beyond his earlier assertion—that authors

impose a debt on society that should be repaid—to claim instead that authors provide a gift that by its very nature cannot be repaid: whereas earlier he spoke of "due recognition and recompense . . . of valuable service
rendered," he now proclaims that "literature and literary men can give,
and do give, much more to the State than the State ever can repay" (491).
By claiming that the state can *never* repay literary men, Forster implies
that there is a qualitative, rather than merely a quantitative, difference between what the two parties have to offer: the worth of literature cannot
be measured by the coin of the realm. Here, then, we hear an echo of that
foundational claim of aesthetic theory, the incommensurability of aesthetic value and exchange value; its incommensurability with exchange
value, one might say, *is* the value of the aesthetic. But whatever the merit
of this notion, an argument against the ready translation between kinds
of value does not readily translate into an argument for paying authors,
just as you cannot demand payment for a gift. Rather than clinching the
case for just compensation, then, this emphasis on incommensurability
militates against it. Forster is saying, in effect, that authors deserve whatever they receive, but his formulation invites the response Thackeray is
only too happy to provide: "The rewards of the profession," the novelist
announces, "are not to be measured by the money-standard."[50]

Despite Forster's evident investment in the uncharitable interpretation of
extramarket authorial support, not even he and his colleagues attempt to
describe any and all monies handed over to authors as not-charity. On
the contrary, they attack the foremost existing institution for aiding authors, the Royal Literary Fund, precisely on the grounds that it "limits its
proceedings . . . to dealing with the followers of Literature as beggars
only."[51] And indeed, just as the newly enriched Mr. Dorrit makes one
final trip around the Marshalsea yard, giving out money and "sa[ying] in
every . . . case, 'it is a donation, not a loan,' "[52] the Literary Fund's regulations expressly seek to rule out uncharitable interpretation, as they
specify that "all relief shall be given as a donation towards the removal of
the distress of the applicant, and not as a loan, nor for the completion of
any literary work."[53] Critics of the Literary Fund, by contrast, believe
that "indigent and deserving followers of Literature" should receive
some form of noncharitable support.[54] Precisely because no institution-
alized mechanism for providing such aid currently exists (with the pos-

sible exception of the civil-list pension, which, as we have seen, is itself viewed as limited and somewhat compromised), they set out to establish one, and to establish its legitimacy by distinguishing it as fully as possible from the RLF. Midcentury efforts to create a professional organization for authors are thus crucially inspired and shaped by dissatisfaction with the eleemosynary character of the few available forms of extramarket support. As a result, this organizational activity involves elaborate exercises in the practice and (one might say) solicitation of uncharitable interpretation. The most elaborate such exercise—which is to say, the most fully formed effort to invent a new system of support—is that undertaken by the Guild of Literature and Art, founded in 1851 by a group led by Dickens, Forster, and Bulwer-Lytton.[55]

According to the Guild's prospectus (written mainly by Forster and Bulwer-Lytton), the "originators and promoters" of the Guild are authors and artists "anxiously desirous to aid those distinguished in pursuits similar to their own; whose youth they have seen prematurely broken by noble struggles for independence, or whose age they have witnessed a suppliant for bounty, so administered as to embitter every memory of service, and humiliate every honest sentiment of pride."[56] Here, as throughout the prospectus, the emphasis falls not simply on the provision of aid to struggling authors and artists, but rather on the provision of aid in such a way as to preserve the recipients' "independence" and "pride." Invoking the cardinal distinction between forms of extramarket support, the organizers of the Guild stress their desire that "whatever aid they may have the power to proffer or suggest . . . should necessitate no degrading plea of poverty—no painful exposition of calamity and want; but that it should bear the character of *a tribute to merit, not of an alms to destitution*" (855; emphasis added).

The Guild seeks to avoid the stigma of charity and the charge of governmental "protection" by cultivating an image of collective independence; this is to be an organization *of* as well as *for* authors, as its name suggests: *guild,* the prospectus notes, is "the name given by old Saxon custom to societies in which the members of a class contributed to the benefit of each other" (856). Dickens, in his *Household Words* article on the Guild, places great weight on this point. Turning on its head the standing accusation that authors are seeking special treatment—as the *Morning Chronicle* asks, "Why is an unsuccessful writer to stand on a different footing from an unsuccessful lawyer or surgeon?" (488)[57]— Dickens says "the real question" at hand is "whether Literature shall continue to be an exception from all other professions and pursuits, in having no resource for its distressed and divided followers but in eleemosynary aid; or whether it is good that they should be provident, united, helpful of one another, and independent."[58] By creating this mutual-aid society, authors are simply bringing their profession in line with "all other[s]"; as such a society, moreover, any money that changes hands will constitute a form of self-help, not charity. The Guild should therefore be understood to enhance, rather than compromise, the independence of its members and, by extension, the respectability of authorship itself as a profession.

While created, then, to address the financial precariousness of authorship, the Guild is also intended to rely on and exhibit the newfound financial strength of authors as a class at a time when unprecedented numbers of individuals are able to earn a living by writing. The promoters therefore propose opening "a Branch Insurance and Provident Society, solely for the Professors of Literature and of Art," with, among authors, "all writers, of either sex, of original works or dramas, or of not less than twenty original papers in Periodicals" eligible for membership (852). Because authors' "distresses . . . have been popularly ascribed" to a lack of "ordinary prudence" (855), this element of the proposal is important to the image of the profession as a whole, as well as to the well-being of individual authors. Rather than stop at this meaningful but relatively modest goal, however, the Prospectus also unveils an ambitious plan to create a nonmarket system of support for worthy authors. The promoters envision "especial resources . . . that would enable them to smooth the earlier path of a future Southey,—to sustain from despair the youth of a future Chatterton,—or, should a new Burns arise, to offer . . . something more suited to the vocation of genius, something more worthy the ornament of an age, than the place of an exciseman" (856). Here the rhetoric of legitimization shifts from the collective nature of the Guild's organization to the selective nature of its awards: the Guild's goal is "to lift *the chiefs of their class* above the chances of famine, or the relief that is bestowed upon a pauper" (857; emphasis added). The proposed aid is distinguished from such relief, moreover, precisely by this restriction to "the chiefs of their class"—or so the Guild's organizers hope. Thus, the

Prospectus stresses the Guild's lack of interest in aiding the "large proportion of authors and artists [who] fail simply because their abilities are not suited to the profession they have embraced"; "a fund applied to the relief of these," the Prospectus explains in a pregnant turn of phrase, "though it might serve as a charity, could not pretend to be a tribute to merit" (855).

In order to offer such tributes, the Guild proposes establishing an "Institute." This Institute, carefully and explicitly designed in such a way as to distinguish its support from "the humiliating charity of an Asylum" (856), will have a warden, members, and associates, who are to receive "salaries" of £100 to £200 a year, some with housing on land donated by Bulwer-Lytton. Individuals insured through the Guild, along with certain "exceptional cases," will be eligible to offer themselves as candidates for these positions, which are to be filled (again with certain exceptions) through a vote of the Guild's members. Institute members will be elected for life from "Writers and Artists of established reputation, and generally of mature years (or, if young, in failing health), to whom the income attached to the appointment may be an object of honourable desire" (854); associates will be chosen either for life or for a fixed term from among those who are "less known to the general public" and those "in earlier life, who give promise of future eminence, and to whom a temporary income of £100 a year may be of essential and permanent service" (854). Applications are required for these positions, but there is no means test; instead, "the application for the office should be held a sufficient presumption that the candidate does not disdain the modest salary attached to it" (855).

The Guild's organizers take special pains to articulate the rationale for these "salaries"—to justify, as it were, their labeling as such. These payments, the prospectus explains, are intended to serve "first, as a means to support those fitted by industry or talent to render service to mankind, in the earlier and ruder steps of their career; and, secondly, and more especially, as an offering of gratitude to those who have made their order illustrious, maintained the renown of their country in Literature and Art, or, even in humbler departments, contributed to the enjoyment and instruction of mankind" (855). In their zeal to strengthen the distinction between these so-called salaries and charity, however, the organizers do not stop at representing them as investments or rewards. Instead, they also require the recipients of this money to take on certain responsibilities, such as delivering occasional lectures to mechanics' institutes, on the principle that "it is . . . desirable to annex to the receipt of a salary the performance of a duty." At the same time, they specify that "it is not intended that such duty should make so great a demand upon the time and labour [of these individuals] as to deprive the Public of their services in those departments in which they have gained distinction, or to divert their own efforts for independence from their accustomed pursuits" (853–54).

In short, the prospectus ends up characterizing the money the Guild plans to distribute as both earned and not earned, both imposing a duty and fulfilling one, both preserving and anticipating its recipients' independence. The prospectus thus reads less as a compelling blueprint for an alternative economic model than a virtual diagram of its drafters' anxieties as they attempt to secure an uncharitable interpretation of their activities. The plan's contradictions and inconsistencies, however, do not reflect a simple failure of logic or imagination on the part of these activists, but rather the ideological constraints under which they operate: to legitimize the Guild's supplementation of the marketplace, literary labor and its products must be shown to have a value the market does not always recognize or reward, but the best way to ensure this supplement's difference from charity is to represent it as a calculated, calibrated payment for goods and services. While these conflicting demands may not be absolutely contradictory, they prove largely irreconcilable.

Matching and indeed exacerbating the conceptual and rhetorical challenges the Guild's organizers face are the material—which is to say, financial—obstacles in their path. For although the Guild trades on an image of collective self-sufficiency, it discounts the possibility of endowing its Institute solely through the collection of dues or pooling of authorial capital. Not only is it therefore necessary to raise funds, but the manner in which they are raised, as much as that in which they are distributed, will play a crucial role in determining the Guild's legitimacy. Indeed, while the failure to win an uncharitable interpretation of the Guild's "salaries" threatens to taint their recipients with the stigma of charity, such a failure with regard to the Guild's fund-raising activities threatens to taint the fund-raisers themselves.

Having already mounted several ad hoc theatrical performances to raise money for individual distressed authors, Dickens and his collaborators now plan another such production "to bring the plan . . . into general notice, and to form the commencement of the necessary fund" (856).[59] Bulwer-Lytton writes a comedy, *Not So Bad as We Seem; or, Many Sides to a Character,* expressly for the purpose, granting copyright to the Guild as well. As Dickens states in his *Household Words* article, however, "no child can suppose that the profits of the comedy alone will be sufficient for such an Endowment as is sought to be established."[60] Instead, "for farther support to the endowment by subscription, and especially by annual subscription, it is intended to appeal to the Public" (856–57). This appeal, it is hoped, will save authors from having to beg.

This turn to subscriptions as a funding mechanism—the very method used by the Royal Literary Fund, no less—would seem to jibe poorly with the Guild's rhetoric of independence. And indeed, this scheme represents a major retreat from that outlined by Dickens three years earlier in the proposed prospectus for a Provident Union of Literature, Science, and Art, a precursor to the Guild which never got past the planning stages. Resolving "to make no appeal to public charity and to canvass no one in behalf of this Society," the earlier organization proposes raising its funds through regular "Amateur Theatrical Representations." To secure an uncharitable interpretation of this arrangement itself, Dickens emphasizes the professionalism of the "Amateur" performances: "The Society will never address itself to the Public as a Charitable Institution, but . . . will always consider that a sufficient return is made for the Money which is received for Tickets," the prospectus insists, because its plays will be "presented with the utmost care, and the most scrupulous attention to accuracy, fidelity, and completeness in all respects." The plays themselves are described as "sterling," as if to insure the equivalence of the exchange: theatergoers will not merely get what they paid for, they will virtually get back what they paid with.[61]

Dickens implicitly presents the Guild's retreat from this fund-raising strategy as a bow to realism ("no child can suppose that the profits of the comedy alone will be sufficient"), and the earlier plan does seem to have been rendered impracticable by its puristic pursuit of uncharitable interpretation—its prospectus even announces that "because the practice of canvassing for relief from public bodies . . . in the monstrous extent to which it has arisen, [is] one of the disgraces of the time, the Committee

will receive no application for relief from any person whomsoever."[62]
Yet the Guild's founders make numerous compromises in order to keep
authors' independence from being compromised, and once having
started down this slippery slope, they accelerate headlong toward the
very sort of behavior they hope to render obsolete. Thus, in order to
raise money and heighten public interest as effectively as possible, Dickens writes to the Duke of Devonshire, who arranges for the first performance of *Not So Bad as We Seem* to be held at Devonshire House, before
Queen Victoria and her Court.[63] As soon as the Guild secures this patronage, moreover, Bulwer-Lytton begins to worry that the Duke will
be offended by the play, a comedy set in the reign of George I and filled
with political and romantic intrigue (including, like *The History of Henry
Esmond,* a Jacobite plot). The play features a Duke of Middlesex who is
satirized for his pride, and much of the action revolves around his agents'
attempts to regain his brother's scandalous memoir. As a result, the playwright fears that the plot may suggest "mystery and gossip about the
Duke [of Devonshire]'s private life," and is anxious as well to remove a
number of jokes that come at the expense of the play's duke.[64]

The rich irony generated by the Guild's lack of capital is hardly less-
ened by the fact that after reading the script the Duke of Devonshire
"thoroughly understands and appreciates the comedy of the Duke," as
Dickens reassures Bulwer-Lytton.[65] Clearly, the beneficent real Duke is
preferable to the "proud Duke" condemned by the play's "Grub Street
Author and Pamphleteer," David Fallen: "Years ago, when a kind word
from his Grace, a nod of his head, a touch of his hand, would have turned
my foes into flatterers, I had the meanness to name him my patron—inscribed to him a work, took it to his house, and waited in his hall among
porters and lackeys—till, sweeping by to his carriage, he said, 'Oh! you
are the poet? take this,'—and extended his alms, as if to a beggar."[66]
Nonetheless, the difference between the Duke of Middlesex and the
Duke of Devonshire is merely that between a bad patron and a good one.
Indeed, the latter's indulgence only punctuates the extent to which the
founders of the Guild, exerting themselves "in the cause of their brotherhood," succeed in incurring a "debt that we can but feebly acknowledge," as Bulwer-Lytton writes in dedicating the play to the Duke (v).

If the need to raise money is by no means the least of the Guild's problems, the compromises and even contradictions this need occasions only

reinforce those already in evidence in the plans for disbursing the money. In a society dominated by laissez-faire doctrines of political economy, all nonmarket transactions threaten to impose debts that can be but feebly acknowledged. Ironically, however, the Guild's difficulties may also be seen to stem from a failure to go *far enough* in challenging the hegemony of the marketplace and its logic of exchange. Instead of adopting the classic professionalizing strategy of seeking to "persuade society to set aside a secure income, or a monopolistic level of fees, to enable [professionals] to perform [their expert] service rather than jeopardize it by subjecting it to the rigours of capitalist competition in the conventional free market,"[67] the Guild advocates this kind of arrangement only in selected instances where the market fails to provide adequate support.[68] This approach would seem less radical and thus more easily advanced than a thoroughgoing rejection of the marketplace, but the very acknowledgment of the market's legitimate role weakens the case for its circumvention; as was already evident in Forster's defense of "encouragement of literature by the state," rapprochement with the marketplace threatens annexation by it. Conversely, and more damagingly, the Guild's efforts to circumvent the marketplace foreground the question of *need*. Ultimately, insofar as economic necessity provides these projects with their raison d'être, no amount of talk concerning worth or justice will put paid to the specter of charity.[69]

Nowhere are these problems more vividly dramatized, appropriately enough, than in the play written and performed to raise funds for the Guild. Seeking to contribute to the Guild's legitimization as well as its coffers, *Not So Bad as We Seem* incorporates the project's concerns into its rhetoric and its action, at first somewhat egregiously but later to remarkable effect. Unsurprisingly, the play stresses the poverty and heroism of authors, and repeats the Prospectus's call for collective action and mutual aid. Thus, the sight of David Fallen moves the politician Mr. Hardman—played in the original production by John Forster—to deliver the following speech:

> A state may but humble by alms; a minister corrupt by a bribe: what Patron then for Letters!—The public?—yes, for the Author, whose talents the Public may chance to appreciate. And for those who, with toils as severe, but with genius less shaped to the taste

of the many, can win not the ear of the day, why perhaps in some far distant age, when eno' of the strong have dropped to death broken-hearted, and eno' of the weak (bowed down by the tyrant Necessity) have veiled in shame and despair the eyes that once looked to the stars; these rival children of light may learn at last, that the tie they now rend should be the bond to unite them, and help one another. (71)

This tentative prophecy suggests that the play cannot provide a representation of the promised land but can only point the way there, since the desired system of collective self-help lies in the future. The speech also suggests, though, that the Guild, and indeed the play itself, as an event, can and do represent this ideal.

A later scene goes further to integrate the Guild's project into the plot of the play itself. Here Bulwer-Lytton constructs a remarkably layered tableau, a palimpsest of the various ways in which authors have historically obtained their livelihood. The scene is thus something of a case study in how to interpret and reinterpret interactions between a man with money and a man with a manuscript (I use the word *man* advisedly here, for the dynamic differs for women writers[70])—and therefore something of an allegory of the Guild itself. Magnifying the scene's symbolic—and ironic—potential is the fact that the man with the money is played by Charles Dickens.

As the scene opens, David Fallen (played by the artist Augustus Egg) is taking "one moment's respite from drudgery" to work on his own poem, which he calls "my grand bequest to my country." A Lord Wilmot appears—disguised, however, as the notoriously unscrupulous bookseller Edmund Curll. When Dickens/Wilmot/Curll announces, "I'm come to buy—," Fallen finishes his sentence: "this poem? it is nearly finished—twelve books—twenty years' labor—twenty-four thousand lines—£10, Mr. Curll, £10!" (104). Here, then, is the scene's first version of authorial income: market exchange, the sale of a text, or rather a copyright, to a publisher. This source of income is portrayed as legitimate, albeit inadequate; ironically, this inadequacy in fact enhances the transaction's legitimacy, by hinting at a fundamental discrepancy between literary value and exchange value. Thus, while it seems odd that Fallen wants to sell something he has just called a "bequest," the low price he seeks suggests that his true interest lies in securing publication, and thereby assuring that his gift will be received. At the same time, however, this scene may be said to hold out hope in the possibility of adequate, and even commensurate, compensation, insofar as Fallen's description of his poem implies that literary value is grounded, at least in part, in the same source as exchange value: the labor of production.[71] In any case, the scene is careful not to allow the possible incommensurability of literary value and market value to function as an excuse for the market's inadequacy, or a justification of authorial poverty—not to allow, that is, Fallen's proposed bargain to serve as a defense of the status quo—as "Curll" immediately rejects this offer. He does so, moreover, by co-opting a chestnut of those who argue for the protection of authors' rights: "Price of *Paradise Lost!* Can't expect such prices for poetry now-a-days, my dear Mr. Fallen" (104).[72]

The purpose of his visit, the disguised lord goes on to explain, is to offer Fallen three hundred guineas for "some most interesting papers" that have come into Fallen's possession (as an erstwhile Jacobite agent), "the private Memoirs and Confessions of a Man of Quality recently deceased . . . Lord Henry de Mowbray" (104). An older version of authorship is invoked here, with authors the suppliers of scandal and with an actual, physical manuscript rather than the right to reproduce a text as the object of the exchange. The fact that Fallen himself has not written this manuscript may suggest the imprecision of this genealogical allegory, but—especially in light of scholarship arguing for the dual invention of authorship and copyright—it may also suggest the "pre-authorial" nature of such writing, the extent to which scandal texts do not invite or entail the investment of authorial personality.[73] Again, though, the proposed deal is not consummated, this time because Fallen rejects the offer as a bribe (a word originally meaning "bread given to a beggar"). "Shame, shame on you, base huckster of conscience!" the poet cries. "I will not sell man's hearth to the public" (106).

At this point in the scene, "Curll" informs the poet that he is employed by "Lord Henry's nearest relation," the Duke of Middlesex, to recover the memoir, and he asks Fallen to name his price (106). When Fallen refuses money—despite the fact that it was this duke who had treated him like "a beggar"—and demands that "Curll" speak to him "not as tempter to pauper; but . . . as man speaks to man," Wilmot sheds his disguise and identifies himself. "Mr. Fallen," he declares, "your works first raised me from the world of the senses, and taught me to believe in such nobleness as I now hope for in you." Since the manuscript he seeks is "priceless," the lord argues, the proper economy in which it should circulate is that of the gift: "Give me this record to take to the Duke—no price, sir; for such things are priceless—and let me go hence with the sight of this poverty before my eyes, and on my soul the grand picture of the man who has spurned the bribe to his honor, and can humble by a gift the great prince who insulted him by alms" (107).

The scene does not, however, end on this note of Maussian triumph for Fallen. Instead, upon receiving the manuscript, Wilmot acknowledges, and seeks to redress, his own indebtedness: "Now you indeed make me twofold your debtor—in your books, the rich thought; in yourself, the heroic example. Accept from my superfluities, in small part of such debt, a yearly sum equal to that which your poverty refused as a bribe." "My Lord—My Lord," stammers the poet, and bursts into tears (108). Thus peeling back historical layers, the play seemingly arrives at a wish-fulfillment version of aristocratic patronage. In producing this model, however, the scene fails to resolve, and indeed may be said to foreground, a crucial ambiguity—perhaps *the* crucial ambiguity: does Lord Wilmot's offer reward David Fallen's independence or compromise it? Are the rich lord and the poor poet speaking to each other now "as man to man, and gentleman to gentleman," or again as "tempter to pauper"? The fact that the proffered annual stipend is equal in value to the spurned bribe, while no doubt intended as a form of poetic justice, threatens to render the two transactions interchangeable, their differences nugatory; what the lord's assertion of indebtedness gives, this exact equivalence takes away. Acknowledging this ambiguity and attempting to dispel it, Wilmot assures Fallen, "Oh, trust me, the day shall come, when men will feel that it is not charity we owe to the ennoblers of life—it is tribute!"; yet the use of the future tense here is hardly reassuring.

If the day Wilmot describes has not come within the play itself, has it come by means of the play—that is, with the advent of the Guild? Dickens, coming close to shedding—or perhaps fully internalizing—the role of Wilmot, goes on to suggest that this is indeed the case. This attempt to envision authors as noble recipients of tribute, however, quickly mutates into an author's fulsome tribute to the nobility, especially the

Queen: echoing the Prospectus's claim that "the day, at least [*sic*], has come when Civilisation should no longer forget the civilisers," Wilmot/ Dickens prophesies that "the day shall come . . . when your Order shall rise with the civilization it called into being; and, amidst an assembly of all that is lofty and fair in the chivalry of birth, it shall refer its claim to just rank among freemen, to some Queen whom even a Milton might have sung, and even a Hampden have died for" (108). Even as this speech evokes the occasion of the play's performance, it works to mystify that occasion's economic component, and the very attempt to finesse the Guild's fund-raising activities in this way suggests that they are less likely to overcome the dangerous ambiguity of the Wilmot/Fallen transaction than to reproduce it. In short, whether the transaction in question is that between Lord Wilmot and David Fallen, between Dickens/the Guild and the David Fallens of the nineteenth century, or between the Guild and its noble benefactors, the Guild's vision of equality and mutuality is nowhere to be seen, and the threat of begging only intensifies. More radically, the scene threatens to discredit the shared basis of charitable and uncharitable interpretation alike, as the sheer speed with which the players move from one transaction to the next—or from one interpretation of a single transaction to the next—calls attention less to the significance of the distinctions in question than to their tenuousness, and perhaps even their artificiality. David Fallen's spectacularly ambiguous response to Wilmot's speech literalizes the impasse reached in the scene: "O dream of my youth! My heart swells and chokes me!" (108). Disambiguating this response, albeit not in the way one might expect, the play ends with an epilogue titled "'David Fallen is Dead!,' or A Key to the Play," in which Mr. Hardman informs Lord Wilmot, "Your annuity killed him!"

> *Wilmot:* How—how? to the point.
> *Hardman:* By the shock on his nerves—at the sight of a joint.
> (158)[74]

However humorous in intent, this exchange does not so much deflect as confirm the dangers of the Wilmot/Fallen encounter and all that it comes to stand for.

The Guild of Literature and Art thus proves markedly more successful at showcasing its dilemmas than resolving them. Not surprisingly, then, the

Guild made little progress toward realizing its ideological or material goals: although the theatrical performances raise over £4,000 by 1854, the Guild's Institute was variously derided as a "literary Soup-Kitchen"[75] and "a system of outdoor relief,"[76] and the parliamentary bill incorporating the organization forbade it to fill its offices for seven years, after which time its structure proved largely unwieldy.[77] The Guild was eventually dissolved, its assets turned over to the very organizations against which it had sought to define itself, the Royal Literary Fund and the Artists' General Benevolent Institution.[78] In retrospect, at least, the dedication to *Bleak House,* written just two years after the play's début, already sounds like an epitaph—"Dedicated as a remembrance of our friendly union to my companions in the Guild of Literature and Art"[79]—and it is soon thereafter, in *Little Dorrit,* that Dickens turns from the frustrations of disavowing begging to the pleasures of parodying this disavowal. To be sure, this parody itself can also be seen as a sophisticated form of disavowal, and Dickens and his colleagues never completely abandoned the search for noneleemosynary alternatives to the marketplace.[80] Yet just as the conceptual and logistical ambition of the Guild remained unsurpassed in the nineteenth century, so too did its conceptual and logistical dead ends.

Intractable as the questions of productivity and payment prove, however, they do not exhaust the challenges that the specter of begging presented to authors—especially novelists, including financially successful ones. For these authors, even more troubling than the spectacle of beggarly authors is that of writerly beggars. Bringing back into play forms of materiality beyond the economic, the figure of the begging-letter writer raises vexing questions about the legitimacy of authorship as a profession and forces a rethinking of the formal workings and cultural work of the novel, as we shall see in the next chapter.

4   Sympathy for the Begging-Letter Writer

INTRODUCING HIS SURVEY entitled "The Street-Sellers of Stationery, Literature, and the Fine Arts" in *London Labour and the London Poor,* Henry Mayhew remarks upon "the self-esteem of the patterers":

> To patter, is a slang term, meaning to speak. To indulge in this kind of oral puffery, of course, requires a certain exercise of the intellect, and it is the consciousness of their mental superiority which makes the patterers look down upon the costermongers as an inferior body, with whom they object either to be classed or to associate. . . . "We are the haristocracy of the streets," was said to me by one of the street-folks, who told penny fortunes with a bottle. "People don't pay us for what we gives 'em, but only to hear us talk. We live like yourself, sir, by the hexercise of our hintellects—we by talking, and you by writing."[1]

This fortune-teller's claim of kinship with Mayhew is certainly piquant, but how much force does it carry? What difference does the distinction he notes between "talking" and "writing" make? Just how comparable are the livelihoods of Mayhew and his informant, not in the latter's eyes but in those of Mayhew and his readers?

The near repetition of Mayhew's own words, "a certain exercise of the intellect," in the very formula the patterer uses to equate himself with his interlocutor—"the hexercise of our hintellects"—seems to reinforce their identification.[2] Yet we would expect authors to object to being classed with London's "street-orators"—authors, too, have their self-esteem—and Mayhew proves no exception to this rule: not only does he refuse to dignify the fortune-teller's claim by responding to it openly, but by transcribing the speaker's errant *h*'s, he foregrounds the patterer's own distinction between spoken and written language and aligns it with a difference in class. The close resemblance of the two statements, in other words, highlights the gulf between the individuals making them. Mayhew himself is too busy appearing to take the patterer's claim lightly to flesh out this point, but implicit in this class distinction is a disparity not only in education but also in bodiliness, or level of implication in the material world:[3] authors, unlike patterers, need not put their own bodies on display in the marketplace, and the product of literary labor, a text, transcends its particular material instantiations (a fact underscored by its mechanical reproduction). Just as the patterers' dismissal of the costermongers as "an inferior body" relies on the perceived inferiority of body to intellect, this same hierarchy thus elevates those who live by writing above those who live by speaking.

Differently inflected, the opposition between writing and speaking may be invoked to distinguish authors from the group Mayhew describes as the worst kind of patterer, and with whom, as we saw in the last chapter, authors are historically associated: beggars, or those who do not "patter to help off their goods" but instead "*do nothing but patter,* as a means of exciting commiseration to their assumed calamities" (1:310). These individuals, Mayhew asserts, "*will* not work or do anything for their living," in contrast to the pattering street-sellers, who, by circulating "goods" as well as words, at least "do *something* for the bread they eat" (1:310). Equating "*do[ing] nothing but patter*" with doing nothing at all, Mayhew links beggars' reprehensible idleness and dependency—in short, their beggarliness—to the immateriality and ephemerality of their characteristic activity. The logic here recalls that of the political-economic doctrine of productive labor discussed in the last chapter: as John Stuart Mill puts it, productive labor encompasses "only those kinds of exertion which produce utilities embodied in material objects."[4] From this perspective, the distinction between writing and talking again serves as the basis for the respectability of authorship, only now the emphasis falls not on the relative disembodiment writing allows, as above, but rather on the greater materiality of the written or printed text as opposed to the spoken word.

Mayhew's treatment of the pattering class thus hints at two ways to found authors' productivity, respectability, or sheer nonbeggarliness on the distinction between exercising one's intellect in speech and in writing. This distinction itself fails, however, in the final section of his survey. In this section, which immediately follows the discussion of those who "do nothing but patter," Mayhew describes "the 'Screevers,' or Writers of Begging-Letters and Petitions" (1:311). "'Screeving'—that is to say, *writing* false or exaggerated accounts of afflictions and privations," he explains, "is a necessary corollary to 'Pattering,' or making pompous *orations* in public." Here, then, the close connection between writing and talking seems more important than any differences, just as the fortune-teller would have it; if anything, Mayhew's formulation implies that writing is derivative of, and hence inferior to, speaking. Mayhew, through his informant, does focus attention on the physical materiality of begging letters, but as evidence of deceptiveness, not productiveness: "Lawyer Joe was up to his trade—he folded the paper in official style—creased it as if it was long written and often examined, attached the signatures of the minister and churchwardens, and dipping his fingers under the fireplace, smeared it with ashes, and made the whole the best representation of a true account of 'a horse in the mad staggers' and 'a child in the measles' that could be desired" (1:313). Paradoxically, this attention to the appearance of a document serves less to anchor that document in the material world than to remove it from that world, as the activation of the document's own semiotic potential transforms it into, or merges it with its text as, a "representation"—indeed, a representation of a representation ("the best representation of a true account").

Given this treatment of writing, it is not surprising that the begging-letter writers' very status as writers does not prevent Mayhew from quickly assigning them "to the class who will *not work*," like those who do nothing but patter. In fact, because begging-letter writers belong to this class, "'economically' considered," he provides only "a brief description of the 'business'" in this section of his survey, while "reserving a more comprehensive and scientific view of the subject till such time as I come to treat of the *professional* beggar, under the head of those who are *able* but *unwilling* to labour for their livelihood" (1:311). Yet despite Mayhew's authoritative tone, this inability to limit discussion of begging-letter writing to one location hints at the problems of categorization that the activity presents. These problems, I suggest, both reflect and magnify those presented by authorship. As I will show, the figure of the begging-letter writer displays an almost uncanny ability to subvert values and blur distinctions dear to mainstream Victorian culture in general and crucial to authorial claims of respectability and cultural authority in particular. Indeed, if the history of Victorian authorship were seen as itself a Victorian novel, the begging-letter writer might well emerge as Our Hero the Author's most formidable doppelganger: in the manner of Jane Eyre's dark double or David Copperfield's unctuous rival, this demonized figure's resemblance to the protagonist threatens to reveal the arbitrariness with which this narrative favors certain characters over others and endorses specific arrangements of status and power.[5]

Unlike resemblances, commonalities, or homologies that only become visible in hindsight, however, the kinship of begging letters and begging-letter writers with ostensibly more legitimate forms of writing and kinds of writers, in particular novels and novelists, is one that Victorian writers themselves recognized, which is to say articulated—if at times by disavowing. As we will see, there is even an actual Victorian novel that deploys a begging-letter writer in much the Heepishly subversive manner envisioned above: Wilkie Collins's *No Name*. The figure of the begging-letter writer thus emerges in the mid–nineteenth century as the Victorian novelist's not-so-secret sharer, raising in acute form questions about the actions of novelists and the experience of novel reading.

The Begging-Letter Writer as Novelist

Although rarely the subject of later scholarly attention, the circulation of written pleas for money or other forms of assistance constituted a frequently noticed feature of the Victorian landscape. Public awareness of this phenomenon—indeed, its construction as a phenomenon—is not surprising, since the practice was in no way confined to neighborhoods where respectable individuals rarely ventured (as was the case, for example, with some of the other occupations documented by Mayhew). On the contrary, the handiwork of begging-letter writers regularly found its way into the homes and offices of the most prominent, influential, and voluble members of Victorian society. Thus, a list that Mayhew includes of "persons known to be charitable" who have been targeted by begging-letter writers begins with "the late Queen Dowager" and includes Sir Robert Peel, the philanthropist Angela Burdett-Coutts, various dukes and marquesses, and a newspaper editor (1:314–15). "The greatest man of his day," the Duke of Wellington, was "the great patron of the class," according to the *Times,* and Queen Victoria herself subscribed to an organization established to investigate the claims of begging-letter writers; this organization, the London Society for the Suppression of Mendicity, collected some 200,000 begging letters over the course of the century.[6] John Ruskin complained that his "desk [was] full of begging letters, eloquently written either by distressed or dishonest people,"[7] and Charles Dickens, who also appears on Mayhew's list, informed one correspondent that he received such "communications . . . not by twos or threes, but by scores upon scores," and wrote to W. H. Wills, the subeditor of *Household Words,* that "I get these letters by hundreds—not counting those that *you* get."[8]

The ubiquity and abundance of begging letters is one of their most abundantly remarked features, not only in private correspondence such as Dickens's but also in the journal articles, government reports, journalistic/sociological accounts, and novels where the letters are described, categorized, reproduced, and, above all, condemned. These various sources provide a fairly consistent (which is not to say reliable) account of the practices and products of begging-letter writing. "Mournful catalogues of all the ills that flesh is heir to," as Mayhew's informant puts it (1:312),[9] begging letters are said to tell tales of blighted prospects and pressing bills, swindles and Chancery suits, invalid parents and hungry children, industrial accidents and natural disasters. They come—or claim to come—from decayed gentlemen, broken-down tradesmen, discharged soldiers, disabled laborers, deserted women, and, not least, distressed authors; they are accompanied by letters of reference, medical testimonies, eviction notices, pawnbrokers' tickets, and, by 1869, photographs.[10] The letters ask for money, of course, but also for clothing and food and other forms of aid. Virtually all begging letters are fraudulent, however, their writers liars, swindlers, and impostors—or so virtually all Victorian writers on the subject would have us believe.

The issue of fraudulence aside, the very existence of begging-letter writing as a recognized practice—indeed, as a coherent concept—would seem not only to drain the distinction between writing and talking of economic significance, as noted above, but also to vindicate those who focus on exchange as the key site for distinguishing authors from beggars. Far from settling these questions, however, the discourse on begging letters, as articulated in *London Labour and the London Poor* and elsewhere, complicates them considerably, while at the same time heightening their urgency. Thus, Mayhew's informant on begging-letter writers no sooner begins to speak than he renders the ostensibly crucial distinction between selling and begging inadequate to the task of differentiating authors from begging-letter writers: he begins his testimony by asserting that begging letters and petitions are "seldom written by the persons who present or send them," but instead are written by "professional begging-letter writers" (1:311). These professionals "sometimes, though seldom, beg themselves," but more commonly are "supported by the fraternity for whom they write" (1:311). In other words, a begging letter can itself be a commodity.

To make matters worse, not only do begging-letter writers, like authors, sell what they write but, also like authors, they write and sell what we might think of as avowedly literary texts: as a price list reproduced by Mayhew indicates, begging-letter writers will provide "manuscript for a broken down author" for ten shillings, or "part of a play" for less (1:313). "Economically considered," as Mayhew would say, the difference between the manuscript written *for* a broken-down author and that written *by* a broken-down author would seem to be that only the former has (or realizes) any exchange value. Although Mayhew himself insists on assigning them "to the class who will *not work*," professional begging-letter writers—unlike broken-down authors—thus appear to satisfy his own definition of workers as those "who perform any act whatsoever that is considered worthy of being paid for by others" (4:9).

As depicted in *London Labour and the London Poor*, then, begging-letter writing undercuts the economic basis for preferring authors to begging-letter writers, or simply distinguishing between the two. In at least one recorded instance, the begging-letter writer's status as authorial double took spectacularly literal form. In 1849, as Mary Howitt recounts in her autobiography, an Edward Youl progressed from writing contributions for *Howitt's Journal* to soliciting contributions in Howitt's name:

> Youl, from York, wrote a begging-letter in my name to Macaulay, and received £10 by return of post. . . . We had immediately in-

stituted an extensive inquiry, and found that, amongst other persons of rank and influence, he had forged my name to Lords John Russell, Lansdown, Denman, Mahon, and Brougham. The latter . . . stated that on receiving an application from me speaking of great pecuniary difficulties, and requiring immediate assistance, he had instantly sent it to Lord John Russell, with a strong recommendation to settle a pension on me, applied on my behalf to Miss Burdett Coutts, and himself forwarded £20. . . . Sir Robert Peel had generously remitted £50.[11]

At a minimum, this episode indicates that it is not inconceivable in the mid-nineteenth century for even established authors to send appeals for money and, furthermore, that the professional writer's skills are transferable to this task. Ironically, Howitt is able to distance herself from her impostor only by publicizing his assumption of her identity: "Impatient of the stigma lying upon me in many unknown quarters, I insisted, in spite of the entreaties of our legal adviser, on sending a statement of the fraud to the daily papers."[12] While she thus manages to put a stop to the deception and to clear her name with those imposed upon, some of the "stigma" she fears perhaps remains, insofar as Youl's very success attests not only to the talent of the con man but also to the aptness of the con. Howitt herself emphasizes the specifically writerly nature of this fraud when she complains that "the forged letters returned to me were written in a crawling, exaggerated strain,"[13] as if to suggest that the insult of the personal imposture is compounded by the stylistic shortcomings of the literary imitation.

The "nefarious Howitt imposition" (as Dickens called it) is no less revealing for its doubtless exceptionality. At the same time, such imposture is not the only way in which the identification of authors with begging-letter writers shaded into identity: numerous authors were in fact reduced to writing self-declared begging letters. This literalization of the equation *author equals begging-letter writer* tends to reinforce the *figurative* equivalence of the two occupations; that is, the actual movement of individuals across the boundary between the writing of books and articles and the writing of begging letters underscores not only the notorious economic precariousness of authorship but the conceptual precariousness of this boundary as well. In his essay "Literature as a Career," for example, Walter Besant recounts this ostensibly true story of an individual who "began life with a fine enthusiasm and soaring ambitions [to] be a great writer":

> He sent a story to a certain editor, who accepted it and gave him a little advice about the *technique* of story-telling—of a kind. He had more stories accepted—and still more. Then he thought himself justified in giving up his clerkship and devoting his whole time to this weaving of conventional and unreal fiction for obscure magazines. . . . He writes all day long and every day; he produces story after story; he is paid £2 10s. for a story of twenty thousand words; he writes the penny "novelettes" that are sold by the ten thousand and bought by factory girls and servant girls. When things are desperate, he sends begging letters to men whose names he knows.[14]

Begging-letter writing appears on the scene here as a logical development in, if not the inevitable result of, an unsuccessful literary career. In fact, when Besant turns from "those who try to earn a livelihood by the production of bad fiction" to "the class which lives by manufacturing books not wanted," the career he sketches traces the same trajectory: "No one knows how or why he ever gets a commission to make any one of his books, but he does: he gets paid for every book—fifty pounds, seventy-five pounds, a hundred pounds. He is always impecunious; he lives from hand to mouth; the 'Royal Literary Fund' regards him as a pensioner, so regular are his applications. When things are very hard, he, too, sends round a begging letter." Besant is clearly interested in distinguishing between more and less successful authors, but he also sees the beggarly fate of the latter as dramatizing the condition of all authors in the literary marketplace, in that the existing system, he argues, allows publishers to treat even the most accomplished author as "a workman without rights, a mendicant, a helpless dependent, the mere recipient of bounty and charity."[15] As the longtime president of the Society of Authors (founded in 1884), Besant of course hopes to change this system, and to dissociate authors from beggars. Yet the very seamlessness of the transition he describes from writing books to writing begging letters serves to locate the two activities along a continuum, and perhaps even to suggest that they are essentially the same activity performed in different circumstances. In short, if the Carlylean gulf between Man-of-Letters Hero in the marketplace and mendicant monk is too great to bridge (as we saw in the last chapter), the Besantian slide from author to begging-letter writer is all too smooth.

One author who took this slide, it happens, was Henry Mayhew, who was imprisoned for debt and forced to write to the Royal Literary Fund (RLF) for aid in 1853, a few short years after the original publication of *London Labour and the London Poor*.[16] Turning to Mayhew's letter to the RLF, we can begin to grasp more fully the ways authorship and begging-letter writing resemble each other not only as forms of economic agency but also as specifically literary endeavors. Understood as a *genre,* that is, the begging letter shares a number of formal characteristics with other, ostensibly more legitimate genres, and this commonality extends begging-letter writing's challenge to the legitimacy of authorship beyond the economic realm to its aesthetic and ethical bases as well. Indeed, the begging letter as a genre so neatly captures certain of the qualities that underwrite claims for the cultural value of literature—especially the novel—that it eventually becomes necessary to ask if begging letters parody these valued literary practices or rather epitomize them.

On 25 June 1853, Henry Mayhew applied for relief from the RLF, listing his present address on the application form as Queen's Bench Prison and his "present means and sources of income, whether from Salary, Annuity, Pension, or other kind of provision; and the amount thereof," as "None."[17] In addition to the obligatory application form, Mayhew submitted a seven-page letter, addressed "To the Committee of the Literary Fund," in which he explains the circumstances that led to his incarceration. Most immediately striking about this letter is its inclusion of so many of the tropes Mayhew himself and others describe as typical of begging letters: the letter reads almost as a composite begging letter, as it blames Mayhew's indebtedness on the combination of a Chancery suit, an attempt to save a friend from transportation, and the misrepresentations of a (supposed) clergyman, while closing with a reference to the writer's ailing wife, who is "only waiting my liberation to withdraw to the country according to the advice of her physician."[18] More important for present purposes, however, are the literary, and especially *novelistic,* qualities of the letter, and the extent to which this literariness and what we might term the letter's begging-letterness are bound up with each other, indeed are in some ways identical. Not only are the aforementioned tropes as novelistic as they are begging-letterly, for example, but Mayhew summons his skill as a writer to craft an engaging, not entirely implausible narrative, one with a clear beginning and middle pointing past existing obstacles toward a desired ending.

Mayhew begins by framing his situation in the most favorable light possible—"Gentlemen, I am unfortunately confined here for a debt incurred with the view of saving a friend from transportation"—before going on to explain, in some detail, how he was persuaded to stand security for a friend who must repay money stolen from a government office, only to have the friend declare bankruptcy, the Catholic priest who had promised to pay the debt if necessary prove penniless, and the profits from *London Labour and the London Poor* tied up by a Chancery suit. Aid from the RLF, Mayhew asserts, will allow him to leave prison, take his ailing wife to the country, and resume his own labors.[19] Minimizing but not denying his own bad judgment, Mayhew portrays himself as a well-meaning individual victimized by the malfeasance of others. A telling sign of the extent to which Mayhew does not simply recount his coherent, linear narrative but rather constructs it may be found in a letter that his publisher, David Bogue, sent to the RLF on his behalf: while ostensibly recommending Mayhew's application, Bogue asserts that "his present unfortunate position in great measure arises from the non fulfilment of an engagement into which he entered with the Crystal Palace Company," a factor that has no place at all in Mayhew's account.[20]

For all its points of resemblance to the begging letters he and others describe, Mayhew's self-serving but emotionally restrained statement downplays a pair of the begging letter's signature features: the cultivation of sympathy and the open appeal to benevolence. This reticence is no doubt intentional, an attempt to preserve the writer's dignity by painting the transaction in the least charitable light (in the manner described in the previous chapter). Yet of the characteristics that the begging letter shares with more legitimate genres, the most vexing—because the most value-laden—are undoubtedly this ethic of sympathy and the literary strategies it entails. Begging letters, as one commentator notes, "dwell with an edifying circumstantiality, and expatiate with an amazing pathos, on . . . cases of distress";[21] in the words of another, they "giv[e] a pleasant impulse to our benevolent affections, and suppl[y] our opportunity of goodness."[22] Such letters thus belong squarely to the genre Thomas Laqueur has described as "humanitarian narrative." Laqueur brings together "the realistic novel, the autopsy, the clinical report, and the social inquiry" as forms that rely on "detail as the sign of truth" and on "the personal body, not only as the locus of pain but also as the common bond between those who suffer and those who would help and as the object of the scientific discourse through which the causal links between an evil, a victim, and a benefactor are forged"; such narrative, he argues, both reflects and contributes to the growth of humanitarian sentiment from the eighteenth century on by "expos[ing] the lineaments of causality and of human agency" so as to represent "ameliorative action . . . as possible, effective, and therefore morally imperative."[23] If a humanitarian narrative is one in which "an analytic of suffering exposes the means for its relief,"[24] then the begging letter represents the form reduced to its very essence: "June 20.—Addressed the Duke of Richmond under the name of John Smith," reads one begging-letter writer's journal, "case, leg amputated, out of work for six months, and wife and seven children starving. Result, 2*l*."[25]

To test this identification of the begging letter as a form of humanitarian narrative against an actual letter, consider this excerpt from an 1861 appeal to the General Committee of the RLF. The letter is from the novelist Emma Robinson, author of *Whitefriars; or, The Days of Charles the Second, Whitehall; or, The Days of Charles the First, Caesar Borgia, an Historical Romance,* and other works:

> On the wages of the severe toil to which I willingly subjected myself while youth and hope and strength remained, I have for a long period supported a Father, now an aged man, and other individuals who had legitimate claims on my exertions—besides myself. To redeem my Father from the consequences of disastrous speculations, I have parted with my most valuable copyrights. . . . The grim foe of Necessity ever gaining upon me, I have struggled long and unweariedly; and I know not that I should yet have yielded my arms, however exhaustedly wielding them, had not an unlucky chance seized them unawares and left me at mercy. An accident, otherwise slight, has directed mischief on organs the most precious to all mankind, but to the zealous littérateur, besides, the

essential instrument of his toils. Not that I state that I am *blind!*—God forbid!—It is with my own pen I write this memorial. But a species of ophthalmia which surrounds every object with glare and sparkle, on any lengthened application of my visual organs, and which my medical friend assures me only requires an interval of rest, after this long dark winter, necessitating so much artificial light, to subside into a normal condition, prevents, and has prevented me, from continuing my usual work.[26]

Notwithstanding its tendency toward periphrasis and departicularizing allegory—rhetorical habits perhaps reflecting the writer's experience as an author of historical romances—this "memorial" supplies a specific account of individualized suffering and physical affliction and points toward a cure. Indeed, as the narrative reaches its climax, Robinson seems to sense the danger of her suffering becoming mere spectacle rather than the occasion for remedial action, and she therefore foreswears the melodramatic revelation she has hinted at ("Not that I state that I am *blind!*"), switching instead into the calmly authoritative, diagnostic idiom of medical discourse ("a species of ophthalmia"). To a cruel advocate of the humanitarian aesthetic, Robinson's letter might even suggest a revision of Walter Besant's narrative of downward mobility, such that for "those who try to earn a livelihood by the production of bad fiction," the writing of begging letters represents less a logical recourse than an aesthetic step up.

Pursuing this last point, I would suggest that some of the best-known and indeed cruelest advocacy of a humanitarian aesthetic, George Eliot's 1856 essays "The Natural History of German Life" and "Silly Novels by Lady Novelists," approaches the admonition "close thy bad novels, open thy begging letters." Robinson herself escapes mention in the latter essay, but the traits noted above, such as periphrasis, an elevated style, and the melodramatic elevation of "very ordinary events of civilized life . . . into the most awful crises," are among those Eliot singles out for censure.[27] On the other hand, given her sarcastic comment that "lady novelists, it appears, can see something else besides matter; they are not limited to phenomena, but can relieve their eyesight by occasional glimpses of the *noumenon*,"[28] Eliot would no doubt approve of the medical explanation Robinson gives for her visionary gleam.

In fact, it requires very little brushing against the grain to read the famous programmatic statement of Eliot's ethico-aesthetic in "The Natural History of German Life" as an apologia for the begging letter:

> The greatest benefit we owe to the artist, whether painter, poet, or novelist, is the extension of our sympathies. Appeals founded on generalizations and statistics require a sympathy ready-made, a moral sentiment already in activity; but a picture of human life such as a great artist can give, surprises even the trivial and the selfish into that attention to what is apart from themselves, which may be called the raw material of moral sentiment. . . . Art is the nearest thing to life; it is a mode of amplifying experience and extending our contact with our fellowmen beyond the bounds of our personal lot.[29]

The begging letter, with its focus on individual suffering, is the antithesis of "appeals founded on generalizations and statistics." Arriving in the morning mail, it surprises readers too trivial or selfish to bother with soi-disant great art into "attention to what is apart from themselves," and does not merely "extend our contact with our fellowmen beyond the bounds of our personal lot" but rather extends the bounds of that lot itself. Why *not* celebrate the begging letter, then? Indeed, why not prefer the begging letter to fiction, which, truth be told, extends the reader's sympathy (in the first instance, at least) to *fictional* persons, not real ones?

These questions are not merely rhetorical, nor the suggested inclusion of the begging-letter writer among Eliot's artistic benefactors solely ironic. Turning to another actual example, we see a begging letter having the very effect Eliot desires. This letter is particularly intriguing because it is addressed to Charles Dickens, the very novelist Eliot discusses immediately after articulating her aesthetic. Dated 10 October 1854 and signed Frederick Maynard, the letter begins, "I hope you will forgive the strange appeal I am about to make to you, but, I shall be very grateful if you will read this letter, and, may I hope, not throw it aside without notice."[30] The writer tells the story of his older sister, who "became acquainted with a gentleman and lived with him 9 years but I regret to say not as his wife." Maynard explains that his sister, Caroline Maynard Thompson, raised him and another sister, articling Frederick to an architect. Caroline's "protector left her," however, and Frederick's articles were canceled, which has prevented him from "returning her that kindness which she showered upon me when I was unable to help myself." Maynard asserts that his sister "must not be judged by her unhappy condition, for I affirm in spite of it—a more virtuous minded woman never lived," and assures Dickens, "You I am sure would not judge her harshly did you know all particulars of her past life." He explains, "The reason of my writing to you is this":

> I have no friends who would interest themselves in her behalf, neither has she, for hers is a peculiar position—I have heard much of your goodness to unfortunate people—and your writings have emboldened me to pray for your advice—There is not a tale, or article of your writing that has not assured me that your disposition is charitable to the misfortunes, and merciful to the faults of others, and that your mind is above the vulgar prejudices of this world.

"Upon you," he continues, "I have placed my hopes of receiving counsel that will enable me to place my sister, who has been a Mother to me, in an honest position." Offering to "enter more fully into the particulars that led to this unhappy state of affairs" at a "later time," and giving the names and addresses of his current and former employers as references, Maynard concludes, "Do not . . . plunge me in despair by refusing me your advice—Hoping for a favorable reply."

This letter's very survival shows that its appeal did not go unheeded, for the letter escaped the fire to which Dickens ultimately consigned virtually all his correspondence only because he forwarded it to his friend Angela Burdett-Coutts, the banking heiress and philanthropist (whose name we saw listed by Mayhew's begging-letter writer); in addition to the formal philanthropic projects the two collaborated on—most famously a House for Fallen Women—Dickens often recommended cases for her assistance, while she regularly forwarded him begging letters to vet (especially those from distressed authors). In the pragmatic terms Laqueur emphasizes, Maynard's letter must be considered a successful example of humanitarian narrative, as it prompted Dickens to act on Caroline's behalf. By his own account, in fact, this letter and the meeting with Maynard it led to had a profound impact on the novelist. Caroline, he explains to Burdett-Coutts, has been forced to become a prostitute, but "although she is what she is, in the very house to which this brother goes home every night of his life, he has an unbounded respect and love for her, which presents one of the strangest and most bewildering spectacles I ever saw within my remembrance."[31] His own letter to Burdett-Coutts thus presents the spectacle of Dickens experiencing the very amplification of experience and extension of sympathy Eliot calls for. "I really had a difficulty," he stresses, "in collecting myself to understand that in the tremendous circumstances of their daily existence, she has not fallen in this brother's *respect*" (with "respect" underlined twice). Dickens himself, moreover, seems to have viewed the story Maynard tells, if not his letter per se, in literary terms, as he concludes his letter to Burdett-Coutts by asserting, "I cannot let it rest; for the position of this brother—his perception of his sister's disgrace, and undiminished admiration of her, and the confidence he has grown up in, of her being something good, and never to be mentioned without tenderness and deference—is a romance so astonishing and yet so intelligible as I never had the boldness to think of."[32]

Given this response on Dickens's part, we might expect a steady diet of begging letters like Maynard's to help the novelist develop his art in the very manner Eliot prescribes: "We have one great novelist," she writes, "who is gifted with the utmost power of rendering the external traits of our town population; and if he could give us their psychological character—their conceptions of life, and their emotions—with the same truth as their idiom and manners, his books would be the greatest contribution Art has ever made to the awakening of social sympathies." Ironically, however, the aspects of Maynard's story that so move Dickens play into the exact tendencies Eliot decries, as she fears that "his frequently false psychology, his preternaturally virtuous poor children and artisans, his melodramatic boatmen and courtesans . . . encourag[e] the miserable fallacy that high morality and refined sentiment can grow out of harsh social relations, ignorance, and want." From Eliot's perspective, in other words, this episode is all too Dickensian. Even if we do not follow Eliot in equating knowledge of the lower classes with knowledge of their viciousness ("We want to be taught to feel . . . for the peasant in all his coarse apathy, and the artisan in all his suspicious selfishness"), we might still agree that Maynard's story is so effective precisely because it out-Dickenses Dickens.[33]

Eliot, intent on carving out a space to step into as the preeminent novelist of the age, would no doubt feel relieved to learn that this space has not already been filled by a begging-letter writer. Yet this notion—or, more generally, the idea that begging letters and novels are ethically and aesthetically cognate—is not so farfetched or whimsical that the future novelist does not move to squelch it: Eliot apotropaically refers to begging letters in the paragraph preceding the one quoted above, in a manner designed to prevent comparison or the possibility of identification from explicitly arising. Neither ignoring the existence of begging letters nor openly addressing their similarity to the art she values, Eliot mentions them in passing, in the course of explaining that peasants are no more honest than educated people, but rather are merely dishonest in different ways: "It is quite true that a thresher is likely to be innocent of any adroit arithmetical cheating," she writes, "but he is not the less likely to carry home his master's corn in his shoes and pocket; a reaper is not given to writing begging-letters, but he is quite capable of cajoling the dairymaid into filling his small-beer bottle with ale." [34] In implying that begging-letter writing, with its prerequisite of literacy, is a misdeed of the educated classes, this passage simply takes for granted its status as a misdeed, a dishonorable act motivated by what Eliot immediately goes on to call "the selfish instincts." Thus dismissed as a trivial act of selfishness, begging-letter writing can bear no resemblance to that which "surprises even the trivial and the selfish into that attention to what is apart from themselves, which may be called the raw material of moral sentiment."

Eliot is hardly unique in attempting to ward off the comparison of novelist and begging-letter writer, as we shall see. Such defensive maneuvering reflects the Victorians' own awareness of the similarities and intersections that we have identified here. In fact, some Victorian commentators even go so far as to discuss begging letters as literary texts and directly compare their writers to novelists. Such comparisons give urgency to novelists' efforts to distance themselves from begging-letter writers, while at the same time complicating this task by raising pointed questions about the efficacy and desirability of the literary cultivation of sympathy.

Yet while some Victorian writers attend to the literariness of begging letters, as we have done here, their attention differs from ours in one crucial respect: those advocating or undertaking a literary-critical approach to begging letters take as their premise the fraudulence of these letters. While this stipulation of fraudulence offers grounds for denouncing begging letters, it also facilitates attention to their literary qualities and the comparison of begging-letter writers to novelists. The notion that begging letters are invariably false helps to produce a conception of begging-letter writing as not simply an action or activity but rather a well-defined (albeit illegitimate) occupation; as we saw earlier, Mayhew even speaks of "professional begging-letter writers" (1:311). This understanding fosters reification of *the begging-letter writer* as a type with particular skills and habits, and the construction of *the begging letter* as a genre with its own conventions and traditions. The presumed falseness of begging letters, in other words, highlights their status as narrative and rhetorical constructs, and that of begging-letter writers as *writers*. This presumption also allows commentators to assign to writers of begging letters specifically literary talents they might not otherwise be seen to possess, such as inventiveness and imagination, as well as valued character traits authors themselves are often said to lack, such as industriousness and entrepreneurship.

Of course, while the assertion of fraudulence facilitates consideration of begging letters' literary qualities and comparison of their writers to authors, it also ensures that such analysis will be overwhelmingly ironic in tone: after all, the most obvious effect of this stipulated fraudulence is to render obvious the illegitimacy of begging-letter writing. Yet this irony does not limit the critical force of the comparison but instead renders it double-edged, as we see in two of the era's most extended, explicit comparisons of begging-letter writing to novel writing, both of which were quoted above at the beginning of the discussion of humanitarian narrative—albeit strategically (and misleadingly, mea culpa) shorn of their emphasis on fraudulence, and thus of their irony. The earlier of these comparisons comes in James Grant's wide-ranging 1838 work *Sketches in London,* which begins with an introduction to what he unambiguously calls "the begging-letter class of impostors."[35] Grant's discussion is marked by a proto-Mayhewian dedication to both statistical data and firsthand testimony and documentation, as he seeks to establish such matters as the actual numbers of begging-letter writers currently at work in London (two hundred fifty, he estimates) and their average income (£200 per annum), on the one hand, and to detail specific practices and actual examples, on the other (3). Unlike most commentators on the subject, Grant's tone is never outraged, but instead is usually one of bemusement, shading at times into amazement, and while he does not defend the schemes he describes, he openly relishes their ingenuity (to use one of his favorite words). Not surprisingly, then, when he turns to examples drawn from actual begging-letter writers' journals and letters (or so he claims), Grant turns literary critic.

After he first cites a begging-letter writer's journal, Grant quickly assures the reader that "the above is, of course, but a mere skeleton or outline of the letters which are addressed." In fact, he explains, "the writers dwell with an edifying circumstantiality, and expatiate with an amazing pathos, on the pretended cases of distress," and he promises that "of the admirable tactics of these epistolarian impostors I shall have occasion to speak at greater length by-and-bye, when I shall give some approved specimens of their correspondence" (7). True to his word, Grant soon offers extended appreciations of his two favorite begging-letter writers, "the notorious Underwood" (17) and his female counterpart, "Harriet Reid, alias Harriet Minette" (22). Not only could Underwood "write every variety of calligraphy," Grant enthuses, "but his intellectual resources were ample even to excess": "He could write on any subject; he had not only the ingenuity to assume every conceivable character, but he could immediately, on assuming such character, sit down and write in that strain which was most consonant to it. . . . His inventive powers were of the first order. If the faculty of creation be one of the principal attributes of genius, Underwood was a genius of the first magnitude. The force and felicity of his imaginative facts were remarkable" (16). The direction in which this paean is moving is clear, and Grant does not disappoint: "Had he turned his attention to novel-writing, instead of to the profession of a begging-letter imposter, there is no saying how high his name might at this moment have stood in the current literature of the country. United as were his inventive powers to great facility and force of composition, he must certainly, had he applied himself to the production of works of fiction, have attained to no ordinary reputation" (16–17).

Carried away, perhaps, by the momentum of his own rhetoric, Grant seems to move beyond irony here; one gets the sense that he means what he says about Underwood's potential as a novelist. After pausing to note that "it can hardly be necessary to say, that a man of so much ingenuity was successful in his profession," and to report, somewhat incongruously, Underwood's recent death in prison (17), Grant backs up his claims by reproducing letters written by the master in "the character of a widow" (17) and of "a young lady, who had been seduced from her 'tender parent's' roof by a gentleman, under promise of marriage" (18). "I am sure my readers will concur with me," he concludes, "that in point of ingenious invention, the above letters might put our modern novelists to the blush" (22). Insofar as this inventiveness is in the service of defrauding the letter's recipient, Grant's praise is hardly devoid of irony. It is less clear whether he really finds the letters ingeniously inventive and really expects his readers to concur. As a commentary on "our modern novelists," however, these niceties hardly matter. The present reader, for example, does not agree with Grant's putative judgment, but instead finds the letters notable for their comically excessive use of humanitarian/novelistic conventions (which may, of course, be Grant's actual judgment as well): "I am become a great cripple, a melancholy spectacle; and but for the kindness of a friend, I and my fatherless children would have been driven into the workhouse, or have become poor houseless wanderers" (18), reads the former; the latter, "I hope to mingle your pity with your censure. I am gradually wasting away through the want of food and nourishment, and without the aid of humanity, must inevitably fall a victim to poverty and starvation" (20). Yet if novelists here see their own favorite tropes banalized or parodied by a begging-letter writer, rather than improved upon, they have no less cause for embarrassment.

While the treatment of begging letters as literary texts thus devalues the latter, Grant's succeeding discussion of Harriet Minette foregrounds a more immediate effect of such treatment, one that reflects on literary texts more indirectly. At first this discussion follows the same pattern as that of Underwood's letters, with Grant regretting that "Mrs. Harriet Minnette did not apply herself to novel writing" and going so far as to suggest that the sample letter he cites (a tale of spousal abandonment and contemplated suicide) shows "dashes of the pathetic . . . which even Goethe himself would have readily admitted into his 'Sorrows of Werter'" (23). Grant's next comment, however, reminds us of both the begging letter's original purpose and the extent to which he has encouraged us to forget that purpose: "Who could resist such an appeal to one's feelings?" he asks. Begging letters solicit a sympathetic interest that will lead to action, not the disinterested interest Grant bestows upon them. Thus, while "the Rev. gentleman to whom it was addressed could not" resist this appeal, Grant, or the Grantian reader—the reader, that is, who approaches the begging letter as critic or connoisseur—surely can. Rarely does an aesthetic stance function so clearly to bracket ethical demands as it does here.[36]

But where does this treatment of begging letters leave the novel itself? Grant argues that by reading begging letters as novels we free ourselves from their moral and affective purchase. He thus implies that the overt fictionality of novels, like the ascribed fictiveness of begging letters, works to circumscribe a narrative's impact on its readers' emotions and actions—or perhaps, if we are not simply noting the pathos of Minette's letter but also feeling it, that this fictionality allows for affective indulgence by making it an end in itself, detached from the question of action (which is to say, the question of ethics). Ironically, however, the one novel Grant names, *The Sorrows of Young Werther*, was notorious precisely for its influence on (or curtailing of) readers' lives. Insofar as Grant is aware of this irony, we may take him to be suggesting not only that begging letters should be read as novels but also that novels should be read as fraudulent begging letters. A stance of ironic detachment protects the reader against the importunities of both genres.

A later, more openly hostile literary-critical treatment of "the" begging-letter writer suggests more fully that the kind of readerly engagement encouraged by novels contributes to a susceptibility to begging letters. This 1867 *Times* leader implies that the novel reader is liable to be fooled by a fraudulent begging letter because of that reader's preexisting foolishness, and the article is scarcely less critical of novelists than of begging-letter writers. Indeed, after beginning with the assertion that "there is a branch of literary enterprise which has hardly received the attention it deserves, either as a matter of curious inquiry or for the proof it affords of the original genius of this country," the article twice figures begging-letter writers and authors as competitors, and both times awards the palm to the former:

The novelists of the circulating library, by dint of huge type and monstrous margin, stretch a simple tale of passion and wickedness into three volumes, nominally priced a guinea and a half. The Begging Letter Writer confines himself to one sheet of note paper, and often gets from the reader two or five guineas. . . . Let us not despise this humble professional, who gives a pleasant impulse to our benevolent affections, and supplies our opportunity of goodness, without seeking the usual guerdon of fame, or aggravating the bitter rivalry of literature. While authors are envying, quarrelling, and starving, the Begging Letter Writer carries off the ready money.[37]

The *Times* is saying, of course, that we *should* despise this humble professional, that begging letters misdirect our benevolent affections, and that the reader does more harm than good by sending along two or five guineas. Yet an appreciation of the article's irony does little to mitigate its criticism of authors. The fact that begging letters are fraudulent hardly negates the suggestion that novels themselves are a rip-off, nor does it qualify the article's impatience with authorial self-promotion. Authors are not worse than begging-letter writers, then: they are just as contemptible.

The article does not develop its explicit criticism of authors and novels, but novels in particular get implicated, I would argue, in its attack on begging letters. The article insistently damns "this truly national literature" with ironic praise:

The Begging Letter Writer has talents which it is impossible not to admire, and a province from which he cannot be expelled. His wide dominion is in the hearts of the sympathetic, the all-believing, and the soft. . . . He is a student of human nature in all its aspects, and without having read the *Rhetoric* of Aristotle, or a single volume of literary correspondence, he is accomplished in the arts of persuasion. . . . Those [recipients of begging letters] who have outlived the more generous class of illusions will bear us out when we say that there is no greater calumny than to charge our country men with want of imagination or inventive power. . . . Hundreds of these compositions have we read, and the more we read admired. . . . All honour to art, even in its most questionable applications! Art deals with fiction, imitation, personation, and whatever adorns or recommends truth, at a slight sacrifice of its essence, or departure from its straightest code.

Clearly, the development here of the conceit of the-begging-letter-as-literature risks none of the ambiguity of Grant's account. The article avoids this risk, however, not simply by continually insinuating the fraudulence of begging letters but also by denigrating the very nature of their appeal and condescending to those open to it. Thus, while Grant was content to invite the reader to join him in his stance of ironic appreciation, this article devotes a good deal of energy to contrasting this stance with, or constructing it in opposition to, one of naiveté. In the passage cited above, for example, "the sympathetic" are also "the all-believing, and the soft," whereas those "who have outlived the more generous class of illusions" are implicitly sage enough to see generosity itself as something of an illusion. If "the Begging Letter Writer enters with ready sympathy and keen appreciation into all forms of misery, all phases of grief," the reader should not make the same mistake. "Good reader,—" the article coos, "simple, confiding reader," although "suspicion is brutal," it is sadly necessary. We must face facts: "The writer of the artless and affecting narrative which has struck a real pang into your breast and raised images you cannot dispel is a drunken sot."

While the *Times* thus justifies its hermeneutics of suspicion on the grounds that "scarcely any" begging letters tell true stories, it also clearly directs its scorn toward readerly sympathy, and not only the credulity to which this sympathy is seen to contribute; sympathy itself comes under suspicion here. This suspicion reflects an increasingly common hostility toward charity itself when it takes the form of "casual" or "indiscriminate almsgiving," rather than an organized, institutional form.[38] Not surprisingly, then, the article winds up promoting the cause of the London Mendicity Society, which both keeps files on fraudulent begging-letter writers and works to "rescue" individuals from mendicancy.[39] It is this hostility toward excessive, unregulated sympathy that seems to catch the novel in the article's net: novels encourage the very reading habits that begging-letter writers exploit. The possibility arises that readerly resistance to begging letters' appeals may require resistance to the appeal of novels as well.

Riches to Wragge: No Name and the Novelists' Begging-Letter Writers

Begging-letter writers thus display, and are seen to display, qualities novelists wish to dissociate themselves from, such as a beggarly dependence on the benevolence of others, as well as qualities they generally continue to embrace but which themselves come under attack, such as the textual cultivation of such benevolence. More subtly, they depend on what would seem to be the same mechanism of sympathetic identification. But just as Victorian writers on begging-letter writing compare begging letters to novels, so too do Victorian novelists respond to such comparisons and the similarities they highlight, as we began to see with George Eliot. The perceived urgency of this challenge differs from novelist to novelist, as does the strategy of differentiation, depending on the author's particular narrative practices and authorial persona.

The Victorian novelist who writes most extensively about begging-letter writing is undoubtedly Dickens, the receptive recipient of Frederick Maynard's moving appeal. Yet rather than extend his rehabilitative efforts from Caroline Maynard Thompson to the debased genre that brings her to his attention, Dickens instead participates actively in its vilification, attacking the practice in both novels and articles. Most famously, Dickens devotes a chapter of Our Mutual Friend, "A Dismal Swamp," to a satiric taxonomy of the countless begging-letter writers who importune the novel's Golden Dustman. This account's hostility is muted by its humor (and perhaps a hint of resignation), but this humor itself is premised on a refusal to take the letters' claims seriously. Emphasizing their brazenness, persistence, and sheer abundance, the novel lampoons "corporate beggars," including those who seek contributions for "the Society for Granting Annuities to Unassuming Members of the Middle Classes," and inventories the many varieties of "individual beggars," such as "the inspired beggars," "the suggestively-befriended beggars," "the nobly independent beggars," "the beggars of punctual business-habits," and "the beggars who make sporting ventures."[40]

Dickens's comically inventive beggars serve as an occasion for the display of his own comic inventiveness, but the possibility of identification between beggar and novelist is deflected by the narrative's strict adherence to the point of view of the letters' recipient. Thus, the account begins by noting that "no one knows so well as the Secretary, who opens and reads the letters, what a set is made at the man marked by a stroke of notoriety," and ends by returning to this figure: "In such a Dismal Swamp does the new house stand, and through it does the Secretary daily struggle breast-high."[41] Begging letters occasion sympathy here, but sympathy for their readers, not their writers. Moreover, in inviting the novel reader to identify with the begging-letter reader, the novel implicitly invites its own readers to identify the novelist himself with, or as, the begging-letter recipient—and not, therefore, its writer.

This identification with the recipient of begging letters is certainly reflective of Dickens's own experience as a favorite addressee of begging-letter writers. This popularity clearly derives from the novelist's perceived sympathy toward the downtrodden and disadvantaged, as noted by Frederick Maynard, combined with his sheer celebrity and financial success. In addition, though, Dickens makes himself all the more approachable by personalizing his relationship with his readers: in both his novels and journalism, he consistently figures this relationship as individualized and intimate, located in the private rather than the public sphere—naming his journal *Household Words,* for example, and using the prefaces to his novels to emphasize "the affection and confidence that have grown up between [him and his readers]"[42] and to "acknowledge the unbounded warmth and earnestness of their sympathy in every stage of the journey we have just concluded."[43] Representing his commerce with his readers as infused with feelings absent from the Smithian or Carlylean marketplace, Dickens blurs the lines between commercial and affective relations and between published work and private correspondence. Dickens's own positioning thus undercuts or renders unavailable distinctions to which he might otherwise appeal in distinguishing himself from the disreputable figure of the begging-letter writer.

This bind accounts for the ferocity and disingenuousness that mark Dickens's most sustained treatment of the subject, a piece titled "The Begging-Letter Writer," which was the leading article in one of the first issues of *Household Words.* As in the later account in *Our Mutual Friend,* the point of view in this piece is that of the begging-letter recipient, only here Dickens openly claims this position as his own: "I, the writer of this paper, have been, for some time, a chosen receiver of Begging Letters," he states.[44] Claiming authority on this basis—"I ought to know something of the Begging-Letter Writer" (228)—Dickens uses the conceit of a biographical sketch to survey the variety of claims and demands begging letters make: "The natural phenomena of which he has been the victim, are of a most astounding nature. . . . He has been the sport of the strangest misfortunes. . . . He has been attached to every conceivable pursuit. . . . He writes in a variety of styles," and so on (229–30). At first, it might seem that the multiplicity of the often contradictory characteristics and experiences Dickens describes reflects this portrait's composite nature; as quickly becomes apparent, however, the point is rather that individual begging-letter writers make multiple and contradictory statements over the course of their careers. For at the heart of this article is the claim that begging letters are invariably fraudulent: "The poor," Dickens asserts flatly, "never write these letters. Nothing could be more unlike their habits" (234). "It is of little use inquiring into the Begging-Letter Writer's circumstances," he writes, for while "he may be sometimes accidentally found out, . . . apparent misery is always a part of his trade"; indeed, "real misery very often is" as well, but this is due to "his dissipated and dishonest life" (232). The begging-letter writer's distress, in other words, is either a lie or the result or reflection of his penchant for lying. It is therefore incumbent upon recipients of begging letters "to be deaf to such appeals" (234).

Dickens's article thus identifies the fraudulence of begging letters as their defining characteristic and the most important factor in determining how individuals and society as a whole should respond to them. The accuracy of this charge aside, its implications are clear: if the begging-letter writer's mendicity is inextricable from his mendacity, then those "who [seek] to do some little to repair the social wrongs, inflicted in the way of preventible sickness and death upon the poor, [are] strengthening those wrongs, however innocently, by wasting money on pestilent knaves cumbering society" (233). At the same time, the assertion of fraudulence is also absolutely crucial to the article's implicit agenda of differentiation, for it allows Dickens to condemn—and thereby distance himself from—begging-letter writers, and to do so without calling into question his own commitment to benevolence and the textual cultivation of sympathy. In fact, the claim of fraudulence enables Dickens to denounce begging-letter writers in the very name of these ideals, as he blasts the impostors for "dirtying the stream of true benevolence" (228), "interpos[ing themselves] between the general desire to do something to relieve the sickness and misery under which the poor were suffering; and the suffering poor themselves" (233), and "pervert[ing] the lessons of our lives" (234). While implicitly acknowledging the resemblance of begging-letter writing to his own practice, then, Dickens frames this resemblance in such a way as to make it the basis for his attack.

Although Dickens refuses to recognize any meaningful correspondence between his correspondents and himself, he does acknowledge that begging-letter writers sometimes claim to be authors. One of the cases he describes, for instance, involves an individual who "introduced himself as a literary gentleman in the last extremity of distress," and who claims to have "had a play accepted at a certain Theatre," but due to a delay in its production is "in a state of absolute starvation" (231). In relating this episode, Dickens uses an analogy parallel to (if more venerable than) that of begging-letter writer to novelist, that of beggar to actor: after the supposed playwright writes to say that his wife has died, Dickens "dispatched a trusty messenger to comfort the bereaved mourner and his poor children; but the messenger went so soon, that the play was not ready to be played out; my friend was not at home, and his wife was in a most delightful state of health" (231).[45] A Grantian, aesthetic appreciation of this individual's prose even emerges here, albeit in heavily circumscribed fashion, as the man is brought before a magistrate who is "deeply impressed by the excellence of his letters" and "compliment[s] him highly on his powers of composition" before discharging him, despite Dickens's testimony (231). Attention to the supposed literariness of begging letters thus occasions—and implicitly stands as—a ludicrous miscarriage of justice, and one that particularly wrongs Dickens, who is here made to feel "a sort of monster" (231).

Yet despite Dickens's efforts, his article also serves to accentuate his vulnerability to comparison to begging-letter writers. The suggestion, for example, that fraudulent begging-letter writers do "immeasurable harm . . . to the deserving" by "muddling the brains of foolish justices, with inability to distinguish between the base coin of distress, and the true currency we have always among us" (228), may again raise questions concerning the value of the novel's *fictional* "currency." The currency of Dickens's aesthetic may itself be debased, moreover, by the article's suggestion that it is not terribly difficult to excite a reader's sympathy, and that there is no shortage of such sympathy available. To make matters worse, the article depends on some of the very rhetorical maneuvers it associates with begging-letter writers, and which Dickens warns his readers against. For instance, while Dickens's appeal to his own experience confers authority on his account and positions him as a recipient (not sender) of begging letters, it also establishes him as an object of the reader's pity. If "the Begging-Letter Writer" has been "the sport of the strangest misfortunes," Dickens himself has been the victim of a ubiquitous, almost Gothic, villain: "The Begging-Letter Writer . . . has besieged my door, at all hours of the day and night; he has fought my servant; he has lain in ambush for me, going out and coming in; he has followed me out of town into the country; he has appeared at provincial hotels, where I have been staying for only a few hours" (228). Like his subject, the writer of "The Begging-Letter Writer" anticipates and attempts to overcome readerly resistance to his account: "I am describing actual experiences," he emphasizes, "the real experience of a real person" (231, 233). In a further irony, just as Dickens asserts that the begging-letter writer's supposed misery is at times real but is the writer's own fault, Dickens's chosen biographer will eventually suggest that the novelist's own misery as a "chosen receiver of Begging Letters" is also real but self-imposed: according to John Forster, in this article Dickens "has described, without a particle of exaggeration, the extent to which he was made a victim by this class of swindler . . . but he had not confessed, as he might, that for much of what he suffered he was himself responsible, by giving so largely, as at first he did, to almost every one who applied to him." [46]

If Dickens's denunciation of begging-letter writers serves as a distancing strategy, the extreme vehemence of this denunciation signals frustration over the difficulty of achieving this distance. This frustration boils over in the article's final paragraph, which deploys an almost incoherent rhetoric of abjection:

> There are degrees in murder. Life must be held sacred among us in more ways than one—sacred, not merely from the murderous

weapon, or the subtle poison, or the cruel blow, but sacred from preventible diseases, distortions, and pains. That is the first great end we have to set against this miserable imposition. Physical life respected, moral life comes next. What will not content a Begging-Letter Writer for a week, would educate a score of children for a year. Let us give all we can; let us give more than ever. Let us do all we can; let us do more than ever. But let us give, and do, with a high purpose; not to endow the scum of the earth, to its own greater corruption, with the offals of our duty. (234)

In a letter to Henry Austin (his brother-in-law and secretary of the General Board of Health), Dickens writes, "You will see next week, that I have turned a paper called 'The Begging Letter Writer,' to sanitary purposes,"[47] but this "turn" here produces a rhetorical muddle (as Stephen Blackpool might say). Indeed, the final sentence is barely legible, as its accumulation of waste products mimics the process of corruption it names; what emerges most clearly is the author's investment in (distancing himself from) his subject. Not surprisingly, this article does succeed in alienating the population it describes, at least according to the reported testimony of one member of "the pattering fraternity"—"Mr. Dickens *was* a favourite," one of Mayhew's informants says, "but he has gone down sadly in the scale since his *Household Words* 'came it so strong' against the begging letter department" (1:250); even here, though, the perceived exceptionality of the attack betrays the novelist's overdetermined relationship to the begging-letter writer.

Novelists less inclined than Dickens to sentimentalize their relationship to their readers, such as William Thackeray and Anthony Trollope, are better positioned to emphasize the difference between a literary commodity and begging letter. Like Dickens, however, Thackeray and Trollope are keen on maintaining their own identification with benevolence, and they too are faced with the similarity of novelistic and begging-letterly mechanisms of sympathetic identification. In a complicated series of maneuvers, then, they work to differentiate themselves from begging-letter writers by separating benevolence from the marketplace while aligning themselves with both. This stance hinges not quite on a sharp distinction between public and private selves, as it first seems, but rather on a constantly endangered yet continually reaffirmed distinction between the two—both of which, paradoxically, must be equally visible to the reader.

Thackeray, like Dickens, represents himself as a recipient of begging letters in "Thorns in the Cushion," one of the series of his essays published in the *Cornhill Magazine* and collected as the *Roundabout Papers*. In a crucial twist, however, Thackeray locates this correspondence in the literary marketplace itself, by writing about the letters he receives in his capacity as the magazine's editor. "Last month," the novelist-cum-editor writes, "we sang the song of glorification, and rode in the chariot of triumph," celebrating the journal's first six months of publication. "But now that the performance is over," he continues, "just step into my private room, and see that it is not all pleasure." [48] Turning from public pleasure to private pain, Thackeray declares that "it is not the fire of adverse critics which afflicts or frightens the editorial bosom"; rather, "the thorn in the cushion of the editorial chair . . . comes with almost every morning's post," in the form of the letters he receives from would-be contributors (212, 213). "This is what I call a thorn-letter," he writes:

> "Sir,—May I hope, may I entreat, that you will favour me by perusing the enclosed lines, and that they may be found worthy of insertion in the *Cornhill Magazine?* We have known better days, sir. I have a sick and widowed mother to maintain, and little brothers and sisters who look to me. I do my utmost as a governess to support them. . . . If I could add but a *little* to our means by my pen, many of my poor invalid's wants might be supplied. . . . Do—do cast a kind glance over my poem, and if you can help us, the widow, the orphans will bless you!" (213)

Through his description of these "thorn-letters," Thackeray raises the possibility of the literary marketplace's infiltration by what he calls the "argument *ad misericordiam*" (214). Under such conditions, the begging letter and the literary commodity emerge as economic complements, not opposites, and if publication signals successful commodification, it can also reflect a prior, successful appeal to benevolence. Thackeray describes this scenario, however, in order to condemn it. Stigmatizing the "true female logic" of such an "appeal to my pity" (213, 214), he argues that such letters do not humanize the marketplace but rather misunderstand or willfully pervert it.

Yet Thackeray does not simply use authorial begging letters to underscore the normal and proper noneleemosynary nature of the literary marketplace, or even his commitment to such a market. At the same time, in an adroit balancing act, he also uses these letters to promote his own association with the very qualities he banishes from the marketplace, such as pity and benevolence. Thus, the letters he receives are *thorns:* they do not anger him, or amuse him, or leave him cold, they *pain* him. "They don't sting quite so sharply as they did [at first]," he writes, "but a skin is a skin, and they bite, after all, most wickedly" (213). While quick to claim that "one of the immense advantages which women have over our sex is, that they actually like to read these letters" (214), Thackeray makes clear that his antipathy is bound up with his own susceptibility: "Ah! it stings me now as I write," he exclaims (213). He locates his vulnerability not only in his body but also in the feminized realm of the home, complaining that would-be contributors write to him there despite the magazine's express instructions not to. Even as he calls for the public to respect the separate spheres of his own life, however, he emphasizes the existence of this private, sympathetic self by putting it on display: "At night I come home, and take my letters up to bed (not daring to open them), and in the morning I find one, two, three thorns on my pillow" (213). Not only should the reader identify Thackeray as the recipient of begging letters, then, and pity his plight as such, one should also feel sympathy for his very ability to—or inability not to—sympathize.

If Thackeray's urbane, ironic tone suggests that his request for pity and sympathy has freed itself from the identificatory taint that overwhelms similar moments in Dickens's sketch, we can attribute this reduced anxiety to the presence here of the moment notably absent in Dickens's writings—the assertion and embrace of the "masculine" logic of the marketplace. We might take it as confirmation of this point that Anthony Trollope, notorious champion of the view that "money payment for work done is the best and most honest test of success,"[49] cites "Thorns in the Cushion" on no fewer than three occasions: in his book on Thackeray, in his *Autobiography,* and in one of the short stories he too wrote in the persona of an editor, always aligning himself with Thackeray's stance of faux regret at his susceptibility to "thorn letters." Trollope goes beyond Thackeray, however, not only in his desire to revisit this scenario over and over but also in his eagerness to represent both men as succumbing to the temptation to use what he evocatively calls "the butterboat of benevolence."[50] In his biographical sketch, for example, Trollope writes that "justice compels me to say that Thackeray was not a good editor," but he accounts for this on the basis of Thackeray's own preference for mercy over justice, with "Thorns in the Cushion" his prime exhibit: "Of a magazine editor it is required that he should be patient, scrupulous, judicious, but above all things hard-hearted. I think it may be doubted whether Thackeray did bring himself to read the basketfuls of manuscripts with which he was deluged, but he probably did, sooner or later, read the touching little private notes by which they were accompanied." Quoting from the "thorn letter" cited above, Trollope writes, "He could not stand this, and the money would be sent, out of his own pocket, though the poem might be—postponed, till happily it should be lost," concluding that "from such material a good editor could not be made."[51]

Returning to "Thorns in the Cushion" in his *Autobiography* when describing the failure of the magazine he edited, *St. Paul's,* Trollope makes clear his identification with Thackeray's supposed "faults" as an editor. He argues that "publishers themselves have been the best editors of magazines," because they are "not so frequently tempted to fall into that worst of literary quicksands, the publishing of matter not for the sake of the readers, but for that of the writer." While he does not specify here exactly whom publishers are less susceptible than, Trollope immediately goes on to state, "I did not so sin very often, but often enough to feel that I was a coward," by "giv[ing] way on behalf of some literary aspirant whose work did not represent itself to me as being good." The novelist-cum-editor presents this action as blameworthy—"as often as I did so, I broke my trust to those who employed me"—and thereby reaffirms his own commitment to the "hard-hearted" standards of the properly functioning marketplace, but he does not wish himself any different. Again citing Thackeray's essay, he writes, "Now, I think that such editors as Thackeray and myself—if I may for the moment be allowed to couple men so unequal—will always be liable to commit such faults, but that the natures of publishers and proprietors will be less soft"—less soft, we may infer, than the natures of novelists.[52]

Trollope performs this same balancing act repeatedly in the stories collected as *An Editor's Tales*. Here the tension between professional responsibility and personal sympathy, judgment and benevolence, virtually defines the narrator-editor's existential condition. "The cowardly professional reader indeed, unable to endure those thorns in the flesh of which poor Thackeray spoke so feelingly, when hard-pressed for definite answers, generally lies,"[53] Trollope writes in one story, and in another recounts that "the butter-boat of benevolence was in our hand, and we proceeded to pour out its contents freely. It is a vessel which an editor should lock up carefully; and should he lose the key, he will not be the worse for the loss."[54] Trollope clearly wants to use his butter-boat and lock it away too, to represent himself as benevolent but the literary marketplace as a realm in which benevolence itself is not the currency, even as the representation or cultivation of benevolent intentions may bestow value on text or author.

Trollope's cultivation of this persona of the benevolent-to-a-fault recipient of the pleas of author-beggars works on one level to keep him from being mistaken for an author-beggar himself. Yet it opens the way for this identification on another level, by undermining the marketplace's status as a legitimate barometer of success—a status, as we have seen, to which Trollope is openly committed. Trollope grapples with this difficulty in the Editor's Tale "Mary Gresley," which seeks to balance the editor's benevolence and his professional responsibility by dividing the two as completely as possible. While the story's narrator-editor offers its eponymous heroine both financial and editorial help (only the latter of which is accepted), he scrupulously separates the two by separating his literary advice from his official "editorial capacity" (79): "We had told her frankly that we would publish nothing of hers in the periodical which we ourselves were conducting. She had become too dear to us for us not to feel that were we to do so, we should be doing it rather for her sake than for that of our readers" (92). The fear of favoritism the narrator expresses here is not explicitly linked to the work's patent unacceptability on its own merit, as it will be in the nearly identical passage in the *Autobiography* (cited above), but it is easy to suspect that the editor's "frankness" in telling Mary that he will not publish her work is not matched in his explanation of this decision. The editor continues by noting, however, that "we did procure for her the publication of two short stories elsewhere" (92), and it is Mary's rapture at this news and the ensuing check that leads to the defense of "money payment for work done" as "the best and most honest test of success." The ambiguity of *procure,* the verb Trollope chooses to describe the editor's intervention here, does not necessarily compromise this transaction, but it does raise questions about the "honesty" of the test itself. Even as Trollope, through his narrator, takes care to highlight the (putatively) nonbeggarly nature of the retail marketplace—"the world" will not "buy your book out of pity," the narrator reminds Mary (92)—he fails to banish the possibility he himself introduces of wholesale contamination.

Although Thackeray and Trollope have somewhat better success than Dickens at rhetorically distancing themselves from begging-letter writers, their efforts do nothing to dispute the scandalous rhetorical, generic, and performative resemblance of novels and begging letters highlighted by James Grant and the *Times.* Those discussions suggest that one way to distinguish novels from begging letters would be to argue that the former, unlike the latter, make nothing happen. As we have seen, however, this protomodernist argument runs directly counter to the ethically based legitimation strategy of leading midcentury novelists. Something like it does emerge, however, in Wilkie Collins's *No Name,* which contains an extended and exuberant portrayal of a fraudulent begging-letter writer—a portrayal that contrasts especially sharply with those by Dickens, Collins's editor, close friend, and rival. The work of a writer keen to position himself as a cultural outsider, *No Name* explores the play of bodies and texts in both fiction and the begging-letter discourse and goes so far as to invite the reader to identify its begging-letter writer with novelists, indeed with Collins himself. Treating the figure of the begging-letter writer less as a threat than a resource, Collins even uses it to script a counternarrative that parodies the main action of the novel while paradoxically heightening the effect of authorial control. Ultimately, as we shall see, *No Name* does circumscribe its bold comparison of writers and genres, but only by foregrounding the limits that the novel's constitutive fictionality places on the range of readerly responses.

Published in weekly installments in Dickens's journal *All the Year Round* from March 1862 to January 1863 and in a three-volume edition at the end of 1862, *No Name* tells the story of Magdalen Vanstone, a spirited eighteen-year-old who learns upon her parents' deaths that she and her sister Norah have been born out of wedlock and have no legal claim to the family property or even the name Vanstone. Presenting this disinheritance as unjust (the girls' mother had saved their father from the dissipation and suicidal despair brought on by his entrapment in a disastrous youthful marriage, and although the two marry as soon as this first wife dies, they themselves die before updating their wills to secure their property for their daughters), the novel recounts, with an unstable mixture of horror and admiration, Magdalen's desperate efforts to regain the home and property she believes is rightfully hers and her sister's. Refusing to accept a future as teacher or governess, as Norah meekly does, Magdalen runs away, planning to use her talent as a "born actress"—recently discovered through her participation in amateur theatricals—to make a living, and to somehow recover the lost inheritance from the uncle, and then the cousin, who inherit it. Aiding Magdalen in her efforts is one Captain Wragge, a self-declared "rogue" and "swindler" who had dunned and possibly blackmailed Mrs. Vanstone on the basis of a tenuous family connection.[55] Magdalen, having seen Captain Wragge once on the road near the family estate of Combe-Raven (in an episode we will return to), encounters him by chance almost immediately after running away from home. Offering Magdalen his services (even while planning to return her home if the price is right), Wragge describes and defends his livelihood, and does so in terms that establish his provocative resemblance to other, ostensibly more legitimate participants in the business of humanitarian narrative: admonishing Magdalen not to be shocked, he says, "I am a Swindler," and explains that "Swindler is nothing but a word of two syllables. S, W, I, N, D—swind; L, E, R—ler; Swindler. Definition: A moral agriculturist; a man who cultivates the field of human sympathy. I am that moral agriculturist, that cultivating man" (152–53). Indeed, he complains, while "narrow-minded mediocrity, envious of my success, calls me a Swindler . . . the same low tone of mind assails men in other professions in a similar manner—calls great writers, scribblers—great generals, butchers—and so on" (153). Explaining that "it entirely depends on the point of view," Wragge goes on to provide his own, asking, "Why am I to be persecuted for habitually exciting the noblest feelings of our common nature?" (153). Against the Dickensian view that the begging-letter writer "dirt[ies] the stream of true benevolence," Wragge defends his "trickery" as necessary to "circumvent sordid man," as farmers "circumvent arid Nature"; in language reminiscent of the sanitation reform Dickens advocates against begging-letter writing, Collins's rogue represents himself as a participant "in the vast occupation of deep-draining mankind" (153). "I have confidence in the future," Wragge announces, sounding like an author advocating an extension in the term of copyright protection: "One of these days (when I am dead and gone), as ideas enlarge and enlightenment progresses, the abstract merits of the profession now called swindling, will be recognized" (154).

The logic of Wragge's argument—"Why am I to blame for making a Christian community do its duty? . . . Is a careful man who has saved money, bound to spend it again on a careless stranger who has saved none? Why of course he is! . . . on the ground that he has *got* the money" (153)—strongly recalls that of Harold Skimpole in *Bleak House* (as well as the speaker in Meredith's "Beggar's Soliloquy"). Unlike Dickens's character, however, Wragge uses this line of reasoning to defend the *active* cultivation of sympathy (as opposed to Skimpole's maddeningly passive reliance on it), a practice he goes on to link specifically to fraudulent begging-letter writing. Describing his "system" in some detail, Wragge explains to Magdalen that "I never plead for myself; and I never apply to rich people," and he shows her his "commercial library," including his "Book of Letters," which contains "my Adopted Handwritings of public characters; my testimonials to my own worth and integrity; my Heartrending Statements of the officer's family, the curate's wife, and the grazier's widow, stained with tears, blotted with emotion; Etcetera, Etcetera" (155–56). Whereas the lazy Skimpole never finishes anything he starts, the energetic Wragge "had reduced his rogueries as strictly to method and system as if they had been the commercial transactions of an honest man" (155).

Given his engagement in the written cultivation of sympathy, on the one hand, and his entrepreneurial drive, on the other, one might expect Wragge to be an even more disturbing presence in *No Name* than Harold Skimpole is in *Bleak House*. On the contrary, however, Wragge is amusing where Skimpole is infuriating—to the reader, I would maintain, but unquestionably to the two novels' respective protagonists. Wragge's defense of swindling is marked as "extravagant," but its "extravagant impudence . . . touched Magdalen's natural sense of humour" (154), and she decides to accept his assistance, although well aware that he will attempt to cheat her. Wragge's "point of view" may not be the novel's, then, but the novel does not seem particularly threatened by its articulation.

Rather than present a parodic version of an ethic of benevolence in order to clarify and reassert the true version, as Dickens does in *Bleak House* or *Little Dorrit,* then, Collins seems content to let this parody stand. To some extent, this reflects that parody's inapplicability to the younger novelist's own "system": unlike Dickens or Eliot, in their different ways, Collins does not identify his own work as "moral agriculture," does not derive his work's value—its legitimacy—from its ability to cultivate the reader's sympathy. Instead, as the prefaces to his novels reveal, Collins seeks to base his authority and merit as an author on an artistry defined not only by its truth to nature (a criterion accepted by virtually all Victorian novelists) and its moral seriousness but also in terms of its craftsmanship. Even as the "Preface" to *No Name* itself expresses a desire to make Magdalen "a pathetic character," for example, it treats this as an aesthetic rather than an ethical imperative, and repeatedly emphasizes the skill and effort necessary for the author to achieve this and the other artistic effects he aims for. Thus, after stating that his book's subject is "the struggle of a human creature, under those opposing influences of Good and Evil"—"the theme of some of the greatest writers, living and dead"—Collins explains that "I have tried hard [to make Magdalen's character "pathetic . . . even in its perversity and its error"] by the least obtrusive and the least artificial of all means—by a resolute adherence, throughout, to the truth as it is in Nature." Choosing perspiration over inspiration (to invoke a later idiom), Collins stresses that "this design was no easy one to accomplish," but asserts that "the object which I had proposed to myself, I might, in some degree, consider as an object achieved," based on readers' responses to the novel's serialization (xxxvi).

Throughout the "Preface," Collins promotes an understanding of his novel as a well-wrought urn, a carefully crafted aesthetic artifact conceived and executed as a whole, in all respects the expression of its author's intentions. He points to the "sharp contrast" between the "more serious passages in the book" and its humorous characters, and defends this artistic decision on the basis of both "the laws of Art" and "experience." Framing his authorial career as a series of "studies in the art of writing fiction," he informs the reader that "the narrative related in these pages has been constructed on a plan" but that this plan "differs from the plan followed in my last novel [*The Woman in White*], and in some other of my works." This new "plan," according to which "the only Secret contained in this book, is revealed midway in the first volume," both reflects and calls attention to the novel's careful construction: "From that point, all the main events of the story are purposely foreshadowed, before they take place—my present design being to rouse the reader's interest in following the train of circumstances by which these foreseen events are brought about" (xxxvi). Ostensibly leaving behind sympathy and readerly identification, the author promotes his novel's purposive self-reflexiveness and uses that reflexiveness for the purpose of self-promotion.[56]

Ironically, however, in positioning himself as a designer of plots rather than a cultivator of sympathy, Collins by no means distances himself from Captain Wragge, but on the contrary lays the groundwork for Wragge's authorial figuration. As G. Robert Stange points out, Collins contrives "to rouse the reader's interest in following the [narrative's] train of circumstances" by making plotting itself the very subject of the novel. *No Name*, Stange argues, "is a tale of trappers trapping trappers, devised by a novelist who, we are continually reminded, is himself an addictive contriver,"[57] and Wragge is the novel's master plotter, carefully planning his cons and recording them in his "Books" (154). In fact, his paean to "moral agriculture" notwithstanding, the schemes in which we see Wragge engaged involve such tricks of the begging-letter writer's trade as fraud, forgery, and disguise, but they do not involve any appeal to benevolence; if Collins aims, as he says in the "Preface," "to vary the form in which I make my appeal to the reader" (xxxvi), so too does Wragge vary his methods. Yet far from seeking to disguise or disavow Wragge's status as an authorial figure—indeed, as a figure not simply of "the author" but of the author of this novel in particular—Collins courts this identification from the very outset. He does so not only by giving the character the author's initials in reverse order (à la *David Copperfield*) but also by in effect signing the first installment of the novel in Wragge's name.[58]

This bold gesture unfolds as follows: entering the novel in the second chapter, Wragge approaches Magdalen, Norah, and their longtime governess, Miss Garth, on the road outside the Vanstone family estate. Looking "like a clergyman in difficulties," this two-faced stranger has "eyes of two different colours—one bilious green, one bilious brown, both sharply intelligent," and speaks "with an easy flow of language, and a strict attention to the elocutionary claims of words in more than one syllable. Persuasion distilled from his mildly-curling lips; and shabby as he was, perennial flowers of courtesy bloomed all over him from head to foot" (14−15). "The persuasive man" (15) engages Miss Garth (who has prudently sent the girls inside) in conversation, and, after learning that Mr. and Mrs. Vanstone have gone to London, he leaves his card for Mrs. Vanstone, explaining that "my name will be quite sufficient to re-call a little family matter" to her (16). The chapter, and along with it the novel's first installment, then concludes with Miss Garth reading the card "in blank astonishment": "The name and address of the clerical-looking stranger (both written in pencil) ran as follows:—*Captain Wragge. Post-office, Bristol*" (16).

The privileged location and italicization of Captain Wragge's name threatens—or promises—to transform a novel "By the Author of 'The Woman in White,'" as the byline reads, into a letter from one of its own characters.[59] This possibility persists and expands over the course of the novel, with Wragge serving to ironize, and thus potentially to undo, the ideological work the novel otherwise seems to be performing.[60] Magdalen's assertion of her supposed property rights to her father's brother, for instance, echoes Wragge's dubious claim on Mrs. Vanstone, a resemblance underscored when Michael Vanstone treats her appeal to his sense of justice as a begging letter. Even this initial appearance by Wragge—that is, the very fact that he appears at Combe-Raven—upsets the opposition that ostensibly organizes *No Name* as well as the begging-letter discourse, that between bodily and textual presence: just as the establishment of the begging-letter writer as a particular category or type obviously depends on a distinction between begging in person and begging in writing, the novel is divided into "Scenes," each identified by geographical location and narrated by a third-person narrator, and sections labeled "Between the Scenes. Progress of the Story through the Post" (or, in one instance, "Between the Scenes. Chronicle of Events: Preserved in Captain Wragge's Despatch Box" [171]), each of which consists in a series of numbered documents, mainly letters. Wragge shows up at the Vanstones' home even though "it had been [Mrs. Vanstone's] practice, for many years past, to assist the captain from her own purse, on the condition that he should never come near the house" (18). As unprecedented as it is unexplained, Wragge's violation of this condition puts new pressure on the opposition between written communication and face-to-face encounter and calls into question its significance. Wragge's appearance at Combe-Raven establishes a pattern, as over the course of *No Name* the distinction between scenes and letters, contact in-person and in-writing, loses not only its importance but also its coherence.

Moreover, the breakdown of the distinction between bodily and textual contact in the novel continues to be associated specifically with Wragge, who calls attention in various ways to a materiality shared by body and text. Wragge's very name, for example, recalls the stuff from which paper is made, and indeed upon his second appearance in the novel we learn that "his dingy white collar and cravat had died the death of old linen, and had gone to their long home at the paper-maker's, to live again one day in quires at a stationer's shop" (134). In addition, the captain has the curious habit (seen above in his definition of "swindler") of spelling words aloud, and the first word he spells in the novel is his own name: "My name is Wragge," he tells Magdalen, "and jocosely spelt his name for her further enlightenment. 'W, R, A, double G, E—Wragge'" (110). Here the graphic excess of the name in relation to its phonetic content underscores the materiality, or materialities, of the signifier itself. Such operations do not nullify the distinction between body and text, but they do deprive it of its self-evidence and force.

This is especially the case in *No Name,* because not only do bodies serve here as signs, as they do in virtually all nineteenth-century novels, but, more unusually, they prove as semiotically malleable and slippery as language itself. Wragge's list of false identities, for instance, is called "Skins to Jump Into" (235). Magdalen's own skin is blemished—or, we might say, is made identifiably hers—by two moles on her neck. Referred to as distinguishing characteristics in the handbill and correspondence of those searching for her, the moles seem likely to prove crucial in revealing her true identity, but they do not: a suspicious Noel Vanstone looks for them, but Wragge manages to conceal them with cosmetics (303). Noel Vanstone's servant Mrs. Lecount eventually succeeds in establishing Magdalen's identity by shifting the focus from her body to her clothing, as she steals a patch of a dress Magdalen wears when disguised as Miss Garth, her own governess, and later matches it to one of Magdalen's. In the matter of identity, then, the body loses its transparency here, and even its primacy starts to seem questionable.

The ontological and epistemological play with bodies and signs in *No Name* points up an unresolved, indeed unacknowledged, contradiction in the begging-letter discourse itself. Portraits of "the" begging-letter writer occasionally go beyond begging-letter writing to the other forms of begging and swindling this figure is said to engage in, and these additional ploys often involve face-to-face encounters. This is the case despite the obvious fact that letter writing is the begging-letter writer's defining modus operandi, and despite the fact that "the quiet agency of the post," as the *Times* puts it, is often seen as particularly appealing to fraudulent beggars precisely because it obviates the necessity of personal contact. For example, at one point in the section on begging-letter writers in the fourth volume of *London Labour and the London Poor,* Mayhew's associate Andrew Halliday (author of this section) describes one group of begging-letter writers without making it immediately clear that they write letters at all: "Among the begging-letter fraternity," he writes, "there are not a few persons who affect to be literary men. They have at one time or another been able to publish a pamphlet, a poem, or a song . . . and copies of these works—they always call them 'works'—they constantly carry about with them to be ready for any customer who may turn up" (4:409).

Paradoxically, then, Wragge's own tendency to "turn up" in the schemes in which he engages in *No Name* (as opposed to those he describes), along with the great care he devotes to his physical appearance, does not diminish his identification as a begging-letter writer. In fact, Collins seems to have borrowed the details of Wragge's appearance from Halliday's account, which was published in the year of *No Name*'s writing: according to Halliday, the typical begging-letter writer exhibits a "general expression of pious resignation," while Wragge "looked like a clergyman in difficulties"; Halliday's beggar's "once raven hair is turning grey, and his well-shaved whiskerless cheeks are blue as with gunpowder tattoo," while Wragge's "hair was iron-grey" and "his cheeks and chin were in the bluest bloom of smooth shaving"; the former "wears a portentous stick-up collar" and "affects white cravats," and the latter's "white cravat was high, stiff, and dingy; the collar, higher, stiffer, and dingier." The captain lives up to Halliday's statement that the begging-letter writer "invariably carries an umbrella," and his "black cotton gloves, neatly darned at the fingers" (14), neatly recall the archetype's "carefully-darned black-cloth gloves" (4:403).[61]

Like Wragge, Halliday's begging-letter writer pays careful attention to his appearance because he does not restrict himself to the writing of begging letters. Halliday singles out begging-letter writers because of the increased potential for deception created by their literacy, but their skill at deception carries over into the realm of performance as well—and thereby undercuts the initial grounds for the begging-letter writer's special treatment. At the same time, Halliday and other commentators pay a great deal of attention to the appearance of begging letters and advocate such attention as a way to detect fraud. The physical features of letters therefore come to serve less as reminders of a vexing absence, as one might expect, than as physical surrogates for, and indexical signs of, their writers.

The begging-letter discourse thus has a way of collapsing the very oppositions that structure it. It has to be said, though, that the discourse seems oblivious to and undeterred by its contradictions. *No Name* itself, however, is fascinated by just this convergence and confusion of bodies and signs, and is much more willing to tease out its implications. In particular, as bodies get revealed as unreliable signs in the novel, and as the ontological difference between signs and their referents blurs, the lines between true identity and impersonation, between being and acting or representing, fray—become Wragged, if you will. "All the world's a stage" (280), as the Captain does not fail to note. Similarly, Magdalen speaks of her ability to "disguise [her]self *in other people's characters*" (453; emphasis added), rather than, say, *as other people*. The theatrical or performative dimension of identity implied by her formulation should not, however, be equated with superficiality—not coming from a character whose parents live for decades "as husband and wife, to all intents and purposes (except that the marriage service had not been read over them)" (93); the novel as a whole is no more willing than Magdalen to dismiss this performance as a sham, a mere impersonation. Indeed, Magdalen's "cool appropriation of Norah's identity to theatrical purposes" (42) early in the novel already suggests the theatricality of personal as well as social identity.[62] That Magdalen herself is a "born actress," then, may have less to do with her talent or even her personal history than with the human condition. And not just human: describing how "gentle" Captain Wragge's wife is, the narrator comments, "If Mrs. Wragge and a lamb had been placed side by side—comparison under those circumstances, would have exposed the lamb as a rank impostor" (146). Whereas the exposure—or even the presumptive exposability—of rank impostors in the begging-letter discourse serves not only to free begging-letter recipients from the letters' claims but also to confirm the solidity of their own sense of identity, in *No Name* such an exposure induces vertigo.

In its final "Scene," Collins's novel seems to pull back from its most radical impulses and dizzying claims. Yet it is here, where the plot is most conventional, that Captain Wragge is most subversive. *No Name* ends with the story of Magdalen's "return to legitimate social identity in marriage," as Deirdre David puts it:[63] Magdalen succeeds in marrying Noel Vanstone, but through Mrs. Lecount's (counter)machinations she does not inherit his property upon his almost immediate death, and her subsequent efforts to locate the Secret Trust governing the property's disposition fail. Then, in the novel's final section, she is saved by a Captain Kirke, who had seen Magdalen once previously and encounters her destitute and ill on a London street. Kirke, who has just returned to England from a voyage on his ship, the *Deliverance*—and who also happens to be the son of the man who prevented Magdalen's father from committing suicide after his disastrous first marriage—nurses Magdalen back to health and proposes to her, even after she confesses her story to him. Meanwhile, Norah, the sister who has accepted her fate, succeeds where Magdalen has failed, as she falls in love with and marries the man who ultimately inherits the property instead of Magdalen.

Margaret Oliphant complained in *Blackwood's* that Magdalen "emerges, at the cheap cost of a fever, as pure, as high-minded, and as spotless as the most dazzling white of heroines"; "after all her endless deceptions and horrible marriage," she continues, "it seems quite right to the author that she should be restored to society, and have a good husband and a happy home."[64] Today, of course, this "restoration" is more likely to be read as Magdalen's recontainment, the final squelching of her remarkable independence and subversive energy. While nominally reaffirming social norms, however, this denouement does not quite assume "conventional narrative form," as David argues, but instead becomes blatantly allegorical, as the foregoing summary suggests.[65] The ostentation with which Collins produces this ending points toward the labor necessary to construct this conventional scenario, and thus toward its arbitrariness. Even more telling, though, is the role played by Captain Wragge in the novel's "Last Scene." This final section of the novel ostensibly offers Magdalen's rescue by Captain Kirke as the undoing or reversal of her earlier "rescue" at the hands of the novel's other captain, with the promised marriage based on love, honesty, and repentance canceling the earlier relationship—itself pointedly sealed with the words "I do" (164)—ruled by deception, revenge, and money. This symmetry is spoiled, however, and the reestablishment of order it represents subverted, by Wragge's unexpected reappearance.

Having dropped out of the story after helping to engineer Magdalen's marriage to Noel Vanstone, Wragge not only returns in "The Last Scene" but returns triumphantly, unchanged in character but having "slightly modif[ied] my old professional habits," as he informs the ailing Magdalen: "I have shifted from Moral Agriculture to Medical Agriculture. Formerly, I prayed on the public sympathy; now, I prey on the public stomach" by selling "a Pill" (525). "Stomach and sympathy, sympathy and stomach . . . come to much the same thing," according to Wragge (at least "when you reach the wrong side of fifty"), only his current livelihood is both legal and wildly successful. He is "a Grand Financial Fact . . . with my clothes positively paid for; with a balance at my banker's; . . . solvent, flourishing, popular" (525). Wragge attributes his success to his advertising campaign, which revolves around his tall, unruly, somewhat dimwitted wife. Rather than attempting to keep Mrs. Wragge hidden away, as he had earlier in the novel, the Captain puts her on display, making her the star of his advertisements. As he explains to Magdalen, "She is the celebrated woman whom I have cured of indescribable agonies from every complaint under the sun. Her portrait is engraved on all the wrappers, with the following inscription beneath it:—'Before she took the Pill, you might have blown this patient away with a feather. Look at her now!!!'" (526). With a brazenness exceeding that of Wragge himself, Collins offers the reader this fraudulent scenario of female recovery even as Captain Kirke is nursing Magdalen back to health from what seems to be "the last stage of illness" (516)—which is to say, even as the novel is staging her moral and ideological recuperation. If, as critics have argued, Collins had to pull back from his attacks on middle-class values in order to ensure his success in the marketplace, or even his ability to get published in mainstream organs, here we see him advertising and satirizing—satirizing by advertising—the work of containment itself.[66]

Strikingly, at the same time that Wragge's encore performance undercuts the denouement of Magdalen's story, Collins reinforces the Captain's status as his own barely alter ego. The openness of this identification is necessary to ensure that Wragge's subversiveness does not subvert but instead enhances Collins's own authority. Not only, then, does Wragge's turn from moral to medical agriculture again confirm his resemblance to his creator, who in 1862 is already credited or blamed with replacing the reigning aesthetic of sympathy with one of sensation, but Wragge starts to sound like Collins as well: while Collins, as we have seen, claims that "my one object . . . [is] to vary the form in which I make my appeal to the reader, as attractively as I can" (xxxvi), Wragge boasts that "there is not a single form of appeal in the whole range of human advertisement, which I am not making to the unfortunate public at this moment" (525). "Hire the last new novel," he says, "there I am, inside the boards of the book" (525). Moreover, just as Collins eschews secrets and directs the reader's attention to the ways in which "foreseen events are brought about" (xxxvi), so too does Wragge embrace transparency and put the labor of production on display: "Behind one counter (visible to the public through the lucid medium of plate-glass), are four-and-twenty young men, in white aprons, making the Pill. Behind another counter, are four-and-twenty young men, in white cravats, making the boxes"; as a result, he says, "The place in which my Pill is made, is an advertisement in itself" (526). If the structure of No Name similarly promotes an awareness of Collins's literary labor and narrative mastery, as I have argued, then here we see Collins promoting an awareness of the self-promotional nature of his own strategy. It is not just plate glass but transparency itself that Collins's reader is invited to see through.

Wragge's last appearance in the novel caps Collins's self-portrait in a con man's mirror. Yet if Collins is willing to explore and exploit the resemblance of his craft to that of the begging-letter writer, real or fraudulent, he ultimately does insist upon one crucial difference between novel and begging letter. This difference retrospectively licenses the sustained comparison Collins undertakes, precisely by putting a limit to the comparability of the two genres, and thus preventing analogy or figurative identification from collapsing into identity. To establish this difference at the end of the novel, Collins surprisingly resurrects the distinction between communication in person and in writing. When Magdalen resolves to tell Captain Kirke her story and demands that he "help me to tell the truth—*force* me to tell it, for my own sake, if not for yours," he asks, "Would it be easier to you . . . to write it than to tell it?" Magdalen agrees to this suggestion, saying, "I can be sure of hiding nothing from you, if I write it" (539). No longer morally or ontologically interchangeable with speech, writing becomes aligned here with truth, and the bodily presence of another—the addressee, the beloved—emerges as a threat to honesty. Magdalen's ensuing demand that Kirke not write back to her—"Wait till we meet; and tell me with your own lips, what you think"—reinforces this new emphasis on the unique power of physical presence: "With a woman's instinctive quickness of penetration," she recognizes "the danger of totally renouncing her personal influence," which is to say the influence of her personal presence, the presence of her person.

Magdalen's instincts here suggest that her rehabilitation is less than complete.[67] Yet rather than pursue this implication, Collins uses this renewed play of bodily and textual presence and absence to a different end, to call attention to the ontological status of his characters—to their status, that is, as all text and no body. In other words, Collins neither takes for granted the novel's constitutive fictionality nor glosses over it as defenders of the genre's humanitarian effects often do (nor treats it as itself a fiction, as we saw Thackeray do in chapter 1). Instead, he insists upon this fictionality. Paradoxically, he does so by recasting the novel as a nonfictional narrative, since in writing the true story of her life Magdalen in essence writes *No Name*. In reading her story, then, Kirke occupies the place of the novel's reader. For Kirke, this is how the reading experience ends and where it leads:

> "Tell me the truth!" she repeated.
> "With my own lips?"

"Yes!" she answered eagerly. "Say what you think of me, with your own lips."

He stooped, and kissed her. (548)

The actual novel reader continues reading, though, for two more words: "The End." Whether or not the reader has identified closely enough with Kirke to want to act as he does, such an option does not exist; instead there is a reminder of its nonexistence—a reminder, that is, of the absoluteness of the fictional character's bodily absence. By calling attention in this way to the ontological gap between real reader and fictional character, Collins suggests the impossibility of directly converting readerly sympathy or identification into action and thus the irreducible difference between novel and begging letter. The reader closes the book on the conflation of novelist and begging-letter writer through the very act of closing the book.

5   Moses and the Advertisement Sheet

Daniel Deronda's Earthly Mixtures

UNEXPECTEDLY THROWN INTO poverty, a spirited young woman is faced with the necessity of earning her livelihood. Horrified at the prospect of becoming a governess, she considers becoming an actress instead. The need to make money is soon obviated, or rather satisfied, by marriage to a rich man. Yet the woman despises her husband and longs for his death. He obliges her by dying. This death comes, however, less as a liberation than as a source of further crisis. Exactly at this woman's moment of greatest extremity, when she is guilt-ridden, sick, possibly delirious, and alone among strangers, a man from her past arrives on the scene. He has just traveled a great distance on unrelated business, but he happens to be thinking about her when he notices a crowd and sees her at the center of it, looking deathly ill. Although his connection to her is difficult to define or explain, he immediately takes charge of the situation, oversees her physical recovery, and aids in her moral renewal.

This admittedly selective plot summary tells the story of *No Name*'s Magdalen Vanstone, discussed in the last chapter. It also tells the story of Gwendolen Harleth, one of the central figures in George Eliot's 1876 novel *Daniel Deronda*.[1] Even granting the limited number of plots available to Victorian-novel heroines—indeed, this limitation is often what drives the plot, not least in these two cases—the parallels here are striking; while it may be, as one of the voices in Henry James's dialogue-review of Eliot's novel puts it, that "as for the Jewish element in *Daniel Deronda* . . . Wilkie Collins and Miss Braddon would not have thought of it,"[2] Collins clearly had already "thought of" many of the plot elements of *Deronda*'s other "half." Of particular interest here is that in *Daniel Deronda,* as in *No Name,* much of this plot—especially its conclusion—

hinges on the relationship between contact in person and contact in writing. Both novels, that is, use this plot to explore what is gained and what is lost, what changes and what stays the same—epistemologically, experientially, ethically—when an individual is in the physical presence of a person as opposed to a text. If the similarities between the two novels suggest Collins's influence on Eliot, then, they also shed light on both novels' treatment of influence itself: the relative power of persons and texts to shape attitudes and actions, and the implied or desired effect of the novels themselves on their readers.

Of course, Eliot's novel does not simply repeat Collins's, and even at the level of abstraction at which I have compared their plots, readers of both novels will have noticed a dramatic difference between the two: Magdalen Vanstone ends up united with the man she regards as her rescuer, whereas Gwendolen Harleth does not. The narrative particulars reinforce this contrast: *No Name* ends with Captain Kirke choosing marriage to Magdalen over a return to sea, but in Gwendolen's final meeting with Daniel Deronda—not, significantly, the final scene in the novel—she learns that he has embraced his newly discovered Jewish heritage, plans to marry another woman, and is leaving England, quite possibly never to see Gwendolen again. Expecting a verbal indication of Kirke's intentions, Magdalen receives a kiss on the lips; Gwendolen, conversely, while finding solace only in Deronda's "presence and touch," is left with his assurance that "we shall not be quite parted," for "I will write to you always, when I can."[3] With this promise from Deronda, Gwendolen's experience diverges from Magdalen's; in the process, however, it comes to resemble, in a heightened key, that of the reader of *No Name,* as described in the last chapter: offered words on paper instead of the face-to-face or bodily contact she craves, Gwendolen, like the reader finishing Collins's novel, is made aware of the difference between textual and physical presence—made aware, that is, of the two as different, with Gwendolen considering herself "forsaken" (805). *No Name*'s formal effect thus becomes *Daniel Deronda*'s narrative event.

Wilkie Collins, I argued, highlights the difference between bodies and texts at the end of *No Name* to make the novel reader's decathexis as jarring and complete as possible. By suggesting the impossibility of directly converting readerly sympathy and identification into action, Collins distinguishes the project of the novelist from that of the begging-letter writer, the disreputable double whose sentimental, sensational, and presumptively fraudulent tales were intended to produce specific actions on the part of readers—namely, the sending of alms. As we also saw in the last chapter, early in her career Eliot too sought to distinguish novelist from begging-letter writer, but without relinquishing the notion that "the extension of our sympathies" is art's "greatest benefit."[4] By the time she writes *Daniel Deronda,* the eminent Eliot is unlikely to feel threatened by any comparison to begging-letter writers. Nonetheless, her final novel does offer a critique of and at least partial retreat from her official ethico-aesthetic: according to the narrator's well-known diagnosis, the indecisive Daniel is hampered by the *over*extension of his sympathies.[5] This reevaluation of sympathy may be seen to register the era's ever-louder condemnation of what it chose to call "indiscriminate alms-giving," and it helps explain *No Name*'s ghostly presence in the novel.

Yet Eliot never completely abandons her commitment to sympathy and its aesthetic cultivation, locating these instead within a dialectical narrative of individual development: although Daniel is too good at sympathizing, Gwendolen's problem remains that she is not good enough. (It is as if Daniel has read too much Eliot, whereas Gwendolen has read too much Collins. Indeed, since *Daniel Deronda* is set in the 1860s, Gwendolen might be imagined as having read *No Name* itself, and even viewing her own life through its lens—hence her surprise when Daniel announces his intentions.)[6] In an oft-cited letter to Harriet Beecher Stowe describing her purposes in writing *Daniel Deronda,* Eliot claims, plausibly enough, that she has sought to "rouse the imagination of men and women to a vision of human claims in those races of their fellow-men who most differ from them in customs and beliefs," and especially the Jews, with whom "western people who have been reared in Christianity, have a peculiar debt and, whether we acknowledge it or not, a peculiar thoroughness of fellowship in religious and moral sentiment."[7] Early and late in her career, then, Eliot stakes the value of her labors as a novelist, even the very legitimacy of the novel as a genre, on an understanding of texts as having a far greater impact on their readers than Gwendolen ultimately envisions or the Collins of *No Name* finally desires. We therefore need to ask whether Gwendolen's fate represents a departure from this stance—or whether, on the contrary, there might be more hope for her future intercourse with Daniel than she (along with virtually all critics) believes. Put more broadly, what understanding of the comparative nature and relative power of bodies and texts does *Daniel Deronda* promote, and to what end?

I want to leave Gwendolen hanging for now—though not, like Eliot, permanently—to approach this larger issue from a different direction. Eliot typically maintains that, just as literature's beneficial influence on its readers justifies the author's entry into the marketplace, so too does the nature of this influence hinge on how well the author resists the influence of the market itself. In this version of what my introduction described as a "dyer's hand" ideology of authorship, Eliot compares the author who "cares for nothing but his income" to "the manufacturer who gets rich by fancy wares colored with arsenic green" (wares, that is, "colored with a green which had arsenic in it that damaged the factory workers and the purchasers"). Such a "man," she continues, "carries on authorship on the principle of the gin-palace; and bad literature of the sort called amusing is spiritual gin." The market's indifference to literature's influence on "the moral taste" of "the public mind," combined with its encouragement of rushed, recycled, inferior work, creates the need for "some regulating principle with regard to the publication of intellectual products, which would override the rule of the market."[8] Eliot demands, in effect, that responsible authors take as their motto the promotional slogan adopted by the Hebrew National brand of kosher meats a century later: "We answer to a higher authority."

In her letter to Stowe, Eliot boasts of having lived up to this market-transcending standard herself when writing *Daniel Deronda* (a work that promotes its own brand of Hebrew nationalism): "I was happily independent in material things and felt no temptation to accommodate my writing to any standard except that of trying to do my best in what seemed to me most needful to be done"—namely, to "treat Jews with such sympathy and understanding as my nature and knowledge could attain to."[9] As Eliot twice stresses to Stowe, the English prejudice and "stupidity" that she has sought to combat led her to expect "resistance and even repulsion." On her own account, then, she is able to write "the Jewish element" of the novel only by resisting—even repulsing— the perceived demands of the marketplace.

The depiction of Jews constitutes a particularly fitting site for Eliot to negotiate her own relationship to the marketplace, because the relationship of Jews themselves to the marketplace is crucially at issue within this depiction. In Victorian England, of course, the figure of the Jew stereotypically stands not for answerability to a higher authority—indeed, Eliot's letter to Stowe expresses disgust at mockery of the laws of kashruth through "small jokes about eating ham"—but for just the opposite, an exclusive commitment to the values of the marketplace. The combating of this stereotype is usually seen as one of the novel's primary objectives; the novel, by this account, seeks to cultivate sympathy for the Jews as a people by showing that not all Jews worship Mammon. Viewed through the lens of the letter to Stowe, then, this distancing of some Jews from the marketplace is made possible by, and thus signals, Eliot's own such distance. Eliot's market-flouting separation of Jews from the marketplace shows that, unlike the dyer's hand, she is not subdued to what she works in.

As if to confirm this alignment, Eliot alludes to the dyer's hand itself in a passage explicitly concerned with Jewishness rather than authorship: according to the narrator, even the good-natured Mrs. Meyrick, who has taken Mirah in, fears that her rediscovered brother Mordecai (also known as Ezra) will "dip Mirah's mind over again in the deepest dye of Jewish sentiment" (567). Struggling to overcome her anti-Jewish attitude, she tells Deronda that "I am as glad as you are that the pawnbroker is not her brother: there are Ezras and Ezras in the world; and really it is a comfort to think that all Jews are not like those shopkeepers who *will not* let you get out of their shops" (567). Mrs. Meyrick thus retains her animus toward the values Jews are seen to represent but learns not to identify all Jews with these values. There are also, as Eliot routinely asserts, authors and authors in the world,[10] and her sympathetic portrayal of nonshopkeeping Jews seems designed to indicate which kind she is.

One of Eliot's standard complaints about the marketplace is that it encourages repetition and recirculation: the author who pursues his vocation "with a trading determination to get rich by it" is liable to "do over again what has already been done, either by himself or others, so as to render his work no real contribution."[11] Ironically, however, not only does one of *Daniel Deronda*'s plots "do over again" *No Name,* but Eliot's very allusion to the dyer's hand closely resembles a passage in one of her own earlier novels: just as Mrs. Meyrick fears that Mordecai will "dip Mirah's mind over again in the deepest dye of Jewish sentiment" (567),

Romola's Tito Melema explains the relationship between his Italian birth and Greek ancestry by saying, "The Greek dye was subdued in me, I suppose, till I had been dipped over again by long abode and much travel in the land of gods and heroes."[12] According to Eliot's own argument, this repetition suggests that she herself has not fully escaped the market's taint. Moreover, since not even the learned and wily Tito could have been familiar with a sonnet written a century after his death, his anachronistic allusion already suggests a lapse on Eliot's part. Through a kind of mimetic contagion, then, both these passages seem to exemplify the damaged authorial agency to which they allude.

The irony here is particularly satisfying to anyone skeptical of the heroic rhetoric of autonomy on display in Eliot's letter to Stowe. And indeed, a starkly different understanding of the connection between *Daniel Deronda*'s representation of Jews and its relationship to the marketplace (as well as the cultivation of sympathy) emerges in a letter written the same day and under the same roof as the Stowe letter. This letter, from Eliot's companion, George Henry Lewes, to her publisher, John Blackwood, deflates the pretensions of Eliot's own letter with comic precision: just as Eliot complains of a widespread English "deadness to the history which has prepared half our world for us," Lewes remarks on "the deadness of so many Christians to that part of the book which does not directly concern Gwendolen"—but Lewes goes on to note that "the Jews seem to be very grateful for Deronda—and will perhaps make up for [this] deadness."[13] "When the cheap edition is issued," he continues, "we shall perhaps see the effect of this Jewish sympathy. The Jews ought to make a good public—as the doctors did for Middlemarch." Just as there are Ezras and Ezras, so too are there Georges and Georges: where Eliot seeks to make the public good, Lewes seeks a good public, and where Eliot opposes her sympathy *for* Jews to a desire for sales, Lewes sees the sympathy *of* Jews as a source of sales. Lewes here recalls *No Name*'s cynical Captain Wragge, who equates moral and medical agriculture, preying on the public's sympathy and its stomach.

It would be wrong, however, to see Lewes's letter as representing the truth that Eliot's mystifies. For one thing, Lewes confirms the riskiness of Eliot's undertaking. More important, the use Eliot makes of Shakespeare's famous simile suggests that the disassociation of Jews and herself from the marketplace may not be her goal after all. In both *Daniel*

Deronda and *Romola,* being dipped in dye figures the strengthening of one's ethnic or national identity, not the degradation of personal or artistic integrity described in the sonnet; and in the later novel, at least, this strengthening is cause for celebration: Eliot uses the phrase to capture Mrs. Meyrick's hostile view of Mirah's anticipated reimmersion in Jewishness, but Mrs. Meyrick's view is decidedly not that of the novel, which celebrates Mirah's reunion with her brother, affirms the dignity of Jewish identity and attachment to that identity, and sets its hero on his life course by dipping him in the very same dye. Eliot's chiastic transformation of an image of the market's negative influence on an author into that of "Jewish sentiment['s]" positive influence on a Jew thus realigns these terms. This realignment is unstable, however, insofar as the earlier image retains its allusive presence. In other words, even as Eliot reworks Shakespeare's simile so that dye no longer figures the market's taint, the very allusion reminds us of this association. At the same time, the reversal of the valence of Shakespeare's image (being dipped in dye goes from bad to good) adumbrates the possible reversal of that attitude toward the marketplace which the image famously captures.

If Eliot's recycled allusion to Shakespeare's sonnet contradicts the claim of distance from the market made in the letter to Stowe, then, it also encourages us to reexamine the novel's very commitment to such distance—or rather, to read the novel itself as such a reexamination. Such a reading will eventually return us to Gwendolen's fate and the questions it raises, as promised. It will do so because *Daniel Deronda*'s treatment of authorship and market activity intersects with its treatment of the comparative nature and power of persons and texts, as both the allusion to the dyer's hand and the echoes of *No Name* should have led us to expect by now. We shall see, in fact, that George Eliot's last novel conducts a remarkably sustained, multifaceted investigation into the implications and imbrications of what we have come to term economic, physical, corporeal, and linguistic materiality. What makes it a particularly appropriate novel with which to conclude the present study, however, will be the questions it ultimately raises concerning the necessity or contingency of this conjunction itself.

The alignment or entanglement of multiple forms of materiality in *Daniel Deronda* is captured with spectacular economy by a passage—

indeed, a phrase—that, even more than the "Ezras and Ezras" passage, seems to announce authoritatively the novel's separation of (some) Jews and Eliot from the debased realm of the marketplace. This passage oc- curs in the opening chapter of book 3, which describes Deronda's thoughts as he "sat up half the night" (205) after saving Mirah Lapidoth from her contemplated suicide in the Thames. Too excited to read, Deronda relives the events of the evening and envisions "possibilities of what had been and what might be" (205) for this young woman of whom he knows little more than that she is Jewish, possesses "exquisite refine- ment and charm" (206), and has come to London to search for the mother and brother from whom she has long been separated. In his mind Deronda sees "rapid images of what might be" if he were to search for Mirah's lost relatives:

> He saw himself guided by some official scout into a dingy street; he entered through a dim doorway, and saw a hawk-eyed woman, rough-headed and unwashed, cheapening a hungry girl's last bit of finery; or in some quarter only the more hideous for being smarter, he found himself under the breath of a young Jew talka- tive and familiar, willing to show his acquaintance with gentle- men's tastes, and not fastidious in any transactions with which they would favour him—and so on through the brief chapter of his experience in this kind. (207)

The narrator pulls up short at the end of this passage, as if these images were too familiar to require elaboration or too offensive to dwell on (or both). The narrator then makes clear how we are to judge Deronda's thoughts by instructing the reader not to judge Deronda for having thought them but instead to "excuse him," because "his mind was not apt to run spontaneously into insulting ideas, or to practise a form of wit which identifies Moses with the advertisement sheet; but he was just now governed by dread, and if Mirah's parents had been Christian, the chief difference would have been that his forebodings would have been fed with wider knowledge" (207).

"*A form of wit which identifies Moses with the advertisement sheet.*" At is- sue here is the relationship between a person, or kind of person (or a name?), and a text, or kind of text. Most obviously, of course, the iden- tification in question is that of Jews with commerce; the *form* of wit in

question, then, is what we would now label anti-Semitic. Yet Eliot's res-
onant phrase evokes additional identifications and other forms of wit also
at issue in the novel. To identify Moses with the advertisement sheet is
to collapse differences between prophecy and puffery, the promotion of
ideas and the selling of commodities: a cynical or narrow-minded
economism, this form of wit denies the existence of a realm of belief and
action not contaminated by or reducible to the values, motives, and logic
of the market economy. In addition, the passage contains a play on
words, as it alludes specifically to the firm of E. Moses & Son, a clothier
that advertised so heavily and flamboyantly in the mid-nineteenth century as to become a Victorian byword for the spread of advertising
(fig. 4).[14] The form of wit that punningly identifies this Moses with the
Bible's is one that foregrounds the materiality of language and exploits
the detachability of sign or name from referent.

Yet another reading emerges when we note that *Daniel Deronda* was
published in eight monthly parts, each of which included pages of advertisements before and after the text of the novel. The mention of an
advertisement sheet occurs on just the seventh page of an almost two-
hundred-page installment (in the third paragraph of its first chapter). It is
therefore well positioned to remind the reader of the novel's own nearby,
recently encountered advertisements for books and other, miscellaneous
commodities. (This attention to the book's format may be further encouraged by the preceding sentence's reference to Daniel's imaginings as
"the brief chapter of his experience in this kind," as these imaginings are
described in the briefest chapter of the novel itself to this point.) Read in
this way—as alluding to the novel's own advertisement sheet—the form
of wit enacted and criticized may be glossed as that which calls attention
to the physical trappings of the text and refuses to distinguish abstract
text from material embodiment.

Daniel Deronda returns again and again to the several forms of wit and
sets of identifications evoked here, all of which it seems to discredit or
disavow:

1. *The anti-Semitic identification of all Jews with commerce.* Contrary to
Daniel's anti-Semitic imaginings, of course, Mirah's brother turns out to
be the spiritual, intellectual, impoverished Mordecai. Eliot does not seek
to disassociate all Jews from commerce—indeed, one is hard-pressed to
find an economic transaction in the novel that does not involve a Jew—

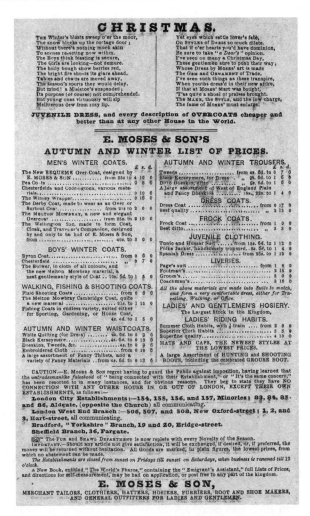

Figure 4. The Moses of the advertisement sheet. Inside back cover of a monthly number of Bleak House *(no. 10, December 1852). (Courtesy of the Poetry Collection of the University Libraries, The State University of New York at Buffalo. Photograph by James Ulrich, University at Buffalo.)*

but rather to distinguish among Jews, dividing them, as many critics have discussed, into two categories, the "refined" and the "vulgar." [15]

2. *The refusal or inability to credit noneconomic values and motives.* Criticism of the blindness and reductionism of a hegemonic market mentality is provided mainly by Daniel himself and the gifted composer and musician Julius Klesmer—both of whom view a commitment to the val-

ues of the marketplace as characteristic of the English rather than the Jews. According to both men, market transactions are inherently selfish, antagonistic, and unfair, a matter of one party gaining advantage at the expense of the other; as a result, they believe, a commitment to the values of the marketplace produces blindness to the power of ideas and deafness to the call of ideals. One of Klesmer's speeches making this case specifically recalls and revises the "form of wit" passage, as he decries "the lack of idealism in English politics, which left all mutuality between distant races to be determined solely by the need of a market: the crusades, to his mind, had at least this excuse, that they had a banner of sentiment round which generous feelings could rally: of course the scoundrels rallied too, but what then? they rally in equal force round your advertisement van of 'Buy cheap, sell dear'" (241). As in the earlier passage, religion and advertising figure idealism and capitalism, respectively, but here a hierarchical distinction between these categories is forcefully reaffirmed.

3. *Exploitation of the gaps between signifier and signified, sign and referent.* The novel explicitly attempts to combat—or, given their inevitability, at least to register and bemoan—the slippages, conflations, and imprecision generated by both the materiality and the abstractness of language: "Heat is a great agent and a useful word," the narrator states, "but considered as a means of explaining the universe it requires an extensive knowledge of differences" (64); and "The word of all work Love will no more express the myriad modes of mutual attraction, than the word Thought can inform you what is passing through your neighbour's mind" (301). Similarly, we can see now that a passage already cited serves as an express corrective to the pun on Moses: it is to distinguish between Mordecai (Ezra) Cohen and the pawnbroker Ezra Cohen with whom he lodges that Mrs. Meyrick says, "There are Ezras and Ezras in the world" (567).

4. *Treatment of the physical appearance or instantiation of a text as intrinsic to its identity and meaning. Daniel Deronda* is not openly hostile toward this approach, and has little to say about the physical materiality of texts, but this relative silence is symptomatic: if neither the narrator nor the characters show a great deal of interest in the physical characteristics of the written and printed documents they come across (especially in comparison to the other novels I discuss), this presumably indicates the insignificance of these characteristics. In general, handwriting in this novel tends

to be as "legible as print" (358), and print tends to be transparent. The experience of reading in *Daniel Deronda* typically resembles Daniel's experience *not* reading as he thinks about Mirah and her imagined family in the "form of wit" chapter: "The printed words were no more than a network through which he saw and heard everything . . . clearly" (205).

The four lines of criticism adumbrated by the "form of wit" passage not only coexist in the novel but reinforce one another in the passage itself. To insist on the detachability of the text from its material instantiation when that instantiation includes and is synecdochically figured by an advertisement sheet virtually amounts to insisting on the text's detachability from the marketplace in which it circulates. Similarly, while Moses & Son is evoked through a pun, the firm itself connotes economic reductionism, as in this passage from a *Household Words* piece by Dickens: complaining of the "base recourse to Money as a healing balm on all occasions" and instancing "the advertising columns of the newspapers" at the time of "the last Thanksgiving Day," he writes, "It was clear to the originators of those advertisements, manifest to the whole tribe of Moses (and Sons) who published those decorous appeals—that we must coin our thankful feelings into Money."[16] Dickens here practices the form of wit that identifies Moses with the advertisement sheet in two senses— punning on *Moses* and identifying Jews with commerce—but does so in order to blame that group for the spread of such "wit" in a third, broader sense, as the tendency to convert motives, feelings, and actions into the currency of the marketplace. The "form of wit" passage in *Daniel Deronda,* by contrast, manages to align and dismiss all the identifications and means of making identifications it evokes. Indeed, each becomes visible as a version of the same basic error: the reduction of the ideal to the material, the privileging of matter over spirit.

Curiously, however, despite the authoritative tone of the "form of wit" passage, Daniel's success in finding Mirah's brother depends upon forms of attention and identifications very much like those which the passage criticizes: Having taken to "rambling in those parts of London which are most inhabited by common Jews" (380), Daniel notices a pawnshop *(Jews and commerce)*. In the novel's only instance of Daniel reading an advertisement, he notices that "a placard in one corner announced—Watches and Jewellery exchanged and repaired" (382); the one who does the repairing, it turns out, is Mordecai *(the prophet and the advertisement sheet)*. Daniel enters the store when he notices that "the name over the shop-window [is] *Ezra Cohen,*" the name Mirah has given as her brother's. Making the acquaintance of Ezra Cohen the pawnbroker leads Daniel to the Ezra Cohen he seeks, not because the pawnbroker is Mirah's brother but, as noted earlier, because the brother lodges with and works for the pawnbroker, whose name he just happens to share *(the prophet Moses/the merchant Moses)*. Something approaching the "form of wit which identifies Moses with the advertisement sheet" gets redeemed, then, in this pawnbroker's shop.

This redemption or reversal is not complete, of course: if it were, the pawnbroker would turn out to be Mirah's brother, and there would just be Ezras in the world, not Ezras and Ezras. Nonetheless, Daniel's reliance in his successful effort to find Mirah's brother on several forms of wit that associate Moses with the advertisement sheet indicates the instability and fluidity of relationship that replaces the confident dualisms of the "form of wit" passage. Mordecai's initial appearance in the novel subtly continues this process, as it destabilizes the very oppositions it seems intended to establish. This episode is narrated immediately after Daniel's discovery of Ezra Cohen's pawnshop, when Daniel returns to actually enter the pawnshop for the first time. On his way there, he stops at a secondhand bookshop, where, "instead of the ordinary tradesman," he sees "a figure that was somewhat startling in its unusualness" (385), a man with an intense gaze and the face of "a prophet of the Exile" (386). The episode revolves around a market transaction, but it does so precisely, it would seem, to show how out of place Mordecai is in the marketplace: he is merely "keeping the shop while [the owner] is gone to dinner," shows little interest in making a sale, let alone obeying the imperative to "sell dear," and treats exchange value as only one possible form or measure of value, and hardly the most important one. Thus, when Daniel, holding a copy of Salomon Maimon's autobiography, asks, "What is the price of this book?" Mordecai asks him what he is disposed to give for it; and when Deronda parries, "Don't you know how much it is worth?" Mordecai pointedly responds, "Not its market-price," and then shifts the verbal exchange to more meaningful terrain, demanding, "Have you read it?" (386). When Daniel claims an interest in Jewish history, "the strange Jew rose from his sitting posture, and Deronda felt a thin hand pressing his arm tightly, while a hoarse, excited voice, not much above a loud whisper, said—'You are perhaps of our race?'" (387). Discovering that Daniel is not Jewish, Mordecai dismissively names a price and completes the sale.

What this episode tells us about Mordecai's relationship to the marketplace is not as clear-cut as it seems. To begin with, in his failure to embody the huckstering spirit of the advertisement sheet, Mordecai in fact resembles "the ordinary tradesman" from whom the passage ostensibly distinguishes him, for there is a "*nonchalance* about sales which seems to belong universally to the second-hand book business" (385), or so Daniel reflects as he enters the shop. Mordecai completes the transaction with an air of "uninterested melancholy" (387), but this hardly marks him as different from secondhand booksellers in general, who are, the narrator reports, typically "morose rather than unctuous in their vocation" (385). Most striking, though, is not Mordecai's uninterest but rather his interest: with its depiction of Mordecai drawing Daniel into conversation, even grasping his arm, the scene undercuts in advance Mrs. Meyrick's blunt but seemingly decisive statement that "there are Ezras and Ezras in the world; and really it is a comfort to think that all Jews are not like those shopkeepers who *will not* let you get out of their shops" (567). The narrator may be unambiguous on the absolute contrast between Mordecai and the Cohen family, but the narrative is not.[17]

As both Daniel's search for Mordecai and their initial encounter suggest, then, *Daniel Deronda* aggressively tests and rethinks its several versions of "Moses"/"advertisement sheet" and ideal/material relations, along with the relationships among these versions, and Mordecai plays a key role in this process, just as he does in Daniel's (and implicitly the reader's) reeducation about Jews. The felt need for this rethinking, in fact, may help account for the novel's shift from Klesmer to Mordecai: Klesmer barely appears in the two-thirds of the novel following his attack on "the lack of idealism in English politics" (241), as Mordecai replaces him as the novel's chief spokesman for an alternative to the values and worldview of the English ruling class. Critical attention to the move from Klesmer to Mordecai has focused all but exclusively on the substitution of Mordecai's race-based nationalism for the cosmopolitanism that Klesmer avows and embodies. (An ethnically ambiguous, self-described "wandering Jew," Klesmer looks forward to a "fusion of races" [242].) Crucially, however, Mordecai also departs from Klesmer's brand of anti-materialism, in particular that hostility to the marketplace which we are quick—too quick—to regard as the novel's own. Along with—indeed, as a key part of—his Zionist vision, Mordecai refuses to oppose the prophet to the merchant. Instead of promoting alternatives to the marketplace, he offers an alternative understanding of how markets work and what they are good for.

The place among the nations that Mordecai envisions for Israel does differ pointedly from Britain's as Klesmer describes it: in contrast to a nation for which "your advertisement van of 'Buy cheap, sell dear'" governs relations between "distant races," Mordecai's Israel will be "a community in the van of the East which carries the culture and the sympathies of every great nation in its bosom" and functions as "a halting-place of enmities" (535). Yet whereas Klesmer invokes the crusades as the antithesis of market-driven action, Mordecai's projected attempt to reclaim the Holy Land depends openly and unapologetically on wealth accumulated by Jews in the marketplace. The founding of "a new Jewish polity," he argues, requires the combined efforts of "the wealthy men, the monarchs of commerce, the learned in all knowledge, the skilful in all arts, the speakers, the political counsellors, who carry in their veins the Hebrew blood" (534). His political vision thus calls for a repetition on a grand scale of his own living arrangements in London, where, as we have seen, he is "nested" (517) by the family of pawnbroker Ezra Cohen. And just as Mordecai is much less eager than are Daniel and the narrator to separate him from the Cohens, so too is he much less anxious to dissociate prophecy from commerce, averring instead that the united labor of the parties he lists will be "hard but glorious like that of Moses and Ezra" (534–35). Describing his earlier efforts to find an audience for his views, Mordecai states that he "went to men of our people—to the rich in influence or knowledge, to the rich in other wealth," but that "scholar and merchant were both too busy to listen" (498–99). His earlier, abortive effort to travel to the East took the form of "going with a merchant as his clerk and companion" (541). When he argues that the Jews have what it takes to build a nation, Mordecai again gives pride of place to finances, and again refuses to contrast this factor with the others he names: the Jews "have wealth enough to redeem the soil from debauched and paupered conquerors; they have the skill of the statesman to devise, the tongue of the orator to persuade. And is there no prophet or poet among us to make the ears of Christian Europe tingle with shame?" (535), he asks. To Mordecai, the inclusion of businessmen in his scheme is not a necessary evil but simply necessary. There is nothing unholy about this alliance.

To see the relationship of prophet to merchant as complementary, rather than contrastive and antagonistic, constitutes a profound break from the position identified with Klesmer. Yet *Daniel Deronda* goes even further, to ally its Hebrew prophet's vision conceptually as well as financially with the marketplace. This is true even of that feature of Mordecai's vision that figures most prominently in the plot and at the same time seems furthest removed from conventional ways of thinking: his belief that Daniel is "the prefigured friend" (493) for whom he has been waiting, the spiritual heir who will be "my new life—my new self" (494), who "will take the sacred inheritance of the Jew" (500). The narrator asserts, for example, that visionaries such as Mordecai, whose "yearnings, conceptions—nay travelled conclusions—continually take the form of images which have a foreshadowing power," are "not always the less capable of the argumentative process, nor less sane than the commonplace calculators of the market" (471). At first, I suspect, one reads the adjective "commonplace" as applying to the entire class of market calculators, but we can also read the adjective restrictively, as distinguishing between commonplace and uncommon—perhaps even visionary—investors and aligning Mordecai with the latter. This reading is encouraged by the paragraph as a whole, which emphasizes the need to make distinctions within categories. Offering an "apology for inevitable kinship," the narrator asserts that every "great mental or social type" subsumes "specimens" ranging from the exalted to the "abject" (471). Even as the passage suggests Mordecai's kinship with expert investors, then, the kinship it apologizes for is not this one but rather that of great visionaries and investors with run-of-the-mill investors. The ostensibly offhand, comic comparison Daniel puts into the mouth of his guardian Sir Hugo in the later passage where Daniel himself "face[s] this question of the family likeness among the heirs of enthusiasm" is thus exactly to the point: "Fanaticism," he imagines Sir Hugo saying, "was not so common as bankruptcy, but taken in all its aspects it was abundant enough" (510). Mordecai, as the novel's denouement will confirm, is unlike a bankrupt, not because he is concerned with spiritual rather than material matters but because he invests well: in more than one sense, Daniel turns out to be the right stock.

Mordecai is so far from a commonplace calculator of the market, in fact, that the very passage in which Daniel ponders his credibility recalls a discussion of the nineteenth century's most influential stockbroker and political economist, David Ricardo. Recounting Daniel's struggles to categorize Mordecai, Eliot writes:

> It was not the first but it was the most pressing occasion on which he had had to face this question of the family likeness among the heirs of enthusiasm, whether prophets or dreamers of dreams, whether the "Great benefactors of mankind, deliverers" [Milton, *Paradise Regained*], or the devotees of phantasmal discovery— from the first believer in his own unmanifested inspiration, down to the last inventor of an ideal machine that will achieve perpetual motion. (510–11)

The rhetoric here bears a strong "family likeness" to a passage in John Cairnes's 1874 work *Some Leading Principles of Political Economy Newly Expounded,* a book Eliot records having read: "Ricardo was considered, and is still considered by some people, a dreamer of dreams, a spinner of abstract fancies; but his dreams and abstractions, when brought to the test of experiment, as commonly happens with the dreams and abstractions of men of genius, have proved to be far more practical, far more closely in accordance with actual occurrences, than the prognostics of so-called 'practical men.'"[18] Even Mordecai's potential status as a "dreamer of dreams," then, marks not his distance from the "real" of the marketplace but rather his resemblance to one of its leading theorists.[19]

A later passage in the chapter that begins with visionaries and market calculators contains perhaps the novel's most explicit fusion of the domains of prophecy and profit. Mordecai's keen sensitivity to the "poetic aspects of London," we are told, leads him to frequent its bridges at sunrise and sunset and drink in "the influences of a large sky":

> Leaning on the parapet of Blackfriars Bridge, and gazing meditatively, the breadth and calm of the river, with its long vista half hazy, half luminous, the grand dim masses or tall forms of buildings which were the signs of world-commerce, the oncoming of

> boats and barges from the still distance into sound and colour, en-
> tered into his mood and blent themselves indistinguishably with
> his thinking, as a fine symphony to which we can hardly be said
> to listen makes a medium that bears up our spiritual wings. (474)

The syntax and imagery of this long sentence are so intricate as to blur
the very blurring of distinctions it describes, but the bottom line, as it
were, is that buildings understood as "the signs of world-commerce . . .
blent themselves indistinguishably with [Mordecai's] thinking." This
process occurs at the very moment when that thinking is at its most
seemingly mystical, as Mordecai yearns for the arrival of "the deliverer
who was to rescue [his] spiritual travail from oblivion" (475). In contrast
to an early passage centering on Klesmer, where the narrator opposes the
English to "a lively, impassioned race, preoccupied with the ideal and
carrying the real as a mere make-weight" (102)—and in contrast to the
"Finale" of *Middlemarch,* with its lament that "the medium in which [the]
ardent deeds [of Saint Theresa and Antigone] took shape is for ever
gone"[20]—here, when "the passionate current of an ideal life strain[s] to
embody itself" (474), "the real" in the form of world commerce emerges
as the ideal's very "medium."

Inverting Marx's famous comment on the mystery of the commod-
ity-form, we might say that Mordecai's theology abounds in economic
niceties. He regularly uses economic models and metaphors when describing Israel's envisaged place in the world: "The life of a people," he
says, "absorbs the thought of other nations into its own forms, and gives
back the thought as new wealth to the world" (526); "Is it rational," he
asks, "to drain away the sap of special kindred that makes the families of
man rich in interchanged wealth?" (528); "Each nation has its own work,
and is a member of the world, enriched by the work of each" (530). In
each of these examples, Mordecai is concerned to show that the benefits
of establishing a Jewish state will not accrue to the Jews alone, nor to the
Jews at the expense of others: "The world will gain as Israel gains," he
insists (535). The "work" and "wealth" he has in mind, of course, are not
economic but rather spiritual as well as political (Israel, he suggests in one
of his less prescient moments, will function as "a halting-place of enmities, a neutral ground" [535]): that is what makes his use of economic
language metaphorical. It is true that these economic metaphors are

moribund if not dead, and thus not as immediately telling as, for example, the pawnbroker Ezra Cohen's rhetorically elaborate (if grammatically faulty) statement that Daniel, in removing Mordecai from the Cohen household, is "taking some of our good works from us, which is a property bearing interest" (575); Ezra's statement may reveal what Mordecai calls the Cohens' "spiritual poverty" (571), but Mordecai's use of that common phrase hardly signals his own. Moreover, Mordecai (perhaps unlike Ezra Cohen) does not translate all phenomena into the language of one master discourse.[21] Nonetheless, his economic vocabulary does indeed reflect a reliance on the logic as well as the language of the marketplace, for his theory of international relations reinscribes with some precision contemporary doctrines of political economy—if not the "real" of world commerce, then at least its ideal, its ideology.

Most obviously, the understanding of exchange that we have seen Mordecai advancing relies on that most basic principle of political economy, the division of labor (which we saw John Forster invoking to describe the supposed mutual dependence of the literary and industrial classes in chapter 3, above). The division of labor makes labor more efficient, which is to say more productive, and thereby creates wealth. As John Cairnes explains in the work cited above, "The necessary means of giving effect to the separation of employments [a phrase Cairnes uses interchangeably with "the division of labor"]" is "trade . . . and the advantages arising from [trade] are the advantages incident to this scheme of things," such as "increased efficiency and economy."[22] Not only does trade make possible a net increase in wealth but it is also mutually beneficial to the parties involved. This view of market exchange is almost too obvious for political economists after Adam Smith to dwell on, but it differs from that of Klesmer and Deronda, who see the marketplace as a site where individuals seek to gain advantage at the expense of others; in such a zero-sum economy one person's gain is another's loss, as Deronda repeatedly argues.

A gain/gain system of exchange based on the division of labor also holds sway, political economists insist, when the parties in question are not individuals but nations. Indeed, it is only when he turns his attention to international trade, three-quarters of the way into his book, that Cairnes feels obliged to "set before our minds in the most general way the fundamental circumstances on which trade, or the interchange of commodities, in all its forms, rests." For Cairnes, the extension of the gain/gain model of exchange to the level of nations rests largely on David Ricardo's theory of comparative cost—precisely the "purely abstract doctrine" that we saw him discussing in the passage that anticipates Eliot's description of Mordecai. According to Cairnes, "The most frequent and important case of all in international commerce" is that in which "each of the trading nations is in the possession . . . of a comparative superiority . . . with reference to the articles which constitute its staples in the trade." He continues, "Any terms of international exchange which are within the limits of that [comparative] advantage will imply a gain . . . for both countries"; if these limits are "transcended," the result is not a trade advantageous to only one party but rather an end to the trade, as "the motive for the trade ceases." The "proper end and only rational purpose" of international trade, Cairnes concludes, is "the greater cheapening of commodities and the increased abundance and comfort which result to the whole family of mankind."[23]

This model of mutually beneficial international exchange underwrites Mordecai's vision of a moral world-system in which "the families of man [are] rich in interchanged wealth" (528) and "the world . . . gain[s] as Israel gains" (535), just as surely as those who have prospered in the commercial economy are to underwrite its accomplishment.[24] This model's emergence in *Daniel Deronda* is particularly striking because it contrasts with Klesmer's and also reverses that adumbrated in the novel's famous opening scene, in which Daniel first observes Gwendolen at a roulette table where individuals representing "very distant varieties of European type" are "absorbed in play" (8). Not only is exchange here zero-sum but it also works to cancel national (and all other) differences, rather than exploit them: "While every single player differed markedly from every other, there was a certain uniform negativeness of expression which had the effect of a mask," because they are all engaged in "the same narrow monotony of action" (9). Explicitly equating gambling at roulette with buying and selling in the marketplace, the narrator describes "a respectable London tradesman['s] . . . well-fed leisure, which in the intervals of winning money in business and spending it showily, sees no better resource than winning money in play and spending it yet more showily" (8). For Mordecai as for Cairnes, however, the roulette table is not exemplary of market (or moral) economies in general, and while the novel does not give up its initial position easily, Mordecai's view gains increasing sway. The novel reflects this disarticulation of the market from gambling by replacing the well-fed tradesman Ezra Cohen (his "flourishing face glistening on the way to fatness" [387]) as Mordecai's ostensible antithesis with Mordecai's father, an assimilationist gambler who at one point thinks back "over old Continental hours at *Roulette*" (778). Indeed, the felt need to find a new foil for Mordecai helps explain Lapidoth's surprising appearance late in the novel.[25]

Mordecai does not embrace all aspects of a market economy, but even when he refuses its logic he can be sufficiently pragmatic to adopt its procedures. In particular, Mordecai views physical appearances and even the body as such as spiritually, which is to say fundamentally, insignificant (a point I return to), yet "experience had rendered him morbidly alive to the effect of a man's poverty and other physical disadvantages in cheapening his ideas" (473). In practice if not in principle, then, Mordecai accepts the lesson preached, as it happens, by E. Moses & Son themselves, in their 1864 pamphlet *The Philosophy of Dress, with a Few Notes on National Costumes:* "The spiritual is not palpable to the sight," this work explains, by way of converting that firm's own practice into principle. "We have no eyes for the inner world. We must therefore judge of the inward man by the outer." [26] Acting accordingly, Mordecai seeks an "accomplished Egyptian" (657) to carry out his vision. In his very desire to make the wealthy and beautiful Daniel his spiritual heir, in other words, Mordecai engages in a "form of wit which identifies Moses with the advertisement sheet."

Noting that "the first office Deronda had to perform for this Hebrew prophet who claimed him as a spiritual inheritor, was to get him a healthy lodging," the narrator remarks, "Such is the irony of earthly mixtures, that the heroes have not always had carpets and tea-cups of their own; and, seen through the open window by the mackerel-vendor, may have been invited with some hopefulness to pay three hundred per cent in the form of fourpence" (546). That with which spiritual grandeur is ironically mixed swerves gratuitously here from physical and material needs to commercial activity. My analysis thus far suggests, however, that by this point in the novel this latter mixture is no longer very ironic, for even as the narrator continues to treat market exchange as vulgar, materialistic, unfair, and dishonest, the novel has been busy charting several forms of traffic between prophet and merchant.

Indeed, such is the irony of textual mixtures that the very image of the mackerel-vendor addressing the prophet recalls and reverses the terms of another striking image, only two paragraphs earlier, where Mordecai is said to address "hearers who took his thoughts without attaching more consequences to them than the Flemings to the ethereal chimes ringing above their market-places" (545). The chiasmus created by the proximity of these two passages about proximity, whereby spiritual sounds ignored by commercial hearers become commercial sounds addressed to spiritual hearers, blurs the distinctions each passage would uphold. Yet it is this blurring, rather than those distinctions, I am arguing, that characterizes the novel as a whole: so persistently does *Daniel Deronda* mobilize the identifications and means of making identifications disavowed in the "form of wit" passage that much of the novel can be understood as the narrative elaboration of the homonyms *prophet/profit*.

Surprisingly, however, Mordecai himself resists the market activity that one might expect him to find most congenial: authorship. First, he brushes aside Daniel's offer to arrange publication of his writings (499), and later he admonishes Daniel to "call nothing mine that I have written" (751). Yet Mordecai makes clear in both instances that his stance has nothing to do with the marketplace per se, but rather is dictated by his desire to maximize his influence over Daniel: in response to the offer of publication, he declares, "You must be not only a hand to me, but a soul—believing my belief—being moved by my reasons—hoping my hope—seeing the vision that I point to—beholding a glory where I behold it!" (499); and he links his wish for "the body that I gave my thought to pass away as this fleshly body will pass" to his hope that "the thought [will] be born again from our fuller soul which shall be called yours" (751). It is not the cash nexus but rather the mediation of the written or printed word—and ultimately that of language itself—that Mordecai disdains.

Yet if Mordecai's lack of interest in the literary marketplace therefore presents no inconsistency with his usual economism, the very dismissal of writing that accounts for this lack of interest generates a stark challenge to the gain/gain model of exchange he advocates, and for which the novel itself had seemed to exchange its initial, gain/loss model. Here we return to *Daniel Deronda*'s rewriting of *No Name:* as this chapter began by noticing, Gwendolen's experience departs from Magdalen Vanstone's at novel's end, when Daniel reveals that he is Jewish, engaged to Mirah Lapidoth, and about to leave England for Palestine. Instead of an affirmation of her ostensible savior's permanent presence such as Magdalen receives, Gwendolen is left with his promise "to write to you always, when I can" (805). Daniel offers an optimistic vision of this textually mediated relationship: "I shall be more with you than I used to be," he asserts, because "if we had been much together before, we should have felt our differences more, and seemed to get farther apart. Now we can perhaps never see each other again. But our minds may get nearer" (805–6). As at the end of *No Name,* however, textual contact seems no match for bodily "presence and touch" (805); if the written word too closely resembles the "fleshly body" (751) to satisfy Mordecai's demands, it is too removed from that body to satisfy Gwendolen's. Devastated, she describes herself as "forsaken," and Daniel himself feels compelled to see her as "the victim of his happiness" (805). Daniel's gain—and Mirah's, and Mordecai's—is Gwendolen's loss.

The novel's narrative economy thus seems to gainsay the gain/gain model of exchange that permeates and legitimizes Mordecai's prophetic nationalism. But this conclusion depends on the authority of Mordecai and Gwendolen's shared sense of writing's ineffectualness, whereas the dominant movement of *Daniel Deronda,* I will argue, is to affirm writing's power. In other words, these characters are wrong about writing. They are wrong about writing because they are wrong about bodies, with Gwendolen overestimating the importance of bodily presence and Mordecai underestimating the role of physicality in his own relationship with Daniel. Neither Mordecai's gain nor Gwendolen's loss can be taken for granted, then—which means, ironically, that the fate of Mordecai's political-cum-moral economy also remains uncertain.

There is a long-standing critical tendency to credit Mordecai with the full influence he claims over Daniel. As John Kucich and Amanda Anderson have shown, however, Daniel never fully adopts Mordecai's beliefs concerning the two things Mordecai cares about most: the nature of their own relationship and that of individual and national identity.[27] What I would add is that Mordecai consistently misconstrues the mechanism or mechanics—and thus the permanence—of the influence he does achieve over Daniel.[28] Disdaining "gross material contact" and "the creeping paths of the senses" (734–35), Mordecai draws on a cabbalistic doctrine of metempsychosis to affirm that a "marriage of . . . souls" (751) with Daniel will occur when death "liberate[s]" his own soul from his body (540): "Death . . . takes me from your bodily eyes and gives me full presence in your soul," he says on his deathbed and the novel's last page (810). Yet bodily contact plays a remarkably prominent role in their relationship. As Jeff Nunokawa in particular has emphasized, Mordecai quite literally cannot keep his hands off Daniel, beginning with their first encounter in a bookshop, where, as we have seen, Daniel feels "a thin hand pressing his arm tightly" as Mordecai asks, "You are perhaps of our race?" (387).[29] But against Nunokawa, who argues for Daniel's continuing aversion to Mordecai's touch and grasp, I would call attention to the increasingly positive role touch plays: for example, even as Daniel shares what the narrator calls "the repulsion that most of us experience under a grasp and speech which assume to dominate," he also overcomes this repulsion and in fact responds to Mordecai's prophetic claim that "you will take the sacred inheritance of the Jew" by "plac[ing] his palm gently on Mordecai's straining hand—an act just then equal to many speeches" (500). When this choreography of touches is explicitly repeated later in the novel, there is no hint of "repulsion"; instead of a resistance to being dominated, now Daniel's "dominant impulse was to do as he had once done before: he laid his firm gentle hand on the hand that grasped him" (543). Mordecai's response at this moment is particularly telling: his hand "relaxed its grasp, and turned upward under Deronda's," we are told, "as if it had a soul of its own" (543). Earlier, Mordecai had declared to Daniel, "You must be not only a hand to me, but a soul" (499), but here we see that dualism breaking down. When Daniel announces that he is in fact Jewish, he is the one who initiates contact, laying his hand on Mordecai's shoulder (747).

Mordecai thus sells short the role of bodily presence and contact in this relationship and as a result overstates the probable strength of his influence over Daniel after his own death: the absence of his body will not complete their union but rather will likely diminish his felt presence for Daniel. Yet even as Mordecai's dualist model of an immaterial essence detachable from its material bearer or instantiation misrepresents the nature of persons, it accurately describes the structure and workings of the medium he deprecates—writing, as represented in the novel. As noted earlier, *Daniel Deronda* pays scant attention to the physical particularities or sheer physicality of writing and print. None of the novel's several crucial letters, for example, is described in any detail as a physical object; this physicality is so inessential to the letters' identity and meaning that when reproducing the text of letters, the narrator uses interchangeably, as if they were synonymous, phrases such as "a letter containing these words" (810) or "it contained these words" (149) and "this was the letter" (15, 617).

In one instance, instead of simply eliding the difference between letter-as-object and letter-as-text, the novel enacts this elision: Lydia Glasher's letter to Gwendolen on her wedding day (accompanying Grandcourt's diamonds) receives narrative attention that is not so much minimal as minimalizing, as the features noted make the document seem barely material in the first place. Thus, while the novel reproduces every word of the letter, the little we learn about the letter-as-object is that Lydia's handwriting is as "legible as print" and the letter itself merely a "bit of thin paper" (358).[30] Like Mordecai, the letter seems to aspire to a condition of immateriality, a condition it quickly achieves in full when, after repeated readings, Gwendolen "stretch[es] out the paper towards the fire," whereupon "it flew like a feather from her trembling fingers and was caught up in the great draught of flame" (359). Crucially, however, the physical destruction of Lydia's letter fails to diminish its efficacy or even, in a sense, to affect its survival: after Gwendolen burns the letter, "those written words kept repeating themselves in her" (359), and, we later learn, "the words had nestled their venomous life within her" (424). The novel even repeats two-thirds of the destroyed letter verbatim, as words that "hung on her consciousness with the weight of a *prophetic doom*" (424; emphasis added). Internalized in this way by Gwendolen, Lydia's letter is the novel's best example of the kind of achieved presence—a presence too present to be called an "afterlife"—that the prophet Mordecai desires when he prays that his life will "'burn, burn indiscernibly into that which shall be, which is my love and not me'" (735). But it is the dualist structure of the text—its nonidentity with or irreducibility to any particular material instantiation, a structure it does not share with persons—that enables it to achieve and sustain this effect.[31]

Daniel's hold over Gwendolen thus looks more lasting, and Mordecai's inspirational role for Daniel less durable, than most readers follow the characters themselves in believing. Soon after *Daniel Deronda*'s publication, however, the implied future I am ascribing to the narrative was in fact spelled out, in *Reclaimed,* an anonymous sequel to Eliot's novel published in the United States in 1878.[32] From a certain perspective, *Reclaimed* is true to—even instantiates a version of—Mordecai's model of absorption without remainder: from the perspective, that is, of the U.S. Copyright Office, where, thanks to the lack of international copyright protection at the time, *Daniel Deronda* exists only insofar as it inhabits *Reclaimed.* But *Reclaimed* itself seems to adopt the model of textual influence I have been teasing out: in its version of events, Daniel—now deprived of Mordecai's presence—quickly sours on his Zionist project, and indeed on Jews in general, whereas Gwendolen remains fixated on Daniel despite his physical absence. Recognizing the power of writing in *Daniel Deronda, Reclaimed* shows Daniel's fascination with Gwendolen being rekindled by his rereading of the letter she sent him on his wedding day, which he has carefully preserved.[33] Having killed off Mirah in childbirth (the child dies too), the novel—undoing *Daniel Deronda*'s undoing of *No Name*—ends with Gwendolen and Daniel together at last, as Gwendolen "s[i]nk[s] beneath gratitude and joy, into the expanded arms of her adored lover,—RECLAIMED."[34]

One might object that *Reclaimed*'s version of events derives more from its author's apparent hostility toward Jews than from any insight into Eliot's novel; one might even argue that *Reclaimed*'s blatant anti-Semitism reflects its author's failure or refusal to understand *Daniel Deronda* on its own terms—after all, not even critics keen on detecting anti-Semitic overtones in Eliot's ostensibly philo-Semitic work see the novel as encouraging us to imagine a future moment when Daniel's growing disgust with Jews will prompt him to have Mirah's corpse dug up from a Jewish cemetery and "placed in Christian sod."[35] Even as *Reclaimed* shockingly transgresses the spirit of *Daniel Deronda,* however, it accurately captures that novel's surprising insistence on the letter.

If *Reclaimed*'s version of Daniel and Gwendolen's future is wrong, and if Mordecai's influence is to persist, it is only because Mordecai and Eliot finally recognize the limitations of his announced strategy: despite Mordecai's rhetorical dismissal of his own writings, he has not only written them but preserved them as well, and leaves his manuscripts to

Daniel. Indeed, in a textbook example of the Derridean logic of supplementarity, Daniel not only meets Mordecai, not only learns that he himself is Jewish, and not only learns that his grandfather had political ideas similar to Mordecai's, but he also receives a chest containing his grandfather's writings.[36] If this is not simply overkill, then Mordecai's claims for an unmediated marriage of souls must be overblown. Writing's mediating or substitutive role restores the possibility of Mordecai's continued influence over Daniel, and does so without foreclosing the possibility of Daniel's continued influence over Gwendolen—along with George Eliot's possible influence over her readers. Although Gwendolen's traumatic sense of abandonment remains too vivid and her future benefits too conjectural for one to see Mordecai's vision of a gain/gain economy as unambiguously vindicated, this reading restores its credibility. Thus salvaging the morality of Mordecai's prophetic economy, the novel also salvages that of the commercial economy upon which he relies and in which the novel itself circulates.

As I have shown, the multiform "form of wit which identifies Moses with the advertisement sheet" comes to dominate *Daniel Deronda:* the discovery of the novel's Jewish prophet depends on the fortuitous sharing of a name; that prophet himself analogizes the promotion of ideas to that of commodities; the novel's legitimation of Zionism relies on the logic of political economy; and, more generally, the realms of spiritual and economic value, while not conflated, are rendered homologous and compatible. Yet the novel persists in refusing one key version of this wit: one way to identify Moses with the advertisement sheet, I suggested earlier, would be to identify George Eliot or *Daniel Deronda* with the advertisements between the novel's own covers; as we have just seen, however, the novel treats texts as fundamentally abstract entities distinct and detachable from their material instantiations, which merit only glancing notice. The novel as a whole thus confirms and extends the operation of the "form of wit" passage, which calls attention to the novel's own material format only to insist on its contingency and transcendability, its nonidentity with the novel itself.

Daniel Deronda's indifference toward the physical materiality of writing sets it at sharp odds with the other works on which I have focused in this study. The contrast with *Bleak House* is particularly striking. As we saw in chapter 2, *Bleak House* pays copious attention to the physical materiality of the written word and uses such attention to model that which the reader is enjoined to pay to the material world in general and the human body in particular. Eliot's novel criticizes "floating among cloud-pictures" (381) and emphasizes the importance of "caring for destinies still moving in the dim streets of our earthly life, not yet lifted among the constellations" (544), but viewed through the lens of *Bleak House,* its lack of interest in—even devaluation of—the physical materiality of writing betokens a more general idealism that threatens to undercut this stance. Similarly, I suggested earlier that for *Daniel Deronda* to seek to distinguish texts from their material instantiation when its own instantiation includes and is figured by pages of advertisements is for the novel to distance itself from the marketplace as well. I have also argued, however, that the novel comes to terms with a market whose terms it comes to borrow. The novel's devaluing of the physical materiality of writing thus threatens to conflict with its treatment of economic as well as corporeal materiality.

Yet the ultimate "irony of earthly mixtures" revealed by *Daniel Deronda* is the compatibility of different mixtures, the mixing of different ways of relating ideal and material. In other words, the neat alignment of materialities and materialisms suggested by the "Moses and the advertisement sheet" passage is too neat. A particular belief about the relationship of mind or soul to body, for example, need not entail a particular understanding of writing or textuality. Thus, whereas *Bleak House* aligns the written word with the human body, *Daniel Deronda* insists on their different structure, and therefore offers no grounds for extending its relative indifference toward the physical materiality of the former to an indifference toward the latter. In fact, the novel's emphasis on the significance of the body actively discourages the notion that the fate of Lydia Glasher's letter predicts the success of Mordecai's parallel vision of "burn[ing] indiscernibly into that which shall be" (735). The novel further discourages this identification of person and text by offering a vivid (and retrospectively quite disturbing) literalization of the kind of self-sacrifice Mordecai envisions: "My dear boy," Sir Hugo glibly but evocatively counsels Daniel, "it is good to be unselfish and generous; but don't carry that too far. It will not do to give yourself to be melted down for the benefit of the tallow-trade" (183–84). Not the sublime(d) but the grotesque: recalling the key event in *Bleak House*'s own treatment of this problematic with uncanny precision, this image, like Krook's death by spontaneous combustion, highlights the ineluctable materiality of the flesh.

Just as the novel's inattention to the physical materiality of writing should not be read as necessarily implying or promoting an unconcern with the materiality of the body, so too should this inattention not be seen as signaling or cultivating the novel's distance from the marketplace—but for the opposite reason. That is, whereas the relationship between the material and immaterial components of texts has no necessary bearing on that between flesh and spirit (they may be either analogous or disanalogous), the literary marketplace does institute and rely upon a particular textual ontology. As discussed earlier, print technology makes possible a sharp distinction between abstract text and material instantiation, a distinction codified in the concept of copyright and thus crucial to the growth of the literary marketplace. A text's transcendence of physical materiality is therefore less a metaphysical operation than a technological, economic, and legal one. This dualistic understanding of textuality is hardly inescapable, as much of this book has gone to show. Nonetheless, it is powerful, and it dominates *Daniel Deronda,* where it applies to unique documents as well as printed books. Even, then, as *Daniel Deronda*'s distinguishing of itself from its material instantiation distances the novel from the advertisements it is bound with and the commercial sphere they openly inhabit, this abstraction of the text conforms to the logic of the market itself. Eliot's novel is detachable from the advertisements with which it was first printed because of, not despite, its nature as property, because of and not despite the commercial activity that also brings them together.

The alignment of materialities promised by the "Moses and the advertisement sheet" passage as well as by the figure of the dyer's hand thus breaks down in *Daniel Deronda,* as reliance on or "subdual" to one kind of materiality makes possible and is signaled by the transcendence of another. A perfect emblem for the paradoxical status of the novel and its author can be found not in the text of *Daniel Deronda* proper but in one of its accompanying advertisements. It is precisely this location, in fact,

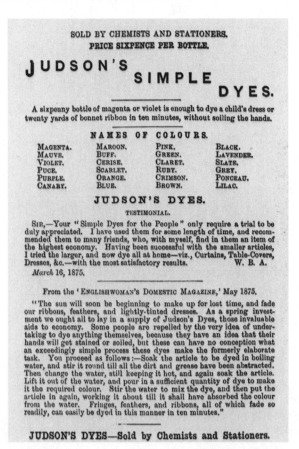

Figure 5. Inside front cover of Daniel Deronda, *book 3:* Maidens Choosing. *(Reproduction by permission of the Buffalo & Erie County Public Library, Buffalo, New York.)*

that makes the image appropriate. "Some people are repelled by the very idea of undertaking to dye anything themselves, because they have an idea that their hands will get stained," states the advertisement printed on the inside cover of the monthly part of *Daniel Deronda* containing the "Moses and the advertisement sheet" passage—but it is easy, the advertisement promises, to use Judson's Simple Dyes "without soiling the hands" (fig. 5).[37] Such is the irony of earthly mixtures.

This book has sought to change what we see when we look at the Victorian novel by changing what we look at. Bringing together materials and materialities usually treated separately if at all, it has shown — to borrow Oscar Wilde's borrowed imagery — that the Victorian novel's own engagement with these materials and materialities "coloured the very texture of [its] nature, . . . dyed it with strange and subtle dyes."[38] Yet if this overarching claim is correct, then no single book on the topic could hope to be comprehensive, however salient the chosen examples. The discovery of more strange and subtle dyes awaits.

Notes

Introduction

1. This trend has been going on for some time, with no sign of abating; as the introduction to a recent collection of essays puts it, "competing idioms, today, . . . claim the term *materialism* in order to authorize themselves" (Cohen et al., "A 'Materiality without Matter'?" in Cohen et al., *Material Events,* viii). For an earlier discussion of the proliferation of self-declared critical "materialisms" and the vagueness of definition attending this proliferation, see Simpson, "Introduction: The Moment of Materialism," 5–8 and passim. For new materialisms that focus on objects or things (sometimes by way of a distinction between the concepts *object* and *thing*), see the essays collected in Brown, *Things.*

2. The materiality of the signifier can be seen either as the phenomenal component of the signifier or as precisely that which renders the signifier nonidentical to its phenomenality, due to its differential nature. As Andrzej Warminski puts it, "A mark as mark, writing as writing, is not something to be heard or seen, it is something to be read. (Just as we can hear [b] and [p], but the difference between them that constitutes one as [b] and the other as [p] is not something we can hear—it is a marking that makes it possible for us to [think we] "hear" [b] and [p])" ("Terrible Reading [Preceded by 'Epigraphs']," 387).

3. Althusser, "Ideology and Ideological State Apparatuses," in *Lenin and Philosophy,* 169: "I shall leave on one side the problem of a theory of the differences between the modalities of materiality." A little earlier, he writes, "Of course, the material existence of the ideology in an apparatus and its practices does not have the same modality as the material existence of a paving-stone or a rifle. But, at the risk of being taken for a Neo-Aristotelian . . . , I shall say that 'matter is discussed in many senses,' or rather that it exists in different modalities, all rooted in the last instance in 'physical' matter" (166). Dorothy Hale discusses the "slippery materialism" of Althusser and others in *Social Formalism,* 12–13 and passim. In *Cultural Capital,* John Guillory similarly complains that "the episteme of literary theory . . . speaks casually and ubiquitously of the materiality of the signifier" without producing any "supporting analysis of the concept of materiality itself, except as that concept is associated with the notion of the signifier. In the absence of such an analysis, 'materiality' is nothing

more than the 'matter' of vulgar materialism, a literalization." Guillory distinguishes
this concept of materiality from that of "historical materialism, for which it may be
said that the world is the totality of relations, not things" (229). Guillory's most specific target is Paul de Man; for de Man's notion of "formal materialism," see his "Phenomenality and Materiality in Kant." Also relevant here is de Man's discussion of the
"unfortunate" mistake of "confus[ing] the materiality of the signifier with the materiality of what it signifies" in the title essay of *The Resistance to Theory,* 11. For a collection of essays that "explore whether de Man's 'materiality' does or does not impact
on or collude with various projects associated with the term *materialism* today" (xv),
see Cohen et al., *Material Events.* Frances Ferguson provides a useful comparison of
"social materialism" and "deconstructive materialism" in *Solitude and the Sublime,*
chap. 1, esp. 10–15. For discussion of the use of "materiality" as "a sign of irreducibility," as well as an analysis of the relationship between the materiality of the
body and the materiality of language, see Butler, *Bodies That Matter,* intro. and chap. 1.

4. This book thus participates in what Eve Kosofsky Sedgwick briefly but cogently describes as the effort to "transmit new ways of knowing . . . that the materiality of human bodies, of words, and of economic production may misrepresent but cannot
simply eclipse one another." I would add the physical materiality of documents and
books to this list—a category that may be captured for Sedgwick by the phrase "the
materiality . . . of words," although I suspect that she means to invoke the deconstructive sense of *materiality* here. See "Paranoid Reading and Reparative Reading,"
in Sedgwick, *Novel Gazing,* 1.

5. For a more philosophically oriented attempt to move beyond the thinness of contemporary invocations of materiality in literary studies, see Tiffany, *Toy Medium.*

6. My emphasis on the Victorians' willingness, indeed eagerness, to address the materialities of writing is modeled on Michel Foucault's demolition of the "repressive hypothesis" of Victorian sexuality, as my use of the Foucauldian phrase "put into discourse" in the preceding sentence is meant to signal. See Foucault, *The History of
Sexuality,* 3–13 and passim. I should also make clear that, while my focus is on mid-
nineteenth-century British configurations of writing's putative materialities, I do not
mean to suggest that earlier periods and other places did not also, if differently, put
these materialities into discourse. For the role of this problematic (articulated in
somewhat different terms) in the development of the eighteenth-century British
novel, see Gallagher, *Nobody's Story,* and Lynch, *The Economy of Character.*

7. Eliot, "Silly Novels by Lady Novelists," *Westminster Review,* October 1856, rpt. in
Eliot, *Selected Essays,* 162.

8. Shakespeare, sonnet 111, *The Riverside Shakespeare,* 1769.

9. D'Israeli published "An Essay on the Manners and Genius of the Literary Character"
in 1798, and he revised and expanded this work through a series of editions over the
course of the next half-century. I quote from an early Victorian version, *The Literary
Character; or, The History of Men of Genius, Drawn from Their Own Feelings and Confessions,* a revision published in 1840 along with a number of D'Israeli's related works
(such as *Quarrels of Authors* and *Calamities of Authors*) as *Miscellanies of Literature;* the
quotation is from 447.

10. Keach, "'Words Are Things,'" 221.

11. Gramsci, *Selections from the Prison Notebooks,* 8–9.

12. Jameson, *The Political Unconscious,* 45.

13. On the hostility of culture to the body, see, for example, Theodor Adorno: "Culture originates in the radical separation of mental and physical work." In good dialectical fashion, though, he continues: "The anti-philistinism of Athens was both the most arrogant contempt of the man who need not soil his hands for the man from whose work he lives, and the preservation of an existence beyond the constraint which underlies all work" ("Cultural Criticism and Society," in *Prisms,* 26–27).

14. On differences in class as differences in levels or degrees of embodiment, see Scarry, *The Body in Pain,* 181–278.

15. Bourdieu, *Distinction,* 44–45. Bourdieu is here discussing reactions to a photograph of an old woman's hands; the most "refined" reading of the photograph he cites begins, "I find this a very beautiful photograph. It's the very symbol of toil. It puts me in mind of Flaubert's old servant woman" (45).

16. Frances Ferguson, summarizing "the de Manian textual turn on the Derridean argument," in *Solitude and the Sublime,* 12.

17. Derrida, *Dissemination,* 97.

18. Jerome McGann, leading theorist of "the textual condition," recommends the pedagogic exercise of having each member of a class bring in a copy of sonnet 111: the likely outcome, he reports, is to end up with as many versions of the text as there are students. Of course, it is only because the text is stable enough to allow a basic, shared understanding of what the poem is "about" that this sonnet makes a particularly telling choice for this exercise (personal communication, November 2002).

19. Carlyle, "The Hero as Poet," *On Heroes, Hero-Worship, and the Heroic in History,* 94.

20. Later in the same lecture series, Carlyle will explain "Cromwell's reputed confusion of speech" by stating that "to himself the internal meaning was sun-clear; but the material with which he was to clothe it in utterance was not there." Language itself here is explicitly "material" ("The Hero as King," 187). This argument and imagery is most fully articulated in *Sartor Resartus.* See James Eli Adams for an insightful analysis of Carlyle's "mistrust of language" and his "allegiance to an essential spirit or form that must be extracted from the crudities of language and the wayward flux of emotion and desire" (*Dandies and Desert Saints,* 37). At the same time, Carlyle is sometimes made anxious by the apparent or comparative immateriality of language, as we will see in chapter 3.

21. The orthographic repetition in Carlyle's sentence was called to my attention by an error I made in transcribing Carlyle's words—typing *sould* for *soul.* It is only fitting that my fingers noticed this pattern before my conscious mind did.

22. D'Israeli, *Miscellanies of Literature,* 447.

23. Byron, *Don Juan,* canto 3, st. 87–88, *The Complete Poetical Works,* 5:192–93.

24. Dickens, *Our Mutual Friend,* 893. For a subtle analysis of the ways in which the novels of Dickens, in particular, may be said to "tell, in one way or another, much of what our recent criticism claims to discover in them," see Bodenheimer, "Knowing and Telling in Dickens's Retrospects" (quotation from 215).

25. Eliot, *Daniel Deronda,* 546.
26. Gissing, *The Nether World,* 31–32.

1. Paratexts and Periwigs

1. Thackeray, *The History of Henry Esmond,* ed. Sutherland and Greenfield, back cover. Except where noted, all further references to *Henry Esmond* will be to this edition, and will be noted parenthetically in the text. This edition is based on the 1858 edition, the last with Thackeray's involvement; differences between the 1858 edition and the 1852 first edition are discussed below.
2. Genette, *Paratexts.*
3. McGann, *The Textual Condition,* 13 and passim.
4. For a thorough discussion of the bibliographic features of the first edition, see Gaskell, *From Writer to Reader,* 156–82. Gaskell identifies the typeface as "Caslon Pica No. 2, originally cut in 1741–2, and probably recast in a small fount for this book" (158). The novel was printed by Bradbury and Evans and published by Smith, Elder.
5. Gaskell, *From Writer to Reader,* 158.
6. [John Forster], *The Examiner,* 13 November 1852, rpt. in Tillotson and Hawes, *Thackeray: The Critical Heritage,* 144.
7. Unsigned review, *United States Review,* March 1853, rpt. ibid., 162.
8. [Samuel Phillips], *Times,* 22 December 1852, rpt. ibid., 157.
9. Even the most extended critical discussion of the book's physical format shares this view, if only to stress the strategy's failure: "On every page," writes Stephen Bann, "the mid-nineteenth-century reader was offered all the outward signs of a text from the earlier period," but "such a degree of historical mimetism was bound to be, in the last resort, self-defeating"; "Thackeray's *framing*—the exceptionally audacious device of a bibliographic replica—sets up the pattern for an authenticity that continually tries too hard, and rebounds upon itself" (*The Clothing of Clio,* 141, 151).
10. Genette, *Paratexts,* 34.
11. Thackeray, *The Virginians,* 29.
12. The novel also contains a dedication by Thackeray to Lord Ashburton. Although not part of the fiction in the way that Esmond's daughter's preface is—the dedication is in Thackeray's own name and is dated "October 18, 1852"—the dedication nonetheless represents itself as an extension of the novel's conceit, as Thackeray writes, "My Dear Lord, The writer of a book which copies the manners and language of Queen Anne's time, must not omit the Dedication to the Patron" (36). Moreover, even as Thackeray's signature foregrounds the nonidentity between memoirist and author, the dedication threatens to collapse this distinction by establishing a parallel between the two: "My volume will reach you," Thackeray writes, "when the Author is on his voyage to . . . America," a voyage Esmond himself makes in the last paragraph of the book. I return below to this question of the relationship between fictional characters and real people, and the novel's management of such relationships.
13. Thackeray to Mrs. T. F. Elliot and Kate Perry, August 1852, in *Letters and Private Papers . . . A Supplement,* 1:480.

14. Thackeray, letter cited in Ritchie, "Introduction," xxiv.

15. Charlotte Brontë to George Smith, 3 November 1852, cited in Chase, "The Kindness of Consanguinity," 224.

16. Ritchie, "Introduction," xxv–xxvi.

17. Thackeray to Harriet Marian Thackeray, 10 September 1852, in *Letters and Private Papers . . . A Supplement*, 1:482.

18. For an influential early articulation of these views, see Anthony Trollope's *Thackeray*, first published in 1879.

19. For a discussion of the "dignity of literature" controversy that Thackeray's treatment of authors in *Pendennis* sparked, see chapter 3, below.

20. Thackeray, *The History of Pendennis*, ed. Hawes, 33. Subsequent references will be to this edition and will appear parenthetically within the text.

21. For more on the ideology of the three-decker, in particular in relation to *Henry Esmond*, see Feltes, *Modes of Production of Victorian Novels*, 18–35.

22. Walter Bagehot, "Sterne and Thackeray," in Tillotson and Hawes, *Thackeray: The Critical Heritage*, 351.

23. Cited in Ray, *Thackeray*, 462.

24. Crosby, *The Ends of History*, 53. See also Chase, "The Kindness of Consanguinity," 222, and Scarry, *Resisting Representation*, 115–17.

25. Elaine Scarry speculates along similar lines in her exhaustive analysis of the novel's many internal inconsistencies: "Because reviewers and friends made Thackeray aware of his own carelessness, it is completely plausible that in *Esmond* he decided to take what had formerly been an unpreventable accident and convert it into a controlled argument—the argument that compositional consistency is unachievable" (*Resisting Representation*, 139).

26. For a somewhat more redemptive view of the sham *Spectator* paper's effect on Henry and Beatrix's relationship, see Carlisle, *The Sense of an Audience*, 18.

27. Crosby continues, "In the sham *Spectator*, Oedipus is a servant to Jocasta and confounded by a riddle, whereas in the classical account he is the King of Thebes and the husband of Jocasta by virtue of his ability to answer riddles, to reply to the Sphinx. As for the relation of this part of *Esmond* to the whole, Oedipus is not Esmond, for Esmond is in the part of Cymon Wyldoats, and Jocasta is not Rachel, but rather Beatrix, the daughter, not the mother" (*The Ends of History*, 65). Crosby's summary, it should be noted, includes a slight but telling mistake: the Oedipus in the sham *Spectator* describes himself as Jocasta's "servant," but the context makes clear that this is meant figuratively, not literally. This mistake, however, is perfectly in keeping with the confusion of letters and figures, literality and figurality, that the novel encourages and explores.

28. Miller, *Fiction and Repetition*, 102.

29. The significance of the attribution of the pun here was suggested to me by D. A. Miller's remark that "Paul de Man would have been the last to claim that puns are personal property" (*The Novel and the Police*, 145).

30. Stephen Bann, J. Hillis Miller, and Elaine Scarry all offer their own examples of patterns in the novel that seem to destroy rather than create meaning, or that lead us to

ask, as Miller does at one point about echoes of the word "moon" in Esmond and Lord Mohun (who plays an important role in the novel), "Is this a senseless accident or does it have meaning?" (*Fiction and Repetition*, 77).

31. These formulations are indebted to Susan Eilenberg's succinct analysis of the competing understandings of literature's relationship to the material world that characterize psychoanalytic and deconstructionist approaches, on the one hand, and new historicist and cultural materialist ones, on the other (*Strange Power of Speech*, xii–xiv).

32. Foucault, "What is an Author?" in *Language, Counter-Memory, Practice*, 138.

33. Indeed, a deconstructive account such as J. Hillis Miller's continues to allow the possibility of (or even requires) the reader's perception of "an implicit circumambient judgment which can only speak indirectly, a judgment which may be called that of 'Thackeray'" (*Fiction and Repetition*, 105–6); the author is dead, long live the author effect!

34. Eisenstein, *The Printing Press as an Agent of Change*, 121. Another of Eisenstein's features of print culture is fixity; ironically, Mark Rose quotes this sentence as reading "the modern game" (instead of "modern games"), as does Catherine Gallagher (citing a different work by Eisenstein, *The Printing Revolution in Early Modern Europe*). Print obviously facilitates "dissemination" in a sense other than Eisenstein's own. See Rose, *Authors and Owners*, 4; and Gallagher, *Nobody's Story*, 62–63.

35. Gallagher, *Nobody's Story*, 65.

36. Rose, *Authors and Owners*, 1. For the abstraction of literary property from its physical basis, see 64–65.

37. Ibid., 2–3.

38. Ong, *Orality and Literacy*, 148.

39. Ong, "From Mimesis to Irony: Writing and Print as Integuments of Voice," in *Interfaces of the Word*, 292. Ong specifically cites Swift's *Battle of the Books* and Sterne's *Tristram Shandy* in this passage.

40. Ibid., 281.

41. Thackeray to George Smith, September/October 1857, in *Letters and Private Papers . . . A Supplement*, 2:827.

42. Rose, *Authors and Owners*, 4.

43. Kernan, *Printing Technology, Letters, and Samuel Johnson*, 4.

44. Scragg, *A History of English Spelling*, 71.

45. Swift, "A Proposal for Correcting, Improving, and Ascertaining the English Language," 35. Swift's proposal, in the form of a letter to the Earl of Oxford, is dated 22 February 1712, and was first published in May 1712. The sham *Spectator* paper is dated 1 April 1712.

46. See, for example, *Spectator* nos. 61 and 62, 10 May and 11 May 1711. Both of these papers are by Addison.

47. Georg Lukács, in his reading of *Henry Esmond*, notes that the *Spectator*'s influence "was largely due to the use of everyday events as a basis for arguing and demonstrating the new, triumphant morality of the rising bourgeoisie." Lukács goes on to criticize the novel's treatment of the *Spectator* on the grounds that Esmond's use of it in an attempt to "exert a beneficent moral influence upon [Beatrix] . . . reduce[s] its historical role to private episodes," thus degrading history "to the level of the trivial

and the private." On Lukács's own reading, however, this putative distortion would seem to be precisely that which the *Spectator* itself promotes. In other words, the novel does not so much analyze the *Spectator*'s historical role as represent it in action, in a manner Lukács should find exemplary (*The Historical Novel*, 204).

48. Rose, *Authors and Owners*, 121.

49. Ibid.

50. Gallagher, *Nobody's Story*, 165, 174–75. "Acquisitive without impertinence" alludes to Edmund Burke's phrase "inquisitive without impertinence."

51. Janice Carlisle sees Beatrix's experience as the reader of the sham *Spectator* paper as a model for that of the novel reader: "Like the reader of one of Thackeray's novels, she experiences the common humanity that she shares with the man who has told her a story." This analogy is undercut, however, by the fact that the story she has just read is her own, an experience quite different from that of the typical novel reader. Ironically, however, Beatrix's relationship to the text does mirror that of some of Thackeray's readers, a point I return to below (*The Sense of an Audience*, 18).

52. Thackeray, *Letters*, 2:784n.

53. Thackeray to Mrs. Carmichael-Smyth, 17–18 (?) November 1851, in *Letters*, 2:815.

54. Thackeray, *Letters*, 2:779–80n.

55. Thackeray's 1857 letter to his publisher on this matter reads, "If the last part of Esmond is not printed please stop[.] I want to cut out a bit concerning the Examinator [*sic*] wh. made the object of the satire very angry, though he said nothing of it for years after" (*Henry Esmond*, ed. Harden, 411).

56. Ibid.

57. Forster, "The Dignity of Literature," *The Examiner*, 19 January 1850, rpt. in Thackeray, *The History of Pendennis*, ed. Shillingsburg, 497. I return to this dispute in chapter 3, below.

58. Forster, review of *Henry Esmond*, in *The Examiner*, 13 November 1852; cited in Tillotson and Hawes, *Thackeray: The Critical Heritage*, 149.

59. Thackeray, *The Virginians*, 720.

2. Reading Matter in *Bleak House* and the "Bleak House Advertiser"

1. Dickens, *The Posthumous Papers of the Pickwick Club*, 67; Dickens, *The Mystery of Edwin Drood*, 280.

2. Dickens, *Great Expectations*, 35.

3. Goux, *Symbolic Economies*, 50. Goux argues that "the increasingly arbitrary medium of exchange, whether economic or signifying, tends to make *matter* indifferent," and finds that "it is impossible not to relate this movement of sublimation and idealization . . . to the history of philosophical idealism."

4. Dickens, *Bleak House*, Norton Critical Edition, 20, 36, 403, 738, 759, 256, 567, 392, 651. Unless otherwise noted, all quotations from *Bleak House* are from this edition, which takes the 1853 first edition as its copy text.

5. Miller, introduction to *Bleak House*, 11.

6. See Miller, *The Novel and the Police*, 66–68.

7. Gissing, *Charles Dickens: A Critical Study*, 61.

8. The monthly numbers of Dickens's novels routinely contained a large number of advertisements—at times more pages of ads than of novel. A good deal of work has been done on the role of serial publication in the determination of both the form of Dickens's novels and his emergence as a cultural phenomenon, but little work has been done on the advertisements, which are at times pointedly ignored. The Norton Critical Edition, for example, while meticulously documenting variations among the manuscript, proofs, and early editions of the novel, never hints at the advertisements' existence. The editors inform the reader that "the first edition appeared in two forms, whose texts are identical: the nineteen monthly installments and the one-volume edition of 1853, which was made up of parts bound together without their green covers" (806). One need not consider the advertisements part of the "text" of the novel to find this assertion, with its leave-nothing-to-be-assumed specificity concerning the green covers, misleading in its failure to mention fully half of what was between those covers. For groundbreaking analyses of Dickens and advertising, see Wicke, *Advertising Fictions*, 19–53, and Curtis, *Visual Words*, 103–41. Bernard Darwin's *The Dickens Advertiser: A Collection of the Advertisements in the Original Parts of Novels by Charles Dickens* is valuable for its reproductions of numerous advertisements, but is a more limited and random "collection" than its title implies.

9. All of these examples first appear in *Bleak House*, no. 1, with the following exceptions: Dakin & Company, purveyor of tea and coffee, takes out large ads beginning with the third number; a sixteen-page advertisement for water-purifying filters appears in the final, double number; and Glover's Superior Inks, which include the Encre à la Violette, are first advertised in the second number.

10. The ad continues: "All persons desirous of testing his art are invited to forward a specimen of their ordinary writing, together with 13 postage-stamps, and a mention of their sex and age, to the above address" (*Bleak House*, no. 1, 17 [Advertiser]).

11. *Bleak House*, no. 1, 17 (Advertiser), 18 (Advertiser).

12. *Bleak House* was published in monthly parts from March 1852 to September 1853. *Henry Esmond* is announced as forthcoming in the first monthly number of *Bleak House*, as "now ready" in the ninth number (November), and as being reprinted in a "second edition" in the tenth.

13. Dickens offers the lines "My nature is subdued / To what it works in, like the dyer's hand: / Pity me then, and wish I were renew'd" as an "apt" commentary on a "Chancery Judge" who, he reports, informed him that whatever "trivial blemish" there was on the Court's "rate of progress" was "entirely owing to the 'parsimony of the public'" (3). Ironically, Walter Bagehot turns sonnet 111 against Dickens's own practice of characterization, which Bagehot sees less as capturing the dehumanizing effects of labor than as effecting a dehumanization of its own: for many of the novelist's characters, Bagehot writes, "not only is human nature in them subdued to what it works in, but there seems to be no nature to subdue; the whole character is the idealisation of a trade," even though "a man's trade or profession in regular life can only exhaust a very small portion of his nature; no approach is made to the essence of humanity by the exaggeration of the traits which typify a beadle or an undertaker" ("Charles Dickens," in *Literary Studies*, 1:197–98, 205).

14. Scarry, *The Body in Pain*, 261, 275.

15. Michael Ragussis similarly connects Caddy's baby's marks to Esther's scars in the course of his argument that in *Bleak House* "the sin of the parents is visited upon the child as a half-intelligible writing that the child's body displays" (*Acts of Naming*, 97).

16. All these quotations are drawn from chap. 32.

17. [George Henry Lewes], *The Leader*, 11 December 1852, 1189. The documentary trail of this debate, as it was conducted in *Bleak House*, *The Leader*, and private correspondence between Dickens and Lewes, has been traced in detail in Haight, "Dickens and Lewes on Spontaneous Combustion." In addition to the columns by Lewes that Haight notes (11 December 1852; and in 1853: 15 January, 5 February, 12 February, 26 March, 3 September), Lewes also raises the subject in his columns of 29 January 1853, where he repeats his promise to investigate the subject further and also invites readers to "furnish their evidence and arguments" for consideration (111); and 2 April 1853, where Lewes comments on the reply he has received from "Ignis," one of the readers whose letter on the subject he has published and discussed the previous week. Lewes comments only briefly, concluding that "we fear our readers have had 'something too much' of this subject" (322), to which his column returns only upon the novel's conclusion, six months later.

18. [Lewes], *The Leader*, 11 December 1852, 1189.

19. George Gissing set an early example of dismissiveness by commenting that "it would, of course, be wide of the mark to begin discussing the possibility of spontaneous combustion" (*Critical Studies*, 149). Oddly enough, such dismissiveness also ultimately characterizes the work of critics who investigate the contemporary scientific standing of spontaneous combustion and the extent of Dickens's own research and knowledge. That is, even when the scientific controversy is thought interesting, it is construed as fundamentally separate from and subordinate to the phenomenon's use as a symbol, and therefore extraneous to its role in the novel. One long discussion of Dickens's use and misuse of "harsh, scientific fact," for example, concludes that "it is necessary for us to suspend our disbelief temporarily and to try to imagine that the phenomenon of spontaneous combustion can actually occur" (Blount, "Dickens and Mr. Krook's Spontaneous Combustion," 210, 211). Another critic interested in the subject suggests that "few readers nowadays would deny that, irrespective of its unlikelihood, the manner of Krook's death is amply justified by its symbolic affirmation of the corruption which permeates the world of *Bleak House*" (Denman, "Krook's Death and Dickens's Authorities," 140). George Levine, in a sympathetic analysis of Dickens's relationship to the scientific thought of his day, similarly finds it "particularly strange that an episode that has such coherent symbolic significances should seem to require from Dickens a defense of its literal truth" (*Darwin and the Novelists*, 133). Other articles largely or entirely devoted to the incident include Wilkinson, "*Bleak House*: From Faraday to Judgment Day," and E. Gaskell, "More about Spontaneous Combustion." For an interesting recent discussion of the relationship between the spontaneous-combustion incident's symbolic aspect, Dickens's truth-claims, and the incident's critical afterlife (partly with reference to an earlier version of this chapter), see Loesberg, "A Fountain, a Spontaneous Combustion, and the Mona Lisa."

20. In the preface to the Cheap Edition of *Martin Chuzzlewit*, published in No-

vember 1849, Dickens writes that "in all my writings, I hope I have taken every possible opportunity of showing the want of sanitary improvements in the neglected dwellings of the poor" (cited in *The Speeches of Charles Dickens,* 104). He expands on this point in the March 1850 preface to the Cheap Edition of *Oliver Twist,* writing that "nothing effectual can be done for the elevation of the poor in England, until their dwelling-places are made decent and wholesome. I have always been convinced that this Reform must precede all other Social Reforms; that it must prepare the way for Education, even for Religion" (*Oliver Twist,* 351). Dickens refers in this preface to the work of the Metropolitan Sanitary Association, founded to extend the provisions of the Public Health Act of 1848 to London. At the Association's first public meeting, on 6 February 1850, Dickens spoke of the need "to cleanse the foul air for the passage of Christianity and education throughout the land" (*Speeches,* 108). At the 10 May 1851 meeting of the same organization, Dickens, echoing his own words from the *Oliver Twist* preface, expressed his conviction that "searching Sanitary Reform must precede all other social remedies . . . and that even Education and Religion can do nothing where the are most needed, until the way is paved for their ministrations by Cleanliness and Decency" (*Speeches,* 129).

21. [Leigh], "Address from an Undertaker to the Trade," 302.

22. For a wide-ranging study of the identification of literality with maternity in nineteenth-century British literature, in particular in women's writing, see Homans, *Bearing the Word.*

23. Dickens, "The Poetry of Science," *The Examiner,* 9 December 1848, rpt. in *Miscellaneous Papers,* 1:135. Further references to this edition will be given parenthetically in the text.

24. In the "Preliminary Word," Dickens writes, "No mere utilitarian spirit, no iron binding of the mind to grim realities, will give a harsh tone to our *Household Words,*" and immediately goes on to speak of fancy as well (*Miscellaneous Papers,* 1:181).

25. Hunt, *The Poetry of Science,* 316.

26. Ibid., 317.

27. Emerson, "Nature," 32–33. Emerson mistakenly attributes this line to Ariel.

28. Ibid., 31.

29. Ibid., 34.

30. Coleridge, *Biographia Literaria,* 174. Coleridge is adapting a poem by John Davies that describes the action of the soul, not the imagination.

31. [Lewes], "Literature," *The Leader,* 12 February 1853, 162.

32. Liebig, *Familiar Letters on Chemistry,* 296. Subsequent references will be to this edition and will appear parenthetically in the text. For more on Liebig's career, see Brock, *Justus von Liebig.* Brock discusses Liebig's debunking of spontaneous human combustion on 284–86.

33. [Lewes], *The Leader,* 26 March 1853, 396.

34. Lewes, "Spontaneous Combustion," 394. This article makes no mention of Dickens.

35. The distance between Dickens's and Lewes's positions is underscored by their curious convergence on the matter adumbrated here. What Jo "can't exactly say" is "what'll be done to him arter he's dead if he tells a lie to the gentlemen here" (148),

while the very item following Lewes's initial discussion of spontaneous combustion in his "Literature" column is a defense of the rights of atheists, in particular the right to testify under oath: we must, he argues, learn "to credit the sincerity of disbelief, and the possibility of an unbeliever not being an unworthy citizen!" Of course, Dickens is most interested in defending the honesty of the ignorant, while Lewes seeks to defend the honesty of the sophisticated; at the same time, each is obviously working to consolidate his own cultural authority.

36. An advertisement for the "New and Cheap Edition" of Liebig's book appears in *Bleak House,* no. 1, 6 (Advertiser). For an account of Liebig's influence on the treatment of contagion in *Bleak House,* see Hamlin, "Providence and Putrefaction."

37. Dickens, *Bleak House,* no. 5 (Advertiser, unpaginated).

38. With one exception, whether canny or slightly daft it is difficult to say: in the fourteenth (April) number, "Harrington Parker, Beer Merchant, 5½ Pall Mall" quotes from the original (6 May) Liebig letter and explains that "influenced by so eminent an authority, I have resolved to sell Allsopp's Ales exclusively."

3.   As Bad as They Seem?

1. Mill, *Principles of Political Economy,* 1:351, 1:48. Further page references to this edition will be included parenthetically in the text.

2. "Prospectus for the Guild of Literature and Art," April 1851, rpt. in Dickens, *Letters,* 6:856. The Great Exhibition ran from 1 May to 11 October 1851; the Guild prospectus is dated 12 April, and the first performance took place on 16 May.

3. Although she does not mention this allusion to the Great Exhibition of 1851 in the Guild's prospectus, Clare Pettitt argues for the importance of the Exhibition as a context for understanding the Guild of Literature of Art and related debates about the professionalization of authorship. Pettitt's interesting account, which focuses on the question of intellectual property (and which also reads *Bleak House* in this context), appeared too late for me to engage with it more fully here. See Pettitt, *Patent Inventions,* 149–203.

4. Smith, *Wealth of Nations,* 352.

5. This maneuver did not escape the notice of at least one Victorian commentator on Mill: "Mr. Mill has somewhat extended the term ["productive labour"] beyond Smith's view of it; for while Smith only allows those to be productive labourers who are directly employed in the production of material products, Mr. Mill includes those also who are indirectly employed in this way. . . . Authors and editors of newspapers take rank as productive labourers; while actors, singers, opera dancers, clergymen and others remain out in the cold as unproductive labourers" (Macleod, *The Principles of Economical Philosophy,* 1:271).

6. Mill himself expresses a wish to replace materiality with permanence as the key criterion of wealth and productiveness, a move he refrains from because of the economy of language itself: "When employing terms which common usage has taken complete possession of, it seems advisable so to employ them as to do the least possible violence to usage; since any improvement in terminology obtained by straining

the received meaning of a popular phrase is generally purchased beyond its value" (*Principles of Political Economy*, 1:48). Mill's expressed dissatisfaction with materiality, however, has different grounds from the unarticulated sense of inadequacy I identify.

7. See Marx, *Theories of Surplus Value*, 152, and below.

8. Ibid., 157.

9. Ibid., 158, 401.

10. Jevons, *The Principles of Economics*, 86, 88.

11. See Adams, *Dandies and Desert Saints;* Clarke, "Strenuous Idleness"; Sussman, *Victorian Masculinities*.

12. Carlyle, "The Hero as Man of Letters," *On Heroes*, 134. All subsequent citations of "The Hero as Man of Letters" refer to this edition.

13. This criticism of the marketplace will find its most famous formulation in Carlyle's next book, *Past and Present*, where he argues that in today's society "our life is not a mutual helpfulness; but rather cloaked under due laws-of-war, named 'fair competition' and so forth, it is a mutual hostility. We have profoundly forgotten everywhere that *Cash-payment* is not the sole relation of human beings; we think, nothing doubting, that *it* absolves and liquidates all engagements of man. 'My starving workers?' answers the rich Mill-owner: 'Did not I hire them fairly in the market?'" (*Past and Present*, 148).

14. Bourdieu, "The Field of Production, or: The Economic World Reversed," in *The Field of Cultural Production*, 40.

15. See Harrison, *Wordsworth's Vagrant Muse*, 121–25.

16. Smith, *Wealth of Nations*, 147, 148.

17. D'Israeli, *Calamities of Authors*, in *Miscellanies of Literature*, 57. In an extended attack on political economists in *The Literary Character*, D'Israeli again quotes this passage from Smith, only this time altered to emphasize its continued relevance; D'Israeli writes: "In a system of political economy it has been discovered, that 'that unprosperous race of men, called men of letters, must necessarily occupy their present forlorn state in society much as formerly, when a scholar and a beggar seem to have been terms very nearly synonymous'" (*Miscellanies of Literature*, 369). John Stuart Mill, with a complacency D'Israeli would no doubt find infuriating, cites the passage from Smith that concludes with this claim as an accurate explanation of the poor remuneration of "bookish occupations" (*Principles of Political Economy*, 1:482–85).

18. Smith, *Wealth of Nations*, 148.

19. Ibid., 18; emphasis added.

20. For a discussion of the beggar as a social category that "delineates the pocket of an indispensable internal exclusion," see Derrida, *Given Time*, 134–35.

21. Meredith, "The Beggar's Soliloquy," lines 49–60, *Poetical Works*, 105. First published in *Once a Week*, 30 March 1861.

22. We should note, however, that the rhetorical question "If people will give, why, who'll refuse?" may invite a response that brushes against the grain of the speaker's intentions: for many readers, the notion that "people will give" was not a given, but rather a problem to be corrected—hence the period's proliferation of attacks on "indiscriminate almsgiving," if not almsgiving tout court, attacks that occasion Meredith's speaker's thoughts in the first place. For those who believe that charity tends to

have pauperizing, demoralizing effects on its recipients, the truth of the speaker's rhetorical question—"who'll refuse?"—therefore constitutes an argument against giving, not an acknowledgment that the beggar will always be with us. I return to this issue, with special reference to the novel, in chapter 4.

23. See Williams, *Culture and Society,* 35 and passim.

24. Ibid., 63.

25. See, for example, Harrison, *Wordsworth's Vagrant Muse,* and Langan, *Romantic Vagrancy.*

26. Wordsworth, *Selected Poems,* 499–500. "The Old Cumberland Beggar" was written in 1797 and published in 1800.

27. Wordsworth, "Preface to Lyrical Ballads (1802)," Coleridge and Wordsworth, *Lyrical Ballads 1798,* 165.

28. The general adherence to orthodox notions of political economy in *Once a Week* reinforces this skeptical reading of the poem, and in fact suggests that the poem's publication there may have depended on the obviousness of this reading. At Christmastime (three months before the publication of Meredith's poem), for example, the journal is careful to qualify even the most insipid expression of Wordsworthian sentiment—"let us all just now make a store of kindly acts, and warm sympathies with our poorer fellow-creatures"—with a warning against "promiscuous alms-giving" ("Last Week," *Once a Week,* 29 December 1860, 28).

29. Sussman, *Victorian Masculinities,* 35, 39; see chap. 1, "The Condition of Manliness Question: Thomas Carlyle and Industrial Manhood," passim.

30. Adams, *Dandies and Desert Saints,* 7.

31. Poovey, *Uneven Developments,* 125.

32. Ibid., 125.

33. As Alexander Welsh notes, Dickens, like most Victorians, was a firm believer in "the eleventh commandment, 'Thou shalt not receive'" (*The City of Dickens,* 97). For Dickens's contradictory attitudes toward charity, see Welsh's chapter entitled "Charity" (86–100), and especially 96–97 for a brief discussion of Dickens's desire to distinguish various forms of aid from charity (a subject to which I return in the second part of this chapter). The primary example Welsh cites is Dickens's speech at a dinner for the General Theatrical Fund, where Dickens asserts, "If you help this Fund you will not be performing an act of charity, but you will be helping those who help themselves" (96; speech of 14 April 1851). Welsh feels compelled to emphasize that this statement comes "in a context devoid of all irony" (96). Yet however unconvincing or embarrassing this implicit apotheosis of the donor may seem to contemporary ears, Dickens himself was sufficiently comfortable with the formulation to use it again a year later, in a letter to Angela Burdett-Coutts: "I have safely received the £10 note, your kind donation to Mrs. Goldsmith, and have remitted it to her. I am glad you think so well of the case. It certainly *is* helping those who help themselves" (8 August 1852, in *Letters,* 6:736). For the purposes of the present discussion, it is also worth noting that the context here is that of authorial support, for Dickens's dealings with this Mrs. Goldsmith are premised on her distant relationship to Oliver Goldsmith.

34. Gallagher, "George Eliot and *Daniel Deronda,*" 42–43.

35. Anson Rabinbach offers a helpful overview of "the traditional emphasis on idleness

as the paramount cause of resistance to work," along with the targeting of beggars this entailed, in chapter 1, "From Idleness to Fatigue," of his *The Human Motor*, 19–44 (quotation from 6).

36. Mayhew, *London Labour and the London Poor*, 4:22–23. I return to Mayhew in chapter 4, below.

37. Carlyle, *Past and Present*, 148.

38. Coleridge's advice to "the youthful literati" is *"never pursue literature as a trade,"* on the principle that inspired writing cannot be produced "mechanically." His rhetoric on this point forms a telling contrast to Carlyle's: "Three hours of leisure, unannoyed by any alien anxiety and looked forward to with delight as a change and recreation," he asserts, "will suffice to realize in literature a larger product of what is truly genial than weeks of compulsion" (*Biographia Literaria*, 127). It is striking how rarely Victorian writers reject authorship as a legitimate means of obtaining one's livelihood (let alone advocate the removal of literature from the marketplace); instead, it is precisely the legitimacy of authorship as a profession that they work to achieve. Thus, among prominent early- and mid-Victorian authors, John Stuart Mill forms the exception when he suggests that there is "something radically amiss in the idea of authorship as a profession" and questions the wisdom of "any social arrangement under which the teachers of mankind consist of persons giving out doctrines for bread" (*Principles of Political Economy*, 1:486–87). Mill offers a similar argument in his *Autobiography,* but there he shifts his focus somewhat to the practical difficulty or impossibility, rather than the moral objectionability, of making a living through the kinds of literary labor he favors (see 51–52). Not even George Eliot, who goes so far as to argue for "some regulating principle with regard to the publication of intellectual products, which would override the rule of the market," joins Mill in preferring that the highest forms of literary labor afford "no remuneration at all"; instead, she rewrites Coleridge's dictum as an ethic of behavior *in* the marketplace: the writer "must make up his mind that he must not pursue authorship as a vocation with a trading determination to get rich by it." Indeed, according to Eliot, if the writer works in this spirit, "it is in the highest sense lawful for him to get as good a price as he honorably can" (Eliot, "Authorship," 234; Mill, *Principles,* 1:486). (I return to Eliot in chapters 4 and 5, below.) In short, while writers clearly want to establish certain perceptions of their involvement in the marketplace, by and large they are not intent on denying or ending this involvement.

39. See Cross, *The Common Writer,* for an informative study of the economic conditions of authors unable or barely able to make a living by writing in the nineteenth century. Cross's book is based largely on the archives of the Royal Literary Fund, an organization I discuss below and in my next chapter.

40. This activity proceeds alongside, and often in conjunction with, efforts to alter the workings of the marketplace itself, especially through various kinds of copyright reform. For discussion of these efforts, see, for example, Vanden Bossche, "The Value of Literature," and Bonham-Carter, *Authors by Profession,* 1:71–100. Carlyle himself, at the time of his lectures on "The Hero as Man of Letters," was actively participating in the campaign to have Parliament extend the term of copyright.

41. Forster, *The Life and Times of Oliver Goldsmith,* 1:195.

42. There is a huge literature on the anthropology and sociology of gift exchange, but for the points made here see Mauss, *The Gift;* Douglas, "Foreword: No Free Gifts"; and Derrida, *Given Time.*

43. Dickens, *Little Dorrit,* 469.

44. While Jeff Nunokawa insightfully reads the economy of *Little Dorrit* as an exaggerated version of the Maussian rule that "anything received must be paid for," he neglects the element of wish-fulfillment this rule represents for the debtor. Thus, he notes that "at the end of his term in debtor's prison, William Dorrit declares his intention to repay all that he owes: 'Everybody . . . shall be remembered. I will not go away from here in anybody's debt [470],'" an intention Nunokawa characterizes as "restoring borrowed money" (30); the point, however, is that the money has not been borrowed, but rather given as charity. As I note later in the chapter, Mr. Dorrit himself chooses to recognize, indeed emphasize, this distinction when the tables are fully turned and he is now handing out money to the remaining prisoners: "He said in every . . . case, 'it is a donation, not a loan'" (475). See Nunokawa, *The Afterlife of Property,* 19–39.

45. The literature on these topics is extensive, but the starting point for discussion of professionalism's relationship to the marketplace remains Larson, *The Rise of Professionalism.* For a compelling analysis of the process whereby market failure came to function, and continues to function, as a source of artistic legitimacy, see Bourdieu, *The Field of Cultural Production.* For the history of nineteenth-century British efforts to create professional organizations of authors and to reform the literary marketplace, see Bonham-Carter, *Authors by Profession.*

46. Illuminating discussions of this controversy include Fielding, "Thackeray and the 'Dignity of Literature'"; Howes, "*Pendennis* and the Controversy on the 'Dignity of Literature'"; and Lund, *Reading Thackeray,* 59–78.

47. *Morning Chronicle,* 3 January 1850, rpt. in Thackeray, *The History of Pendennis,* ed. Shillingsburg, 487. Subsequent references will be to this edition and will appear parenthetically in the text.

48. Forster, "Encouragement of Literature by the State," *The Examiner,* 5 January 1850, rpt. in Thackeray, ibid., 489. Subsequent references will be to this edition and will appear parenthetically in the text.

49. Mr. Dorrit falteringly explains to Arthur Clennam that "it does sometimes occur that people who come here desire to offer some little—Testimonial—to the Father of the place. . . . sometimes—hem—it takes one shape and sometimes another; but it is generally—ha—Money" (*Little Dorrit,* 123).

50. Thackeray, Letter to the Editor of the *Morning Chronicle,* 12 January 1850, rpt. in *The History of Pendennis,* ed. Shillingsburg, 493.

51. *The Case of the Reformers in The Literary Fund stated by Charles W. Dilke, Charles Dickens, and John Forster,* 1858, cited in Fielding, "Dickens and the Royal Literary Fund—1858," 388. On Dickens and the Royal Literary Fund, see also Cross, *The Common Writer,* 30–37, and Fielding, "Dickens and the Royal Literary Fund: 1855."

52. Dickens, *Little Dorrit,* 475.

53. The wording and details of the regulations change slightly over time; I cite the form dated March 1849, from Henry Mayhew's file. For the history of the Royal Literary Fund, see Cross, *The Common Writer.*

54. "Proposed Prospectus for the Provident Union of Literature, Science, & Art, [November] 1847," rpt. in Dickens, *Letters,* 5:700.

55. For an informative, if unduly hostile, overview of the Guild of Literature and Art, see Cross, *The Common Writer,* 70–76.

56. "Prospectus for the Guild of Literature and Art," April 1851, rpt. in Dickens, *Letters,* 6:855. Subsequent references will be to this edition and will appear parenthetically in the text.

57. Compare Thackeray's similar statement in the conclusion to his 1853 lectures *The English Humourists of the Eighteenth Century:* "With what difficulty had [young authors] to contend, save that eternal and mechanical one of want of means and lack of capital, and of which thousands of young lawyers, young doctors, young soldiers and sailors, of inventors, manufacturers, shopkeepers, have to complain?" (188).

58. Dickens, "The Guild of Literature and Art," *Household Words,* 10 May 1851, rpt. in Dickens, *Miscellaneous Papers,* 328.

59. Edgar Johnson recounts the story of the Guild's theatrical efforts in *Charles Dickens,* 2:719–39.

60. Dickens, "The Guild of Literature and Art," in *Miscellaneous Papers,* 328.

61. "Proposed Prospectus," in Dickens, *Letters,* 5:702, 700, 701, 700, 702.

62. Ibid., 702. Even this "uncharitable" purism, it should be noted, runs into conceptual as well as practical difficulties, for although the Union refuses to be solicited, its transactions will still be guided by charitable impulses, as its Committee "will make it their business to inform themselves . . . of such cases as may seem to have the most deserving claim upon their sympathy" (700).

63. The very decision to put on a new play rather than a classic, while obviously intended to heighten interest in the project, may be seen as jeopardizing any claim to provide "a sufficient return" to the purchasers of tickets: a hostile article in the *Times* notes that Bulwer-Lytton is "an author the intermission of whose dramatic labours the public has acquiesced in . . . without any very visible symptoms of discontent" (*Times,* 28 April 1851, cited in Dickens, *Letters,* 6:373). Dickens himself, in the privacy of a letter to Angela Burdett-Coutts, refers to *Not So Bad as We Seem* as "the dismal Comedy" (2 September 1852, in *Letters,* 6:753).

64. Edward Bulwer-Lytton to John Forster, in Dickens, *Letters,* 6:369.

65. Dickens to Bulwer-Lytton, 28 April 1851, ibid., 6:368.

66. Bulwer-Lytton, *Not So Bad as We Seem; or, Many Sides to a Character,* 106. Subsequent references to this edition will appear parenthetically in the text.

67. Perkin, *The Rise of Professional Society,* 117.

68. For a more general discussion of the ways in which conventional notions of professionalization do and do not apply to authorship in the nineteenth century, see Patten, "'The People have set Literature free'"; see also Feltes, *Modes of Production of Victorian Novels,* 36–56. For a nuanced analysis of the development of an ideology of literary professionalism later in the century, see Freedman, *Professions of Taste.*

69. Thackeray, in particular, argues that an emphasis on the economic precariousness of

authorship, far from being an effective strategy for improving authors' conditions, contributes to—is perhaps even responsible for—their degradation and impoverishment. He complains that Alexander Pope, by "revel[ing] in base descriptions of poor men's want . . . contributed, more than any man who ever lived, to depreciate the literary calling. It was not an unprosperous one before that time. . . . The profession of letters was ruined by that libel of *The Dunciad*." Thackeray continues: "If authors were wretched and poor before; . . . if three of them had but one coat between them, the two remained invisible in the garret, the third, at any rate, appeared decently at the coffee-house, and paid his twopence like a gentleman. It was Pope that dragged into light all this poverty and meanness, and held up those wretched shifts and rags to public ridicule. It was Pope that has made generations of the reading world . . . believe that author and wretch, author and rags, author and dirt, author and drink, gin, cow-heel, tripe, poverty, duns, bailiffs, squalling children, and clamorous landladies, were always associated together" (*The English Humourists*, 128–29). Thackeray clearly sees the series of projects climaxing in the founding of the Guild as a continuation of this misguided tradition. Ironically, *Not So Bad As We Seem* itself excoriates Pope for his attacks on fellow authors, but, not surprisingly, not for the association of authorship with poverty that so exercises Thackeray.

70. The specific perils and attractions that the literary marketplace held for women demand (and have received) separate treatment. Most obviously, though, if the scene of exchange described here involved a female author rather than a male one, the potential association of publication with prostitution would loom large. For the trope of the author as prostitute, see Gallagher, "George Eliot and *Daniel Deronda*." For an especially wide-ranging analysis of the conditions and contours of Victorian women writers' participation in the literary marketplace, see Mermin, *Godiva's Ride*.

71. It is curious to note, however, that the lines we see David Fallen writing, borrowed from Dryden's *Indian Emperor* (1.1.27–28)—"Me thinks we walk in dreams on fairy land / Where golden ore lies mixed with common sand"—can be read as an image of poetic inspiration as opposed to labor. That, at any rate, is how the anonymous author of a *Westminster Review* article on "The Profession of Literature" reads them in criticizing would-be authors who "believe writing to be a matter of inspiration": "The world does not look for leviathans in shallows, nor expect to discover, in the works of writers who are 'unaware' of *what* their work requires, the unexpected treasures of Mr. David Fallen's miraculous region—'Where golden ore lies mixed with common sand'" (*Westminster Review* 58 [October 1852]: 524). The fact that the article does not identify this allusion to *Not So Bad as We Seem*, nor even mention the Guild itself, may be taken as a sign of the play's familiarity among the *Westminster's* elite readership.

72. Peter Lindenbaum describes the economic arrangements attending the publication of *Paradise Lost* and briefly analyzes the polemical invocation of these arrangements in the early eighteenth century in "Milton's Contract."

73. See Rose, *Authors and Owners*, esp. chap. 7, "Property/ Originality/ Personality," on the development of the notion of the literary work as "the objectification of a writer's self, . . . the record of a personality" (113–29, 121).

74. It seems likely that the epilogue was omitted in the play's opening performance (and

perhaps thereafter as well), at least partly because of the play's length. See Dickens to Bulwer-Lytton, 1 May 1851, in *Letters,* 6:372.

75. Thackeray's comment, as reported in *The Critic,* 15 March 1852, cited in Dickens, *Letters,* 6:560.

76. *Times,* 28 April 1851, cited in Dickens, *Letters,* 6:373.

77. The Guild made its first grant in 1868, to the dying Peter Cunningham. See Cross, *The Common Writer,* 70–76.

78. Ibid., 75. Despite its failure, the Guild can also be seen as a precursor to the twentieth century's more successfully established mechanisms for providing extramarket, noncharitable support to authors and intellectuals, from state and private endowments to artists' colonies and humanities centers. See Johnson, *Charles Dickens,* 2:739.

79. Dickens, *Bleak House,* Norton Critical Edition, 806.

80. On Dickens's continuing efforts to reform the Royal Literary Fund, see Fielding, "Dickens and the Royal Literary Fund—1858."

4. Sympathy for the Begging-Letter Writer

1. Mayhew, *London Labour and the London Poor,* 1:213. Subsequent references to this edition will appear parenthetically in the text.

2. One might argue, of course, that this convergence also renders the authority or accuracy of the quotation suspect. For present purposes, however, the possibility that the quotation or even the speaker may be a figment of Mayhew's imagination hardly diminishes their interest, as the identification would be no less real for being a projection—on the contrary. In other words, if the quotation is manufactured, it tells us less about the lives of London's street-folk, but that much more about the anxieties of its authors.

3. On class distinctions as distinctions between levels of embodiedness, see Scarry, *The Body in Pain,* 256–77. Catherine Gallagher discusses Mayhew's emphasis on the "complete physicality" of working-class bodies (costermongers in particular) in "The Body versus the Social Body in Malthus and Mayhew," 104.

4. Mill, *Principles of Political Economy,* 1:76. Productive labor, as Mill explains, is distinguished from "unproductive labour," which "ends in immediate enjoyment, without any increase of the accumulated stock or permanent means of enjoyment" (1:77).

5. It is worth noting in this context that Pecksniff, whom Alexander Welsh and others have viewed as a double for Dickens—with, for Welsh, Pecksniff's hypocrisy a version of the hypocrisy that the novelist himself was charged with for his advocacy of an international copyright agreement during his first trip to the United States—is described at the very end of *Martin Chuzzlewit* as "a drunken, begging, squalid, letter-writing man" (832). (This passage reads "drunken, squalid, begging-letter-writing man" in the 1867 Charles Dickens edition, but it is not known who made the change.) See Welsh, *From Copyright to Copperfield,* 18–42. I return to Dickens below.

6. Rose, *"Rogues and Vagabonds,"* 36. Founded in 1818, the Mendicity Society started its begging-letter department in 1820. See Roberts, "Reshaping the Gift Relationship," 221. Roberts also notes that the 1815 Select Committee on Mendicity refers to the "growing problem" of begging letters (221).

7. Ruskin, *Fors Clavigera*, letter 1, in *Works*, 27:12.

8. Dickens to Thomas Roscoe, 23 November 1849, in *Letters*, 5:657; Dickens to W. H. Wills, 29 April 1852, in *Letters*, 6:654.

9. Accounts of begging letters can in fact be extremely consistent; the article in the *Times* cited below notes that the begging-letter writer's "opportunities and his continual study are . . . all the ills that flesh is heir to" (7 October 1867, 6).

10. For the use of photographs by begging-letter writers, see Greenwood, *The Seven Curses of London*, 164. For a brief but informative overview of Victorian begging-letter writing, see Rose, *"Rogues and Vagabonds,"* 33–36.

11. Howitt, *An Autobiography*, 2:53–54. Several of the individuals mentioned here appear on Mayhew's list of frequent recipients of begging letters. It also turns out that Youl had a history of begging-letter writing in his own name as well, as Dickens notes in a letter to Angela Burdett-Coutts: "The man who alone executed the whole of the nefarious Howitt imposition is, I have ascertained, one Mr. Youls [*sic*]. He wrote a begging-letter to you once, in his own name, and I made some enquiries about him for you. I am afraid you gave him some money then. He is a most abandoned and wicked thief, but he had not begun this career at that time" (Dickens to Burdett-Coutts, 7 December 1849, in *Letters*, 5:667).

12. Ibid., 2:53.

13. Ibid., 2:54. She continues, "In acknowledging a donation from the Bishop of Oxford (Wilberforce), I was made to say: 'I went down on my knees and thanked God, Who had moved his lordship's heart to such noble kindness to me.'"

14. Besant, "Literature as a Career," *Essays and Historiettes*, 329–30.

15. Ibid, 330–31, 312.

16. Here I part company with Audrey Jaffe's insightful account of the ways in which "the figure of the 'false beggar' [serves as] a figure for the writer" in the work of Mayhew and Arthur Conan Doyle. According to Jaffe, Mayhew "may be said to have detached himself from his subjects precisely through the act of writing about them," in that "the sympathy and identification which enable his work in fact keep away the possibility that he will actually occupy the beggar's place." We see here, however, that this strategy fails for Mayhew, and I take this failure as indicative of the strategy's fundamental inadequacy. That is, whereas Jaffe maintains that for Mayhew "an identification with illegitimate production is legitimated in a form of production—writing—that allows for vicariousness, for both imaginative participation and professional 'disinterest,'" I would argue the reverse, that the illegitimacy of begging-letter writing calls into question the legitimacy of writing for publication, and in particular its status as a form of "production." As we shall also see, writings about begging letters often begin to resemble the texts they describe in several telltale ways (Jaffe, "Detecting the Beggar," 108–9).

17. Henry Mayhew, file no. 1327, Archives of the Royal Literary Fund.

18. The *Times* leader discussed below, for example, states that "the Court of Chancery . . . stands pre-eminent in the crowd of diabolical agencies peopling these painful records" (7 October 1867, 6).

19. To recount this complicated story in more detail: Mayhew stands security for a friend who is threatened with transportation when "unable to balance his accounts" as a pay

clerk in the government coal-shippers office: although not worth the £200 owed, Mayhew is "induced to place my name on the back of the bills," believing it to be "a mere matter of form," as the clerk will be allowed to work off the debt and the acceptor of the bills, a Catholic priest named "J. Moore," assures Mayhew that "he was ready and able to meet the bills in case the clerk should fail to do so"; in the event, Mayhew explains, the clerk, "finding his income considerably diminished by the stoppage of half his salary . . . took the benefit of the Act for Insolvent Debtors and freed himself of the *debt*," while "the Revd. J. Moore turned out to be possessed of no property whatever, and I was ultimately left to pay the whole." At first, Mayhew emphasizes, he continued paying off the debt, "but at length 'London Labour' was thrown into Chancery [in a dispute with his printer] and my income ceased," at which point he was imprisoned. The RLF granted Mayhew £50. He was again imprisoned for debt, and again aided by the RLF, in 1868.

20. D. Bogue to Octavian Blewitt, 5 July 1853; from Mayhew's RLF file.
21. Grant, *Sketches in London*, 7. The first edition of *Sketches* was published in 1838.
22. *Times*, 7 October 1867, 6.
23. Laqueur, "Bodies, Details, and the Humanitarian Narrative," 177, 178.
24. Ibid., 178.
25. Grant, *Sketches in London*, 7.
26. Emma Robinson to the General Committee of the Royal Literary Fund, undated, accompanying application form dated 5 June 1861, RLF file no. 1558.
27. Eliot, "Silly Novels by Lady Novelists," *Westminster Review*, October 1856, rpt. in *Selected Essays*, 151.
28. Ibid., 148.
29. Eliot, "The Natural History of German Life," *Westminster Review*, July 1856, rpt. ibid., 110–11.
30. Frederick Maynard to Charles Dickens, 10 October 1854, in Dickens, *Letters*, 7:915. The entire letter is on 915–16.
31. Dickens to Burdett-Coutts, 17 November 1854, ibid., 7:467.
32. Ibid., 7:467, 468–69.
33. Eliot, "The Natural History of German Life," 111.
34. Ibid., 109–10.
35. Grant, *Sketches in London*, 1. Subsequent references to this edition will appear parenthetically in the text.
36. Grant ends his account of begging-letter writers with the ironic exception that proves the rule of aesthetic appreciation as the refusal of sympathy: "Of all the begging-letter impostors of whom it has been my fortune to hear there is none for whose fate I ever felt the slightest compassion, with the exception of one of the name of David Jones. This poor fellow had a world of spirit and enterprise in the pursuit of his self-chosen avocation, but nature never intended him for it; for he possessed no variety of mental resources, nor could he in any case disguise his hand-writing" (24).
37. *Times*, 7 October 1867, 6.
38. The institutionalization and professionalization of charity in the second half of the nineteenth century has been widely remarked; for very different accounts of this process, see Jones, *Outcast London*, 239–349, and Himmelfarb, *Poverty and Compassion*.

39. Ironically, the article's endorsement of the Mendicity Society ends up posing the Society not as a more discerning and effective benefactor than the individual almsgiver but rather as a more worthy recipient of charity than the begging-letter writer: "So long as the tender-hearted throw away their sovereigns on Begging Letter Writers, and their pence on the first man that holds out the palm, the Mendicity Society must always be straitened from want of means, and must finds its work hindered rather than forwarded by the casual almsgiver." Given that the article also provides the Mendicity Society's address, we might even begin to see the article itself as something of a begging letter on its behalf.

40. Dickens, *Our Mutual Friend*, 259–61.

41. Ibid., 259, 261.

42. Dickens, preface to *Little Dorrit*, 36.

43. Dickens, preface to *Dombey and Son*, 41.

44. Dickens, "The Begging-Letter Writer," *Household Words*, 18 May 1850, rpt. in *The Amusements of the People and Other Papers*, 228. Subsequent references will be included in the text. This article is nominally anonymous, but it contains internal indications of Dickens's authorship, such as the statement that the writer has been receiving these letters regularly "for fourteen years" (228)—which is to say, since 1836, when *The Pickwick Papers* began publication. In addition, the appearance of Dickens's name on every page of *Household Words* ("conducted by Charles Dickens"), combined with its policy of unsigned articles, ensured that all social or political commentary in the journal was closely identified with Dickens.

45. For the history of the association of actors with beggars, see Carroll, *Fat King, Lean Beggar*.

46. Forster, *Life of Charles Dickens*, 64. As noted above, this phenomenon, whereby discussions of begging letters come to resemble begging letters, is by no means exclusive to Dickens. At times, this resemblance begins to look less like that of analogy than that of identity, as writers oppose begging letters' financial appeals with their own. In classic begging-letter fashion, for example, the anonymous author of an 1855 *Quarterly Review* article on "The Charities and Poor of London" not only solicits contributions but frames the request as an exception to his or her usual course of action, one resorted to only because of the urgency of the situation: "We had not intended, in giving this sketch of London charities," the author writes, "to say a word to bias the reader's decision in favour of any one, but we must be allowed to depart so far from our reserve, as to urge that no one who wishes to walk in the streets of London, with the entire right to disregard the importunities of its mendicant population, should refrain from contributing his mite to the Mendicity Society" ("The Charities and the Poor of London," 426).

47. Dickens to Henry Austin, 12 May 1850, in *Letters*, 6:99.

48. Thackeray, "Thorns in the Cushion," *Roundabout Papers*, 210. Subsequent references to this edition will appear parenthetically in the text.

49. Trollope, "Mary Gresley," *The Spotted Dog and Other Stories*, 92; published in 1870 as *An Editor's Tales*.

50. Trollope, "The Turkish Bath," *Spotted Dog*, 64.

51. Trollope, *Thackeray*, 54–55.

52. Trollope, *Autobiography*, 240–41.
53. Trollope, "Josephine de Montmorenci," *Spotted Dog*, 105–6.
54. Trollope, "The Turkish Bath," *Spotted Dog*, 64.
55. Collins, *No Name*, 152. Subsequent references to this edition will appear parenthetically in the text. Wragge is the child from another marriage of Mrs. Vanstone's mother's first husband. Mrs. Vanstone claims to have "assist[ed] the captain from her own purse" over the years in order to keep him from approaching Mr. Vanstone and taking advantage of his generosity (18). Mr. Pendril, the family lawyer, later explains that Wragge, as the only survivor of Mrs. Vanstone's family, had "privately extorted the price of his silence" from her (92). There is no indication in the novel from Wragge himself, however, that he knows the truth about Mr. and Mrs. Vanstone, and indeed he reacts with "profound bewilderment" when Magdalen tells him the story of her disinheritance (162).
56. On Collins's use of his preface to call his readers' attention to his technique, see Stange, review of *No Name*, 97. Tamar Heller and John Kucich both explore Collins's ongoing attention to his public image as a professional author, with Kucich in particular emphasizing Collins's interest in positioning himself outside "mainstream bourgeois culture." See Heller, *Dead Secrets*, and Kucich, *The Power of Lies*, 77, 75–118.
57. Stange, review of *No Name*, 97.
58. Dickens, by contrast, combats his own potential identification with Harold Skimpole by making him a thinly veiled portrait of *another* author, the improvident Leigh Hunt.
59. I do not mean to suggest, however, that Wragge is the only authorial double in the novel. On the contrary, as noted above, he is only one of its several plotters, all of whom figure each other and the author. This potential identification often comes to involve not simply a talent for plotting but also a facility with language. Wragge's "easy flow of language," for example, may or may not align him with Collins, but it immediately aligns him with Magdalen herself, as the first chapter saw her father "sit down composedly under his daughter's flow of language, like a man who was well used to verbal inundation from that quarter" (8). Wragge is also explicitly paired with Mrs. Lecount, the formidable servant of Noel Vanstone (the man Magdalen contrives to marry, with Wragge's help). Thus, the narrator compares Mrs. Lecount's "daring ingenuity" to Captain Wragge's (297), as does Mrs. Lecount herself (421), and Wragge quickly recognizes her as a worthy rival in the arts of deception and manipulation. In light of the care with which Collins establishes and calls attention to this chain of associations, I must disagree with Joseph Litvak, who, both with specific reference to Mrs. Lecount and more generally, reads Collins's resemblance to his characters as "unwitting implication rather than conscious identification." See Litvak, *Caught in the Act*, 137. On the importance of doubles in the novel, see Blain, "Introduction," xiv.
60. Here I depart from Deirdre David, who also sees Wragge as a "parodic narrator," but who sees him as an "emblem of convention, order, and legitimacy," the embodiment of the conventions Collins is putatively rebelling against, in particular "the fictionally omniscient/omnipotent narrator" (190–92). David attributes to Collins an "unrelenting insistence on diegetic relativism" (190) and sees the novel's use of interpolated diary entries, letters, and the like as a sign of its Bakhtinian dialogism (192).

Not only are these interpolations contained "Between the Scenes," however, with the "Scenes" themselves all characterized by omniscient narration, but these various materials always serve to forward the narrative and never to problematize it. That is, they never contradict each other or create uncertainty as to what has "really" happened, and thus hardly serve to reveal "the subjective, arbitrary nature of fictional representation," as David claims (191). Whereas David points to Wragge's carefully kept "Books" to argue that he "performs a kind of burlesque of Victorian narrative discourse, of the sovereign omniscience that dominates the period" (192), I locate these Books in the more specific context of a humanitarian narrative parodically embodied in the practice of begging-letter writing. Finally, "despite his raffish demeanor and picaresque career," David argues, Wragge's "attitudes . . . represent conformity and conservatism" (194), but I would argue that his "raffishness" stands as a challenge to such categories, and especially to conventional notions of legitimacy. See David, "Rewriting the Male Plot."

61. Collins seems to have gotten additional details and perhaps even the seed for Wragge's name from Halliday, who stresses that the begging-letter writer's "great stock-in-trade is his register" (4:403), and describes "the cleverly organized swindling" of "the Kaggs family" (4:404).

62. For a reading of the novel focusing on theatricality, see Litvak, *Caught in the Act,* 134–37.

63. David, "Rewriting the Male Plot," 194.

64. Margaret Oliphant, unsigned review, *Blackwood's Magazine,* August 1863, rpt. in Page, *Wilkie Collins: The Critical Heritage,* 143.

65. David, "Rewriting the Male Plot," 194.

66. Deirdre David also notes the resemblance between the fates of Magdalen and Mrs. Wragge, but fails to consider the powerfully ironic effect of this resemblance: "Just as Magdalen's story of return to legitimate social identity in marriage assumes conventional narrative form, so Mrs. Wragge's story of respectable celebrity puts an end to her disruption of parodic omnipotence" (ibid., 194). In addition, David overestimates the "respectability" of this celebrity, and of Wragge's Pill: she claims that Wragge "goes legit," but the marketing and sale of such commodities was widely seen as illegitimate; one thinks of Carlyle's attack on "Morrison's Pills" in *Past and Present,* for example. For an informative survey of Victorian quacks and patent-medicine sellers in fact and fiction (including Wragge), see Altick, *The Presence of the Present,* 545–61.

67. Anna Jones argues similarly that at the end of the novel "Magdalen achieves happiness because she avows and does not repent her past life"; Jones's emphasis, however, is on the masochistic pleasure Magdalen takes in accepting the possibility of Kirke's punitive discipline. See Jones, "A Victim in Search of a Torturer."

5.   Moses and the Advertisement Sheet

1. *No Name* was published in 1862. Catherine Peters notes the resemblance of Gwendolen's personality to Magdalen's, though not the narrative similarities between the two novels, in *The King of Inventors,* 249.

2. Cited in Litvak, *Caught in the Act,* 147.

3. Eliot, *Daniel Deronda* (Penguin), 805. Further page references to this edition will be included parenthetically in the text.

4. Eliot, "The Natural History of German Life," *Westminster Review,* July 1856, rpt. in *Selected Essays,* 110.

5. Much has been written about Eliot's treatment of sympathy in *Daniel Deronda.* See, for example, Jaffe, *Scenes of Sympathy,* 121–57, and, for a reading that emphasizes the novel's kinship to sensation fiction (without mentioning *No Name*), Cvetkovich, *Mixed Feelings,* 128–64.

6. Janice Carlisle is one of the critics who observes that "Deronda seems to be a young man brought up on the novels [Eliot] wrote" (*The Sense of an Audience,* 216).

7. Eliot to Harriet Beecher Stowe, 29 October 1876, in *The George Eliot Letters,* 6: 301–2.

8. Eliot, "Authorship," 234–36.

9. Eliot to Stowe, in *The George Eliot Letters,* 6:301–2.

10. In the novel's "apology for inevitable kinship," for example—a passage overtly motivated by a desire to distinguish Mordecai from "abject specimens of the visionary"—the narrator asks, "What great mental or social type is free from specimens whose insignificance is both ugly and noxious?" and avers that "one is afraid to think of . . . the elbowing there might be at the day of judgment for those who ranked as authors, and brought volumes either in their hands or on trucks" (471).

11. Eliot, "Authorship," 236. For an analysis of Eliot's attitude toward the marketplace as reflected in the "Authorship" note and *Daniel Deronda,* see Gallagher, "George Eliot and *Daniel Deronda.*" While greatly indebted to Gallagher's account of the ways in which "the commercial definition of authorship, . . . [while] established as a *fact* [in Eliot's discourse], creates the necessity for its own transcendence in the realm of *value*" (46), my analysis ends up arguing for a rather different understanding of this dynamic. On Eliot's more general "fears of repetition," see Bodenheimer, *The Real Life of Mary Ann Evans,* 174–75.

12. Eliot, *Romola,* 74.

13. George Henry Lewes to John Blackwood, 29 October 1876, in *The George Eliot Letters,* 6:303.

14. An 1847 *Punch* piece, for example, caps its complaint against a proposal to permit advertisements inside omnibuses by pleading archly, "As we have pantomimes, papers, broadsides, circulars, handbills, and fashionable stories, for advertising, do in mercy allow us to ride for a day's pleasure to Richmond, or to go to the Bank to receive our dividends, without compelling us to sit *vis-à-vis* to Moses & Son" ("A Nation of Advertisers," 31).

15. See, for example, Meyer, "'Safely to Their Own Borders,'" 745; Cheyette, *Constructions of "the Jew" in English Literature and Society,* 47; and Ragussis, *Figures of Conversion,* 278–79.

16. Dickens, "A Slight Depreciation of the Currency," *Household Words,* 3 November 1855, rpt. in *"Gone Astray" and Other Papers,* 337.

17. According to the narrator, "there could hardly have been a stronger contrast" be-

tween Mordecai and the Cohen family: "It was an unaccountable conjunction—the presence among these common, prosperous, shopkeeping types of a man who, in an emaciated threadbare condition, imposed a certain awe on Deronda" (400). As far as I can tell, critics have been unanimous in accepting this contrast at face value.

18. Cairnes, *Some Leading Principles of Political Economy*, 315.

19. In the hands of a writer less sympathetic to Ricardo than Cairnes—and less sympathetic to Jews than Eliot—this comparison can run in the opposite direction: speaking of English economists, Alfred Marshall argues that "as to their tendency to indulge in excessively abstract reasonings, that, in so far as the charge is true at all, is chiefly due to the influence of one masterful genius, who was not an Englishman, and had very little in common with the English tone of thought. The faults and the virtues of Ricardo's mind," he explains, "are traceable to his Semitic origin; no English economist has had a mind similar to his" ("The Present Position of Economics [1885]," 153). For what it is worth, Ricardo was in fact born in London, to Jewish parents who had emigrated from Holland. Raised Jewish, he later converted to Unitarianism. This information is included in Ricardo's entry in the *Dictionary of National Biography*, and discussed more fully in Weatherall, *David Ricardo*.

20. Eliot, *Middlemarch*, 838.

21. For the presence of contemporary physiological theory in Mordecai's organicist discourse, see Shuttleworth, *George Eliot and Nineteenth-Century Science*, 189.

22. Cairnes, *Some Leading Principles of Political Economy*, 298.

23. Ibid., 298, 351, 406.

24. Moreover, while the "gain" Mordecai speaks of is of another order than economic benefit, this distinction does not distinguish him from the political economists as much as it might seem, for they too emphasize such noneconomic benefits. Thus, John Stuart Mill concludes a chapter on international trade by arguing that "the economical advantages of commerce are surpassed in importance by those of its effects which are intellectual and moral." "Commerce," he states, "first taught nations to see with good will the wealth and prosperity of one another," and the growth of international trade is "the principal guarantee of the peace of the world" (*Principles of Political Economy*, 1:581–82).

25. For a very interesting treatment of Lapidoth, whom critics often do not know what to do with, see Hertz, *George Eliot's Pulse*, 122–37.

26. E. Moses & Son, *The Philosophy of Dress*, 6.

27. Kucich emphasizes "each character's autonomous conception" of their "friendship," while Anderson details Daniel's consistent refusal to abandon his reflective, dialogic stance in favor of Mordecai's "subsuming organicism." See Kucich, *Repression in Victorian Fiction*, 177, and Anderson, *The Powers of Distance*, 136.

28. Here is where I part ways with Garrett Stewart's acute analysis of writing and influence in *Daniel Deronda*. Whereas Stewart maintains that Mordecai's "yearning beyond the confines of textuality" is "the novel's own," I argue that the novel calls into question the strategic wisdom of Mordecai's desired "abdication from textual embodiment" (an abdication, as I later note, that Mordecai himself ends up qualifying). See Stewart, *Dear Reader*, 301–28 (quotations from 313 and 310).

29. Nunokawa, *The Afterlife of Property,* 112. See also Press, "Same-Sex Unions in Modern Europe," which argues that "Mordecai initiates Deronda into a homosocial brotherhood that reconciles the identity categories of 'Jew' and 'man'" (306).

30. The first note from Lydia to Gwendolen occasions the novel's most prolonged attention to handwriting: "The address was in a lady's handwriting (of the delicate kind which used to be esteemed feminine before the present uncial period)" (149). It is interesting to note that the parenthetical specification here is a careted insertion in the manuscript, as is another of the novel's rare descriptions of writing: when Gwendolen receives Daniel's anonymous note with her necklace early in the novel, the manuscript reads, "<Underneath the paper> it was wrapt in a cambric handkerchief and within this was a scrap of <torn-off> note-paper on which was written <with a pencil> in clear but rapid handwriting." Yet even these additions—"delicate," "torn-off," "pencil"—seem to call attention less to the materiality per se of these documents than to the scantness of this materiality.

31. One might argue that physical contact can be remembered just as easily as the words of a letter. The difference, though, is between remembering a past event and having an ongoing or repeated experience in the present. The letter's presence for Gwendolen, in other words, is not vitiated by its physical destruction, not simply because she has memorized the letter but because the memorized letter *is* the letter, just as much as the written copy is. It is the letter's essential reproducibility that gives it its staying power, its lasting hold.

32. The copy of the novel I consulted reads "Gwendolen. A Sequel to George Eliot's Daniel Deronda" on the title page, but has the title "Reclaimed" on the page where the first chapter begins and as the running header throughout the book.

33. *Reclaimed,* 188–89.

34. Ibid., 312.

35. Ibid., 74. For an analysis that finds significance in the very fact that *Daniel Deronda* encourages us to imagine future moments, see Tucker, *A Probable State,* 119–21.

36. Here I supplement Cynthia Chase's classic deconstruction of the novel, "The Decomposition of the Elephants: Double-Reading *Daniel Deronda.*" Chase argues that "it is not the event of Deronda's birth as a Jew that is decisive for his story, but the knowledge or affirmation of it. This disclosure, as far as the plot is concerned, is the event with causative powers; yet it appears, too, as a mere effect of the account of Deronda's emerging vocation" (218). I am questioning the decisiveness of each of these moments, in part on the basis of the novel's further efforts (overlooked by Chase) to cement Daniel's sense of vocation.

37. Eliot, *Daniel Deronda,* book 3, "Maidens Choosing" (1876), inside front cover.

38. I adapt here Oscar Wilde's ironic suggestion in "The Portrait of Mr. W. H." that one can be "subdued" to Shakespeare's sonnets themselves: the narrator finds in the sonnets "the record of a romance that, without my knowing it, had coloured the very texture of my nature, had dyed it with strange and subtle dyes" (*The Artist as Critic,* 210).

Bibliography

Adams, James Eli. *Dandies and Desert Saints: Styles of Victorian Masculinity.* Ithaca, NY: Cornell Univ. Press, 1995.

Adorno, Theodor. *Prisms.* Trans. Samuel and Shierry Weber. Cambridge, MA: MIT Press, 1981.

Althusser, Louis. *Lenin and Philosophy and Other Essays.* Trans. Ben Brewster. New York: Monthly Review Press, 1971.

Altick, Richard D. *The Presence of the Present: Topics of the Day in the Victorian Novel.* Columbus: Ohio State Univ. Press, 1991.

Anderson, Amanda. *The Powers of Distance: Cosmopolitanism and the Cultivation of Detachment.* Princeton, NJ: Princeton Univ. Press, 2001.

Arac, Jonathan. *Commissioned Spirits: The Shaping of Social Motion in Dickens, Carlyle, Melville, and Hawthorne.* 1979. New York: Columbia Univ. Press, 1989.

Bagehot, Walter. *Literary Studies.* Ed. Richard Holt Hutton. 2 vols. London: Longmans, Green, 1891.

Bann, Stephen. *The Clothing of Clio: A Study of the Representation of History in Nineteenth-Century Britain and France.* Cambridge: Cambridge Univ. Press, 1984.

Barthes, Roland. *Image-Music-Text.* Trans. Stephen Heath. New York: Noonday Press, 1977.

Benjamin, Walter. *The Origin of German Tragic Drama.* Trans. John Osborne. London: NLB, 1977.

Besant, Walter. *Essays and Historiettes.* London: Chatto & Windus, 1903.

Blain, Virginia. Introduction to *No Name,* by Wilkie Collins, vii–xxi. New York: Oxford Univ. Press, 1986.

Blount, Trevor. "Dickens and Mr. Krook's Spontaneous Combustion." *Dickens Studies Annual* 1 (1970).

Bodenheimer, Rosemarie. "Knowing and Telling in Dickens's Retrospects." In *Knowing the Past: Victorian Literature and Culture,* ed. Suzy Anger, 215–33. Ithaca, NY: Cornell Univ. Press, 2001.

———. *The Real Life of Mary Ann Evans: George Eliot, Her Letters and Fiction.* Ithaca, NY: Cornell Univ. Press, 1994.

Bonham-Carter, Victor. *Authors by Profession.* 2 vols. London: Society of Authors, 1978.

Bourdieu, Pierre. *Distinction: A Social Critique of the Judgement of Taste.* Trans. Richard Nice. Cambridge: Harvard Univ. Press, 1984.

————. *The Field of Cultural Production.* Ed. Randal Johnson. New York: Columbia Univ. Press, 1993.

Brock, William H. *Justus von Liebig: The Chemical Gatekeeper.* New York: Cambridge Univ. Press, 1997.

Brown, Bill, ed. *Things.* Chicago: Univ. of Chicago Press, 2004.

Bulwer-Lytton, Edward. *Not So Bad as We Seem; or, Many Sides to a Character.* New York: Harper & Bros., 1851.

Burke, Kenneth. *A Grammar of Motives.* Berkeley: Univ. of California Press, 1969.

Butler, Judith. *Bodies That Matter: On the Discursive Limits of "Sex."* New York: Routledge, 1993.

Byron, Lord (George Gordon). *The Complete Poetical Works.* Ed. Jerome J. McGann, 5 vols. Oxford: Clarendon Press, 1980–86.

Cairnes, John. *Some Leading Principles of Political Economy Newly Expounded.* 1874. New York: Augustus M. Kelley, 1967.

Cameron, Sharon. *The Corporeal Self: Allegories of the Body in Melville and Hawthorne.* New York: Columbia Univ. Press, 1991.

Carlisle, Janice. *The Sense of an Audience: Dickens, Thackeray, and George Eliot at Mid-Century.* Athens: Univ. of Georgia Press, 1981.

Carlyle, Thomas. *The French Revolution: A History.* 1837. Oxford: Oxford Univ. Press, 1989.

————. *On Heroes, Hero-Worship, and the Heroic in History.* 1841. Berkeley: Univ. of California Press, 1993.

————. *Past and Present.* 1843. New York: New York Univ. Press, 1965.

Carroll, William C. *Fat King, Lean Beggar: Representations of Poverty in the Age of Shakespeare.* Ithaca, NY: Cornell Univ. Press, 1996.

"The Charities and the Poor of London." *Quarterly Review* 97 (1855): 407–50.

Chase, Cynthia. "The Decomposition of the Elephants: Double-Reading *Daniel Deronda.*" *PMLA* 93 (1978): 215–27.

Chase, Karen. "The Kindness of Consanguinity: Family History in *Henry Esmond.*" *Modern Language Studies* 16 (1986): 213–26.

Cheyette, Bryan. *Constructions of "the Jew" in English Literature and Society.* Cambridge: Cambridge Univ. Press, 1993.

Clarke, Norma. "Strenuous Idleness: Thomas Carlyle and the Man of Letters as Hero." In *Manful Assertions: Masculinities in Britain since 1800,* ed. Michael Roper and John Tosh. New York: Routledge, 1991.

Cohen, Tom, J. Hillis Miller, and Barbara Cohen. "A 'Materiality without Matter'?" In *Material Events: Paul de Man and the Afterlife of Theory,* ed. Tom Cohen, Barbara Cohen, J. Hillis Miller, and Andrez Warminski, vii–xxv. Minneapolis: Univ. of Minnesota Press, 2001.

Coleridge, Samuel Taylor. *Biographia Literaria, or Biographical Sketches of My Literary Life and Opinions.* 1817. Ed. George Watson. London: Dent, 1975.

Coleridge, Samuel Taylor, and William Wordsworth. *Lyrical Ballads 1798.* Ed. W. J. B. Owen. 2nd ed. Oxford: Oxford Univ. Press, 1969.

Collins, Wilkie. *No Name*. 1862. Ed. Virginia Blain. New York: Oxford Univ. Press, 1986.

Crosby, Christina. *The Ends of History: Victorians and "The Woman Question."* New York: Routledge, 1991.

Cross, Nigel. *The Common Writer: Life in Nineteenth-Century Grub Street*. New York: Cambridge Univ. Press, 1985.

Culler, Jonathan. "Literary History, Allegory, and Semiology." *New Literary History* 7 (1976): 259–70.

[Cunningham, Peter]. "What We Do with Our Letters." *Household Words,* 23 October 1852, 139–42.

Curtis, Gerard. *Visual Words: Art and the Material Book in Victorian England*. Burlington, VT: Ashgate, 2002.

Cvetkovich, Ann. *Mixed Feelings: Feminism, Mass Culture, and Victorian Sensationalism*. New Brunswick, NJ: Rutgers Univ. Press, 1992.

Darwin, Bernard. *The Dickens Advertiser: A Collection of the Advertisements in the Original Parts of Novels by Charles Dickens*. New York: Macmillan, 1930.

David, Deirdre. "Rewriting the Male Plot in Wilkie Collins's *No Name:* Captain Wragge Orders an Omelette and Mrs. Wragge Goes into Custody." In *Out of Bounds: Male Writers and Gender(ed) Criticism,* ed. Laura Claridge and Elizabeth Langland, 186–96. Amherst: Univ. of Massachusetts Press, 1990.

de Man, Paul. *Allegories of Reading: Figural Language in Rousseau, Nietzsche, Rilke, and Proust*. New Haven, CT: Yale Univ. Press, 1979.

———. *Blindness and Insight: Essays in the Rhetoric of Contemporary Criticism*. 2nd rev. ed. Minneapolis: Univ. of Minnesota Press, 1983.

———. "Phenomenality and Materiality in Kant." In *Hermeneutics: Questions and Prospects,* ed. Gary Shapiro and Alan Sica, 121–44. Amherst: Univ. of Massachusetts Press, 1984.

———. *The Resistance to Theory*. Minneapolis: Univ. of Minnesota Press, 1986.

Denman, Peter. "Krook's Death and Dickens's Authorities." *The Dickensian* 82 (1986): 130–41.

Derrida, Jacques. *Dissemination*. Trans. Barbara Johnson. Chicago: Univ. of Chicago Press, 1981.

———. *Given Time: 1. Counterfeit Money*. Trans. Peggy Kamuf. Chicago: Univ. of Chicago Press, 1992.

———. *Of Grammatology*. Trans. Gayatri Chakravorty Spivak. Baltimore: Johns Hopkins Univ. Press, 1976.

Dickens, Charles. "The Begging Letter Writer." *Household Words,* 18 May 1850. Rpt. in *The Amusements of the People and Other Papers: Reports, Essays and Reviews, 1834–51,* ed. Michael Slater. The Dent Uniform Edition of Dickens' Journalism, vol. 2. Columbus: Ohio State Univ. Press, 1996.

———. *Bleak House*. London: Bradbury & Evans, 1852–53 (monthly parts).

———. *Bleak House*. Ed. George Ford and Sylvère Monod. Norton Critical Edition. New York: Norton, 1977.

———. *Dombey and Son*. 1846–48. London: Penguin, 1970.

———. *Great Expectations*. 1860–61. London: Penguin, 1985.

———. "The Guild of Literature and Art." *Household Words,* 10 May 1851. Rpt. in Dickens, *Miscellaneous Papers,* vol. 1.

———. *Letters.* Ed. Madeline House, Graham Storey, and Kathleen Tillotson. 12 vols. Oxford: Clarendon Press, 1965–2002.

———. *Little Dorrit.* 1855–57. London: Penguin, 1967.

———. *Martin Chuzzlewit.* 1843–44. Oxford: Clarendon, 1982.

———. *Miscellaneous Papers.* 2 vols. London: Chapman & Hall, 1909.

———. *The Mystery of Edwin Drood.* 1870. London: Penguin, 1988.

———. *Oliver Twist.* 1838. Oxford: Oxford Univ. Press, 1982.

———. *Our Mutual Friend.* 1864–65. London: Penguin, 1971.

———. "The Poetry of Science." *The Examiner,* 9 Dec 1848. Rpt. in Dickens, *Miscellaneous Papers,* vol. 1.

———. *The Posthumous Papers of the Pickwick Club.* 1836–37. London: Penguin, 1986.

———. "A Preliminary Word." *Household Words,* 30 March 1850. Rpt. in Dickens, *Miscellaneous Papers,* vol. 1.

———. *Reprinted Pieces and Others.* London: Dent, 1921.

———. "A Slight Depreciation of the Currency." *Household Words,* 3 November 1855. Rpt. in *"Gone Astray" and Other Papers from Household Words, 1851–59,* ed. Michael Slater. The Dent Uniform Edition of Dickens' Journalism, vol. 3. London: J. M. Dent, 1998.

———. *The Speeches of Charles Dickens.* Ed. K. J. Fielding. Oxford: Oxford Univ. Press, 1960.

D'Israeli, Isaac. *Miscellanies of Literature.* London: Edward Moxon, 1840.

[Dodd, George]. "Books for the Blind." *Household Words,* 2 July 1853: 421–25.

Douglas, Mary. "Foreword: No Free Gifts." In Mauss, *The Gift,* vii–xviii.

Eilenberg, Susan. *Strange Power of Speech: Wordsworth, Coleridge, and Literary Possession.* New York: Oxford Univ. Press, 1992.

Eisenstein, Elizabeth. *The Printing Press as an Agent of Change: Communications and Cultural Transformations in Early-Modern Europe.* New York: Cambridge Univ. Press, 1980.

Eliot, George. "Authorship." *Leaves from a Notebook: Essays.* Illustrated Sterling Edition. Boston: Dana Estes, n.d.

———. *Daniel Deronda.* Edinburgh: Wm. Blackwood and Sons, 1876 (monthly parts).

———. *Daniel Deronda.* 1876. London: Penguin, 1995.

———. *The George Eliot Letters.* Ed. Gordon S. Haight. New Haven, CT: Yale Univ. Press, 1955.

———. *George Eliot's* Daniel Deronda *Notebooks.* Ed. Jane Irwin. New York: Cambridge Univ. Press, 1996.

———. *Middlemarch.* 1871–72. London: Penguin, 1994.

———. *Romola.* 1863. London: Penguin, 1980.

———. *Selected Essays, Poems, and Other Writings.* Ed. A. S. Byatt and Nicholas Warren. London: Penguin, 1990.

Ellman, Richard. *Oscar Wilde.* New York: Knopf, 1988.

Emerson, Ralph Waldo. "Nature" (1836). *Collected Works of Ralph Waldo Emerson.* Vol. 1, 7–45. Cambridge: Harvard Univ. Press, 1971.

Feltes, N. N. *Modes of Production of Victorian Novels*. Chicago: Univ. of Chicago Press, 1986.

Ferguson, Frances. *Solitude and the Sublime: Romanticism and the Aesthetics of Individuation*. New York: Routledge, 1992.

Fielding, K. J. "Dickens and the Royal Literary Fund: 1855." *TLS*, 15 and 22 October 1954.

———. "Dickens and the Royal Literary Fund—1858." *Review of English Studies*, n.s. 6, no. 224 (1955): 383–94.

———. "Thackeray and the 'Dignity of Literature.'" *TLS*, 19 and 26 September 1958.

Forster, John. "Encouragement of Literature by the State." *The Examiner* [London], 5 January 1850. Rpt. in Thackeray, *The History of Pendennis*, ed. Shillingsburg, 488–91.

———. *Life of Charles Dickens*. London: Chapman & Hall, 1892.

———. *The Life and Times of Oliver Goldsmith*. 2nd ed. 2 vols. London: Bradbury & Evans, 1854.

Foucault, Michel. *The History of Sexuality: volume 1, An Introduction*. Trans. Robert Hurley. New York: Vintage, 1980.

———. *Language, Counter-Memory, Practice*. Ed. Donald F. Bouchard. Trans. Bouchard and Sherry Simon. Ithaca, NY: Cornell Univ. Press, 1977.

Freedman, Jonathan. *Professions of Taste: Henry James, British Aestheticism, and Commodity Culture*. Stanford, CA: Stanford Univ. Press, 1990.

Gallagher, Catherine. "The Body versus the Social Body in Malthus and Mayhew." In *The Making of the Modern Body: Sexuality and Science in the Nineteenth Century*, ed. Gallagher and Thomas Laqueur, 83–106. Berkeley: Univ. of California Press, 1987.

———. "George Eliot and *Daniel Deronda*: The Prostitute and the Jewish Question." In *Sex, Politics and Science in the Nineteenth-Century Novel*, ed. Ruth Bernard Yeazell, 39–62. Baltimore: Johns Hopkins Univ. Press, 1986.

———. *Nobody's Story: The Vanishing Acts of Women Writers in the Marketplace, 1670–1820*. Berkeley: Univ. of California Press, 1994.

Gaskell, E. "More about Spontaneous Combustion." *The Dickensian* 69 (1972): 25–35.

Gaskell, Philip. *From Writer to Reader: Studies in Editorial Method*. Oxford: Oxford Univ. Press, 1978.

Genette, Gérard. *Paratexts: Thresholds of Interpretation*. Trans. Jane E. Lewin. New York: Cambridge Univ. Press, 1997.

———. *The Work of Art: Immanence and Transcendence*. Trans. G. M. Goshgarian. Ithaca, NY: Cornell Univ. Press, 1997.

Gissing, George. *Charles Dickens: A Critical Study*. Port Washington, NY: Kennikat Press, 1966.

———. *Critical Studies of the Works of Charles Dickens*. New York: Greenberg, 1924.

———. *The Nether World*. 1886. London: Dent, 1973.

Goux, Jean-Joseph. *Symbolic Economies: After Marx and Freud*. Trans. Jennifer Curtiss Gage. Ithaca, NY: Cornell Univ. Press, 1990.

Gramsci, Antonio. *Selections from the Prison Notebooks*. Ed. and trans. Quintin Hoare and Geoffrey Nowell Smith. New York: International Publishers, 1971.

Grant, James. *Sketches in London*. 1838. 3rd ed. London: William Tegg, 1850.

Greenwood, James. *The Seven Curses of London*. 1869. Oxford: Basil Blackwell, 1981.

Guillory, John. *Cultural Capital: The Problem of Literary Canon Formation*. Chicago: Univ. of Chicago Press, 1993.

Haight, Gordon. "Dickens and Lewes on Spontaneous Combustion." *Nineteenth-Century Fiction* 10 (1955–56): 53–63.

Hale, Dorothy J. *Social Formalism: The Novel in Theory from Henry James to the Present*. Palo Alto, CA: Stanford Univ. Press, 1998.

Hamlin, Christopher. "Providence and Putrefaction: Victorian Sanitarians and the Natural Theology of Health and Disease." *Victorian Studies* 28 (1985): 381–411.

[Hannay, James]. "Graves and Epitaphs." *Household Words*, 16 October 1852, 105–9.

Harrison, Gary. *Wordsworth's Vagrant Muse: Poetry, Poverty and Power*. Detroit: Wayne State Univ. Press, 1994.

Heller, Tamar. *Dead Secrets: Wilkie Collins and the Female Gothic*. New Haven, CT: Yale Univ. Press, 1992.

Hertz, Neil. *George Eliot's Pulse*. Stanford, CA: Stanford Univ. Press, 2003.

Himmelfarb, Gertrude. *Poverty and Compassion: The Moral Imagination of the Late Victorians*. New York: Vintage Books, 1992.

Homans, Margaret. *Bearing the Word: Language and Female Experience in Nineteenth-Century Women's Writing*. Chicago: Univ. of Chicago Press, 1986.

Howes, Craig. "*Pendennis* and the Controversy on the 'Dignity of Literature.'" *Nineteenth-Century Literature* 41 (1986): 269–98.

Howitt, Mary. *An Autobiography*. Ed. Margaret Howitt. 2 vols. London: William Isbister, 1889.

Hunt, Robert. *The Poetry of Science; or, Studies of the Physical Phenomena of Nature*. 3rd ed. London: Henry G. Bohn, 1854.

Jaffe, Audrey. "Detecting the Beggar: Arthur Conan Doyle, Henry Mayhew, and 'The Man with the Twisted Lip.'" *Representations* 31 (1990): 96–117.

———. *Scenes of Sympathy: Identity and Representation in Victorian Fiction*. Ithaca, NY: Cornell Univ. Press, 2000.

Jameson, Fredric. *The Political Unconscious: Narrative as a Socially Symbolic Act*. Ithaca, NY: Cornell Univ. Press, 1981.

Jevons, W. Stanley. *The Principles of Economics*. London: Macmillan, 1905.

Johnson, Edgar. *Charles Dickens: His Tragedy and Triumph*. 2 vols. New York: Simon & Schuster, 1952.

Jones, Anna. "A Victim in Search of a Torturer: Reading Masochism in Wilkie Collins's *No Name*." *Novel: A Forum on Fiction* 33, no. 2 (Spring 2000): 196–211.

Jones, Gareth Stedman. *Outcast London: A Study in the Relationship between Classes in Victorian Society*. New York: Pantheon Books, 1984.

Keach, William. "'Words Are Things': Romantic Ideology and the Matter of Poetic Language." In *Aesthetics and Ideology*, ed. George Levine, 219–39. New Brunswick, NJ: Rutgers Univ. Press, 1994.

Kernan, Alvin. *Printing Technology, Letters, and Samuel Johnson*. Princeton, NJ: Princeton Univ. Press, 1987.

Kincaid, James R. "Performance, Roles, and the Nature of the Self in Dickens." In *Dramatic Dickens*, ed. Carol Hanbery MacKay, 11–26. London: Macmillan, 1989.

Kucich, John. *The Power of Lies: Transgression in Victorian Fiction*. Ithaca, NY: Cornell Univ. Press, 1994.

———. *Repression in Victorian Fiction: Charlotte Brontë, George Eliot, and Charles Dickens*. Berkeley: Univ. of California Press, 1987.

Langan, Celeste. *Romantic Vagrancy: Wordsworth and the Simulation of Freedom*. New York: Cambridge Univ. Press, 1995.

Laqueur, Thomas. "Bodies, Details, and the Humanitarian Narrative." In *The New Cultural History*, ed. Lynn Hunt, 176–204. Berkeley: Univ. of California Press, 1989.

Larson, Magali Sarfatti. *The Rise of Professionalism: A Sociological Analysis*. Berkeley: Univ. of California Press, 1977.

The Leader [London], 1852–53.

[Leigh, Percival]. "Address from an Undertaker to the Trade (Strictly Private and Confidential)." *Household Words*, 22 June 1850, 301–4.

[Lemon, Mark, and Charles Dickens]. "A Paper Mill." *Household Words*, 31 Aug 1850. Rpt. in *Charles Dickens' Uncollected Writings from* Household Words, *1850–1859*, ed. Harry Stone, 2 vols., 1:137–42. Bloomington: Indiana Univ. Press, 1968.

Levine, George. *Darwin and the Novelists: Patterns of Science in Victorian Fiction*. Cambridge: Harvard Univ. Press, 1988.

Lewes, George Henry. "Spontaneous Combustion." *Blackwood's Edinburgh Magazine* 89 (1861): 385–402.

Liebig, Justus von. *Familiar Letters on Chemistry, in Its Relations to Physiology, Dietetics, Agriculture, Commerce, and Political Economy*. 4th ed. London: Walton & Maberly, 1859.

Lindenbaum, Peter. "Milton's Contract." In *The Construction of Authorship: Textual Appropriation in Law and Literature*, ed. Martha Woodmansee and Peter Jaszi, 175–90. Durham: Duke Univ. Press, 1994.

Litvak, Joseph. *Caught in the Act: Theatricality in the Nineteenth-Century English Novel*. Berkeley: Univ. of California Press, 1992.

Loesberg, Jonathan. "A Fountain, a Spontaneous Combustion, and the Mona Lisa: Duchamp's Symbolism in Dickens and Pater." *Studies in the Literary Imagination* 35, no. 2 (Fall 2002): 53–77.

Longxi, Zhang. "Historicizing the Postmodern Allegory." *Texas Studies in Literature and Language* 36 (1994): 212–31.

Lukács, Georg. *The Historical Novel*. Trans. Hannah and Stanley Mitchell. Lincoln: Univ. of Nebraska Press, 1983.

Lund, Michael. *Reading Thackeray*. Detroit: Wayne State Univ. Press, 1988.

Lynch, Deidre Shauna. *The Economy of Character: Novels, Market Culture, and the Business of Inner Meaning*. Chicago: Univ. of Chicago Press, 1998.

Macleod, Henry Dunning. *The Principles of Economical Philosophy*. 2nd ed. London: Longmans, Green, Reader, & Dyer, 1872.

Marshall, Alfred. "The Present Position of Economics (1885)." In *Memorials of Alfred Marshall*, ed. A. C. Pigou. New York: Kelley & Millman, 1956.

Marx, Karl. *Capital: A Critique of Political Economy.* Vol. 1. Trans. Ben Fowler. London: Penguin, 1990.

———. *A Contribution to the Critique of Political Economy.* Trans. S. W. Ryazanskaya. New York: International Publishers, 1970.

———. *Theories of Surplus Value, Part 1.* Trans. Emile Burns. Moscow: Progress Publishers, 1969.

Mauss, Marcel. *The Gift: The Form and Reason for Exchange in Archaic Societies.* Trans. W. D. Halls. New York: Norton, 1990.

Mayhew, Henry. *London Labour and the London Poor.* 1861–62. 4 vols. New York: Dover, 1968.

McGann, Jerome J. *The Textual Condition.* Princeton, NJ: Princeton Univ. Press, 1991.

Meredith, George. "The Beggar's Soliloquy." [*Once a Week* (London), 30 March 1861.] *The Poetical Works of George Meredith.* New York: Charles Scribner's Sons, 1928.

Mermin, Dorothy. *Godiva's Ride: Women of Letter in England, 1830–1880.* Bloomington: Indiana Univ. Press, 1993.

Meyer, Susan. "'Safely to Their Own Borders': Proto-Zionism, Feminism, and Nationalism in *Daniel Deronda.*" *ELH* 60 (1993): 733–58.

Mill, John Stuart. *Autobiography.* Ed. Jack Stillinger. Boston: Houghton Mifflin, 1969.

———. *Principles of Political Economy; with Some of Their Applications to Social Philosophy.* 5th ed. 2 vols. New York: D. Appleton, 1896.

Miller, D. A. *The Novel and the Police.* Berkeley: Univ. of California Press, 1988.

Miller, J. Hillis. *Fiction and Repetition: Seven English Novels.* Cambridge: Harvard Univ. Press, 1982.

———. Introduction to *Bleak House,* by Charles Dickens. Harmondsworth: Penguin, 1971.

Morning Chronicle [London]. [Untitled article]. 3 January 1850. Rpt. in Thackeray, *The History of Pendennis,* ed. Shillingsburg, 485–88.

Moses, E., & Son. *The Philosophy of Dress, with a Few Notes on National Costumes.* London: E. Moses & Son, 1864.

"Nation of Advertisers, A." *Punch* 12 (1847): 31.

Newsom, Robert. *Dickens on the Romantic Side of Familiar Things: Bleak House and the Novel Tradition.* New York: Columbia Univ. Press, 1977.

Nunokawa, Jeff. *The Afterlife of Property: Domestic Security and the Victorian Novel.* Princeton, NJ: Princeton Univ. Press, 1994.

Once a Week [London], 29 December 1860.

Ong, Walter J. *Interfaces of the Word: Studies in the Evolution of Consciousness and Culture.* Ithaca, NY: Cornell Univ. Press, 1977.

———. *Orality and Literacy: The Technologizing of the Word.* New York: Routledge, 1988.

Page, Norman, ed. *Wilkie Collins: The Critical Heritage.* London: Routledge & Kegan Paul, 1974.

Patten, Robert L. "'The People have set Literature free': The Professionalization of Letters in Nineteenth-Century England." *Review* 9 (1987): 1–34.

Perkin, Harold. *The Rise of Professional Society: England Since 1880.* New York: Routledge, 1989.

Peters, Catherine. *The King of Inventors: A Life of Wilkie Collins.* Princeton, NJ: Princeton Univ. Press, 1993.

Pettitt, Clare. *Patent Inventions: Intellectual Property and the Victorian Novel.* New York: Oxford Univ. Press, 2004.

Poovey, Mary. *Uneven Developments: The Ideological Work of Gender in Mid-Victorian England.* Chicago: Univ. of Chicago Press, 1988.

Press, Jacob. "Same-Sex Unions in Modern Europe: *Daniel Deronda, Altneuland,* and the Homoerotics of Jewish Nationalism." In Sedgwick, *Novel Gazing,* 299–329.

"The Profession of Literature." *Westminster Review* 58 (1852): 507–31.

"Proposed Prospectus for the Provident Union of Literature, Science, & Art, [November] 1847." In Dickens, *Letters,* 5:700–702.

"Prospectus for the Guild of Literature and Art," April 1851. In Dickens, *Letters,* 6: 852–57.

Rabinbach, Anson. *The Human Motor: Energy, Fatigue, and the Origins of Modernity.* Berkeley: Univ. of California Press, 1992.

Ragussis, Michael. *Acts of Naming: The Family Plot in Fiction.* New York: Oxford Univ. Press, 1986.

———. *Figures of Conversion: "The Jewish Question" and English National Identity.* Durham, NC: Duke Univ. Press, 1995.

Ray, Gordon. *Thackeray: The Age of Wisdom.* New York: McGraw-Hill, 1958.

Reclaimed. Boston: Ira Bradley, 1878.

Richardson, Ruth. *Death, Dissection, and the Destitute.* London: Penguin, 1988.

Ritchie, Anne Thackeray. "Introduction." *The History of Henry Esmond, &c.,* by William Makepeace Thackeray. Biographical Edition, vol. 7, xiii–xlvi. New York: Harper & Bros., 1898.

Robbins, Bruce. "Telescopic Philanthropy: Professionalism and Responsibility in *Bleak House.*" In *Nation and Narration,* ed. Homi K. Bhabha, 213–30. New York: Routledge, 1990.

Roberts, M. J. D. "Reshaping the Gift Relationship: The London Mendicity Society and the Suppression of Begging in England 1818–1869." *International Review of Social History* 36 (1991): 201–31.

Rose, Lionel. *"Rogues and Vagabonds": Vagrant Underworld in Britain 1815–1985.* London: Routledge, 1988.

Rose, Mark. *Authors and Owners: The Invention of Copyright.* Cambridge: Harvard Univ. Press, 1993.

Ruskin, John. *Works of John Ruskin.* London: George Allen, 1907.

Scarry, Elaine. *The Body in Pain: The Making and Unmaking of the World.* New York: Oxford Univ. Press, 1985.

———. *Resisting Representation.* New York: Oxford Univ. Press, 1994.

Scragg, D. G. *A History of English Spelling.* New York: Harper & Row, 1974.

Sedgwick, Eve Kosofsky, ed. *Novel Gazing: Queer Readings in Fiction.* Durham, NC: Duke Univ. Press, 1997.

———. "Paranoid Reading and Reparative Reading; or, You're So Paranoid, You Probably Think This Introduction Is about You." In Sedgwick, *Novel Gazing,* 1–37.

Shakespeare, William. *The Riverside Shakespeare.* Ed. G. Blakemore Evans. Boston: Houghton Mifflin, 1974.

Shuttleworth, Sally. *George Eliot and Nineteenth-Century Science: The Make-Believe of a Beginning.* New York: Cambridge Univ. Press, 1984.

Simpson, David. "Introduction: The Moment of Materialism." In *Subject to History: Ideology, Class, Gender,* ed. Simpson, 1–33. Ithaca, NY: Cornell Univ. Press, 1991.

Smith, Adam. *An Inquiry into the Nature and Causes of the Wealth of Nations.* 1776. Chicago: Univ. of Chicago Press, 1976.

Stange, G. Robert. Review of *No Name,* by Wilkie Collins. *Nineteenth-Century Fiction* 34 (1979): 96–100.

Stewart, Garrett. *Dear Reader: The Conscripted Audience in Nineteenth-Century British Fiction.* Baltimore: Johns Hopkins Univ. Press, 1996.

———. "The New Mortality of *Bleak House.*" *ELH* 45 (1978): 443–87.

Sussman, Herbert. *Victorian Masculinities: Manhood and Masculine Poetics in Early Victorian Literature and Art.* Cambridge: Cambridge Univ. Press, 1995.

Swift, Jonathan. "A Proposal for Correcting, Improving, and Ascertaining the English Language." 1712. Excerpted in *Proper English? Readings in Language, History and Cultural Identity.* Ed. Tony Crowley. New York: Routledge, 1991.

Thackeray, William Makepeace. *The English Humourists of the Eighteenth Century.* 1853. Rpt. in *The English Humourists of the Eighteenth Century, The Four Georges, etc.* London: Macmillan, 1924.

———. *The History of Henry Esmond.* London: Smith, Elder, 1852.

———. *The History of Henry Esmond.* Ed. Edgar F. Harden. New York: Garland, 1989.

———. *The History of Henry Esmond.* Ed. John Sutherland and Michael Greenfield. New York: Penguin, 1985.

———. *The History of Pendennis.* 1848–50. Ed. Donald Hawes. Harmondsworth: Penguin, 1986.

———. *The History of Pendennis.* Ed. Peter L. Shillingsburg. New York: Garland, 1991.

———. Letter to the Editor of the *Morning Chronicle.* 12 Jan 1850. Rpt. in Thackeray, *The History of Pendennis,* ed. Shillingsburg, 491–95.

———. *Letters and Private Papers of William Makepeace Thackeray.* Ed. Gordon Ray. 4 vols. London: Oxford Univ. Press, 1945–46.

———. *The Letters and Private Papers of William Makepeace Thackeray, A Supplement.* Ed. Edgar F. Harden. 2 vols. New York: Garland, 1994.

———. *Roundabout Papers.* Biographical Edition of the Works of William Makepeace Thackeray. Vol. 12. New York: Harper & Bros., 1898.

———. *The Virginians.* 1857–59. London: Collins' Clear-Type Press, 1908.

Tiffany, Daniel. *Toy Medium: Materialism and Modern Lyric.* Berkeley: Univ. of California Press, 2000.

Tillotson, Geoffrey, and Donald Hawes, eds. *Thackeray: The Critical Heritage.* New York: Barnes & Noble, 1968.

Times [London]. 7 October 1867.

Trollope, Anthony. *An Autobiography.* Berkeley: Univ. of California Press, 1947.

———. *An Editor's Tales.* 1870. Rpt. as *The Spotted Dog and Other Stories.* Phoenix Mill, UK: Alan Sutton, 1983.

————. *Thackeray.* 1879. London: Macmillan, 1906.

Tucker, Irene. *A Probable State: The Novel, the Contract, and the Jews.* Chicago: Univ. of Chicago Press, 2000.

Vanden Bossche, Chris R. "The Value of Literature: Representations of Print Culture in the Copyright Debate of 1837–1842." *Victorian Studies* 38 (1994): 43–67.

Warminski, Andrzej. "Terrible Reading (Preceded by 'Epigraphs')." In *Responses: On Paul de Man's Wartime Journalism,* ed. Werner Hamacher, Neil Hertz, and Thomas Keenan, 385–96. Lincoln: Univ. of Nebraska Press, 1989.

Weatherall, David. *David Ricardo: A Biography.* The Hague: Martinus Nijhoff, 1976.

Welsh, Alexander. *The City of Dickens.* 1971. Cambridge: Harvard Univ. Press, 1986.

————. *From Copyright to Copperfield: The Identity of Dickens.* Cambridge: Harvard Univ. Press, 1987.

Wicke, Jennifer. *Advertising Fictions: Literature, Advertisement, and Social Reading.* New York: Columbia Univ. Press, 1988.

Wilde, Oscar. *The Artist as Critic: Critical Writings of Oscar Wilde.* Ed. Richard Ellman. New York: Random House, 1969.

Wilkinson, Ann Y. "*Bleak House:* From Faraday to Judgment Day." *ELH* 34 (1967): 225–47.

Williams, Raymond. *Culture and Society: 1780–1950.* New York: Columbia Univ. Press, 1983.

Wordsworth, William. *Selected Poems and Prefaces.* Ed. Jack Stillinger. Boston: Houghton Mifflin, 1965.

Index

RECENT BOOKS IN THE VICTORIAN LITERATURE AND CULTURE SERIES

Linda Dowling/ *The Vulgarization of Art: The Victorians and Aesthetic Democracy*

Tricia Lootens/ *Lost Saints: Silence, Gender, and Victorian Literary Canonization*

Matthew Arnold/ *The Letters of Matthew Arnold*, vols. 1–6
Edited by Cecil Y. Lang

Edward FitzGerald/ *Edward FitzGerald, Rubáiyát* of Omar Khayyám:
A Critical Edition
Edited by Christopher Decker

Christina Rossetti/ *The Letters of Christina Rossetti*, vols. 1–4
Edited by Antony H. Harrison

Barbara Leah Harman/ *The Feminine Political Novel in Victorian England*

John Ruskin/ *The Genius of John Ruskin: Selections from His Writings*
Edited by John D. Rosenberg

Antony H. Harrison/ *Victorian Poets and the Politics of Culture:
Discourse and Ideology*

Judith Stoddart/ *Ruskin's Culture Wars:* Fors Clavigera *and the
Crisis of Victorian Liberalism*

Linda K. Hughes and Michael Lund/ *Victorian Publishing and Mrs. Gaskell's Work*

Linda H. Peterson/ *Traditions of Victorian Women's Autobiography:
The Poetics and Politics of Life Writing*

Gail Turley Houston/ *Royalties: The Queen and Victorian Writers*

Laura C. Berry/ *The Child, the State, and the Victorian Novel*

Barbara J. Black/ *On Exhibit: Victorians and Their Museums*

Annette R. Federico/ *Idol of Suburbia: Marie Corelli and
Late-Victorian Literary Culture*

Talia Schaffer/ *The Forgotten Female Aesthetes: Literary Culture
in Late-Victorian England*

Julia F. Saville/ *A Queer Chivalry: The Homoerotic Asceticism of
Gerard Manley Hopkins*

Victor Shea and William Whitla, Editors/*Essays and Reviews: The 1860 Text and Its Reading*

Marlene Tromp/*The Private Rod: Marital Violence, Sensation, and the Law in Victorian Britain*

Dorice Williams Elliott/*The Angel out of the House: Philanthropy and Gender in Nineteenth-Century England*

Richard Maxwell, Editor/*The Victorian Illustrated Book*

Vineta Colby/*Vernon Lee: A Literary Biography*

E. Warwick Slinn/*Victorian Poetry as Cultural Critique: The Politics of Performative Language*

Simon Joyce/*Capital Offenses: Geographies of Class and Crime in Victorian London*

Caroline Levine/*The Serious Pleasures of Suspense: Victorian Realism and Narrative Doubts*

Emily Davies/*Emily Davies: Collected Letters, 1861–1875*
Edited by Ann B. Murphy and Deirdre Raftery

Joseph Bizup/*Manufacturing Culture: Vindications of Early Victorian Industry*

Lynn M. Voskuil/*Acting Naturally: Victorian Theatricality and Authenticity*

Sally Mitchell/*Frances Power Cobbe: Victorian Feminist, Journalist, Reformer*

Constance W. Hassett/*Christina Rossetti: The Patience of Style*

Brenda Assael/*The Circus and Victorian Society*

Judith Wilt/*Behind Her Times: Transition England in the Novels of Mary Arnold Ward*

Daniel Hack/*The Material Interests of the Victorian Novel*